Transitional Justice and Agrarian Conflict

José A. Gutiérrez

Transitional Justice and Agrarian Conflict

palgrave
macmillan

José A. Gutiérrez
Department of Politics
Centre of Applied Human Rights (CAHR),
University of York
York, UK

ISBN 978-3-032-25227-2 ISBN 978-3-032-25228-9 (eBook)
https://doi.org/10.1007/978-3-032-25228-9

Cover Credit text: Maram_shutterstock

This Palgrave Macmillan imprint is published by the registered company Springer Nature Switzerland AG.
The registered company address is: Gewerbestrasse 11, 6330 Cham, Switzerland

Foreword

To Pilar and Ignacio, the beekeeper

We live in strange times. The liberal order that created and nurtured transitional justice is in what's possibly a terminal crisis, propelled by multiple crises: environmental, social, economic, even moral—judging by the shameful silence that has been characteristic of various liberal institutions in the face of some of the worst atrocities witnessed in decades, despite the loud proclamations of 'Never Again'. Why then a book on transitional justice and agrarian conflict in the current circumstances? Because it is necessary. Not only because much of our crises and conflicts have an agrarian dimension to it, but also because the agrarian mobilisation around justice and its insistence on the need for transformative change, of a transition to a more equitable and sustainable future, gives us hope. And hope is the only thing that can keep us going amidst uncertainty and despair.

This book started to take shape in a series of discussions in the context of the Transformative Justice Network in 2021. A first attempt to synthesise some of our discussions came in the form of the Spanish-language book *Justicia Transformativa y Conflicto Agrario. Elementos para un Debate Necesario* [Transformative Justice and Agrarian Conflict. Notes for a Necessary Debate] (Bogotá: Ediciones USTA), which counted with the collaborations of Eric Hoddy, Dáire McGill, Irene Vélez-Torres, Rocio del Pilar Peña-Huertas, Diana Marcela Muriel and me. Of course, some of our main concerns when we came up with the idea of writing this contribution were the very concrete problems faced by the implementation of the 2016 peace agreement in Colombia and the persistence of the agrarian question in its aftermath, despite the very prominent recognition of the centrality of this question to the armed conflict in this country.

Therefore, Eric Hoddy and I felt the need to develop this project further, this time to an English-speaking audience, expanding our reflections to incorporate a more systematic evaluation of transitional justice in settings of agrarian conflict and what agrarian movements themselves are doing to foster transitions towards agrarian justice. More than re-inventing the wheel, we felt that, in the true vein of the transformative critique of transitional justice, we needed to start from the experience on the ground. Thus, the aim of this project was to synthesise and to bring together a broad range of theoretical and practical developments to help articulate a transitional/transformative justice perspective on agrarian conflict and peasants (as a distinct and specific social category).

While Eric came up with the original idea and plan for this book, a number of personal reasons prevented him from participating in it, and I was therefore tasked with advancing this book by myself. Of course, 'by myself' is a very relative term in academia. I have the privilege of counting on a very supportive, stimulating and encouraging intellectual environment where I work, at the Centre for Applied Human Rights (CAHR) and the Department of Politics at the University of York. Therefore, the list of people that I need to thank is truly enormous; alas, because of word-count restrictions, I can only express my most sincere gratitude to only a few people—Paul Gready, Simon Robins, Tecla Namachanja, Eric Dante Gutierrez, Mónica Parada, Maria Carmen (Ica) Fernandez, Sofía Macher, Piergiuseppe Parisi, Emma Murphy and Álvaro Pastor—who had a read of various parts of this draft and provided most valuable feedback based on their expertise on this topic. I am especially indebted to Camilo Tamayo Gómez, who gave me detailed feedback on the whole manuscript and helped me to improve it decisively with his excellent ideas.

York, United Kingdom José A. Gutiérrez

Competing Interests The author has no competing interests to declare that are relevant to the content of this manuscript.

Contents

CHAPTER 1

Transitional Justice: Its Blind Spots, the Transformative Turn and Peasants

Abstract Since the end of the Cold War, transitional justice has become a dominant lens to engage with the complex transitions from conflict or repressive settings into more equitable, democratic and peaceful societies. In its orthodox form, however, transitional justice has been criticised on numerous grounds, including its failure to deal with social and economic issues and to address the structural root causes of conflict, including colonial legacies. These failures reflect a problem of design, based in the strong association between transitional justice and the liberal peacebuilding paradigm and its companion notion of state-building. This association has rendered invisible a wide range of 'transitional' movements from the ground that articulated rights and justice-based visions in terms different to merely electoral democracy and very often in opposition to the liberalisation of markets. The transformative critique of transitional justice and its critiques below have expanded this narrow orthodox vision and have created room for engagement with socio-economic and cultural rights and with more grassroots forms of mobilisation for justice. Despite this, agrarian conflicts and the situation of peasants, in particular, remain a blind spot for most transitional justice processes.

Keywords Transitional justice • Peacebuilding • State-building • Liberal peace • Transformative justice

J. A. Gutiérrez, *Transitional Justice and Agrarian Conflict*,
https://doi.org/10.1007/978-3-032-25228-9_1

Transitional justice has become a dominant, 'normalised', lens to understand the complex processes of transition from conflict settings or repressive governments into more equitable, peaceful and democratic societies (de Greiff, 2020). Transitional Justice origins can be traced to the end of the Cold War and the subsequent hegemony of political and economic (neo)liberalism as the only legitimate social model, with important landmarks in the Latin American democratisation processes, the post-Soviet transitions in Eastern and Central Europe, the international trials of the former Yugoslavia and the experience of post-Apartheid South Africa (Arthur, 2009). It is often described as 'a set of practices, mechanisms and concerns that arise following a period of conflict, civil strife or repression, and that are aimed directly at confronting and dealing with past violations of human rights and humanitarian law' (Roth-Arriaza & Mariezcurrena, 2006, p. 2).

These mechanisms are based on the so-called four pillars of transitional justice: prosecutions, truth-telling, reparations and guarantees of non-repetition (usually understood as institutional reform and/or vetting). These pillars have been consecrated in a number of UN documents that define the orthodox view of transitional justice, together with principles such as compliance with international norms, victim-centricism and fostering community ownership (UN, 2004, 2023). While the view is supposed to be holistic, the transitional justice outlook has tended to privilege prosecutions—with the International Criminal Court (ICC) as a strong centre of gravity—over restorative measures or over reconciliation, which tend to appear as an afterthought drowned under the powerful flow of a normative 'justice cascade' (Olsen et al., 2010; Lambourne, 2014). This emphasis in prosecution is a defect of birth, all too present in the work of Kritz (1995), one of the earliest works to engage with the topic of transitional justice as such.

1.1 Transitional Justice's Blind Spots

Transitional justice (or rather, the transitional justice orthodoxy) has been critiqued on a number of grounds, which include its failure to deal with social and economic issues and to address the structural root causes of conflict, including colonial legacies (Arbour, 2007; Muvingi, 2009; Sharp, 2013; Gready & Robins, 2014; Evans, 2019; Browne, 2023; Sehmi, 2024). Social and economic rights are insufficiently dealt with and most of the time simply ignored by orthodox transitional justice. Although the

UN adopted the 'Pinheiro Principles' on the issue of the rights of refugees to reparations, addressing socio-economic rights and issues (UN, 2005a), just like the UN right to remedy and reparation framework, they do not go beyond the idea of restitution as to 'restore the victim to the original situation before the gross violations of international human rights law or serious violations of international humanitarian law occurred' (UN, 2005b: article 19). Needless to say, very often that situation was far from rosy and idyllic. Despite more recent transitional justice guidelines insisting on the transformative nature of the UN approach to deal with root causes and structures (UN, 2023), those same documents do not go beyond addressing policy change.

In fact, much of this orthodox transitional justice literature and practice has been actually quite blind about important transformative struggles, led from below, that have articulated a language of transformation, transition to a more equitable and inclusive society, and rights, while relying on über-legalistic tools that only inadequately deal with the roots of conflict (Evans, 2019, 2022; Gready & Robins, 2019). Take, for instance, the seminal work of Ruti Teitel (2000), widely regarded as a foundational book in the field of transitional justice. When she discusses some of the basic tenets of transitional justice, she illustrates her points with examples from all over the world, but most notably from Eastern and Central Europe and Latin America. A bit later, she wrote another paper in which she discusses the genealogy of transitional justice, in which she starts (oddly) with the Nuremberg trials in the aftermath of World War II, and then leaps into the 1980s and 1990s with the post-Soviet transitions, the former Yugoslavia tribunals and the democratisation wave in Latin America, which again here is a prominent example (Teitel, 2003). However, the Latin American examples are drawn primarily from the struggle against the military dictatorships of the Southern Cone, and even those are reduced to liberal pro-democracy movements, not engaging with the political complexity within them and the fact that many of these movements were openly left-wing, had overt socialist leanings and articulated notions of social justice that were at odds with liberal orthodoxy (see, for instance, the account of Arthur, 2009).

But leaving aside the one-sided depiction of the anti-dictatorship struggles as liberal crusades, Teitel completely ignored other movements that around the same time she wrote her book were mobilising millions of people in Bolivia and Ecuador against neoliberalism, corruption and structural racism (Lucas, 2001; Olivera, 2008; Paige, 2020). These movements managed to topple neoliberal governments and articulated, in their own terms, the need for a transition to a more equitable model that guaranteed the welfare of the citizens, the respect of social, economic and cultural rights, the rights of indigenous populations and the peasants' access to land; they pioneered issues related to environmental rights, and articulated their view often in an open model called *Sumaj Kawsay* (alternatively *Sumak Kawsay*, often translated as good life from the original Quechua into English), where development was not to be measured in numbers, but in the satisfaction of the citizens (Artaraz et al., 2021). These movements articulated a view of a transition to a different model, and articulated, quite explicitly, their demands in the language of rights: the right to life, the right to water, the right to development, the right to a clean environment and the right to social and economic inclusion. The language of the mass protests in Bolivia and Ecuador was undeniably a language of transition and transformation, but also one of justice, which, needless to say, is often conceptualised very differently by lawyers and by ordinary people.

Why were the cases of Bolivia or Ecuador not considered in Ruti Teitel's book? This is particularly strange since the movements of both countries were arguably much larger and certainly more visible at the time that she was writing her book than any of the other cases she engaged with in Latin America. Quite possibly the answer lies in the fact that she could not see these movements for what they were, and neither could she perceive the transitional promise in these movements, because her book articulates transitional justice as a 'liberal democratic response to the illiberal state' (Teitel, 2000, p. 9), a response that leaves aside many other notions of justice, of potential transitions,[1] of rights and which is blind to the (direct, structural and systemic) violences of liberalism. These movements in Latin America, instead, were not articulated in the language of the liberal peacebuilding paradigm that has dominated transitional justice. As a matter of fact, these movements toppled governments that were not dictatorships,

[1] Let us remember that for nearly a century before the irruption of transitional justice, the problems of 'transition' were mostly discussed in left-wing circles concerned about the challenges in the transit from capitalism to socialism. Today we are talking of other transition that do not necessarily share the liberal market-oriented orthodoxy: to a post-neoliberal society, to a sustainable economic model or a post-fossil fuel, post-carbon society, to a post-colonial world, etc. Note how the word 'post' has become ubiquitous over the last two decades when discussing about alternative, potential futures, indicating a feeble inclination towards over-prescriptive formulas.

but the personification of the liberal values that the prophets of neoliberalism had promised would bring peace to the post-Cold War world: electoral democracy and market-led economy. The promises of peace and stability in places like Ecuador and Bolivia turned into hunger, environmental degradation, precarity, lack of opportunities and the systematic privatisation of every single right that people had fought over for years. The neoliberal wave of the 1990s had a dreadful impact on the lives of millions, many of them in the countryside, who were brought into poverty and came hand in hand with the destruction of the social fabric and the infrastructure to support their economic and social rights (Simmons, 2016). But it also forced these millions to articulate new grievances against these prevalent forms of injustice in societies which were now mostly open and democratic, perfectly liberal, sometimes even more liberal than Europe or the US, at least when it came to electoral politics and markets.

This blind spot derives also from the fact that structural violence is one area in which transitional justice has been particularly weak, precisely because of its liberal bias, despite the fact that armed conflict and human rights violations are often very closely linked to economic inequality, dispossession and the denial of basic social and economic rights (Nagy, 2013; McGill, 2017). The exploration of the root causes of conflict and of the historical dimensions behind dictatorship, authoritarianism and organised violence, predominantly in the form of truth commissions, has opened up a space to understand better the intersection between direct forms of violence with structural ones (Gready, 2011; McGill, 2017). Through these cracks in the edifice of transitional justice, built mostly with materials borrowed from criminal justice and largely focused on prosecutions, some have started to investigate the role that economic and social rights should play in transitional processes that have an eye in long-term peacebuilding and in truly eliminating the root causes of conflict and oppression in order to make the promise of non-repetition a reality (Hecht & Michalowski, 2012). With historical enquiry and peace process like those of Colombia, where the link between war and the mass violation of social economic rights, including land dispossession on a massive scale, the role of economic/business actors has received a renewed attention, opening further space to factor in structural violence and the role of non-direct participants in the conflict, but also the role of the (market) economy as a driver of conflict. With transitional justice still being mostly about prosecution, this has become an ever more important topic to debate in terms of the justice pillar (cf., Michalowski et al., 2018; Wesche, 2019).

1.2 Transitional Justice and Liberal Peace and State-Building

These blind spots are not a coincidence, they are a problem of design. As we will discuss later, the field is far from monolithic and homogenous, but transitional justice orthodoxy is intrinsically linked to the twin concepts of liberal peacebuilding and liberal state-building. The former concept refers to the belief that societies that have a competitive electoral system and a free-market economy are likely to be more peaceful than those who are not. The latter refers to building the institutional framework of a state that facilitates both a free-market economy and competitive electoral politics. These twin concepts—which are a mutually reinforcing paradigm—were first developed with the post–Cold War ideas on peacebuilding (Boutros-Ghali, 1992), in which the big socio-economic problems of the 1970s developmentalist discourses had disappeared into a concern for 'minorities' and 'vulnerable' groups (not classes) and were later developed into the full liberal peacebuilding paradigm. Even when showing a degree of caution about the potentially destabilising effects of sudden liberalisation of politics and markets without solid institutions and proper state-building (e.g., Paris, 2004), this paradigm exposed a blind faith in the long-term pacifying effects of electoral politics and privatised markets:

> privatisation and related commodity governance schemes are meant to bring economic gains for individuals, groups and the state in a fair and neutral way, diminishing the possibility that economic resources will become a source of violent contestation (…)The goal is to ensure that the struggle over resources occurs in the regulated and "peaceful" private sphere and not the complex and self-interested political sphere. (Peterson, 2014, p. 115)

That markets and business actors could be a driver of conflict (cf., Castel-Branco et al., 2001; Wesche, 2019) was anathema or even unthinkable for the most orthodox liberal school of transitional justice. In a way, aligned with the post–Cold War neoliberal optimism, the idea that in post-conflict societies socio-economic rights magically re-establish themselves (Unruh & Abdul-Jalil, 2021), therefore relegating them to the background of peacebuilding, echoes the (neo)liberal utopia that a rising tide will lift all the boats. Thus, peace came to be understood through the same dominant lens of the neoliberal macro-economy.

Of course, these liberal preconceptions about how to have a peaceful society and a functional state have been robustly criticised by those who have argued that the paradigm as such is more linked to the realities of power in post–Cold War society, 'the push for privatisation [being] part of a wider set of goals which will complete and confirm the victory of capitalism' (Peterson, 2014, p. 122). In fact, this premise was particularly promoted in the transitions of post-socialist countries of Eastern Europe after the fall of the Berlin Wall:

> Thus, while often portrayed as a neutral economic policy, privatisation is in fact an inherently political tool through which liberal peace is installed. (…) Privatisation is a key tool in keeping communists, socialists and actors with leftist sympathies out of power and keeping regimes friendly to the developed liberal nations in control of transitioning states. (Ibid., p. 121)

It is therefore linked to the particular agendas of global economic and political elites, rather than genuine humanitarian considerations or solid evidence about the pacifying effects of this approach. Colombia, for example, is a country that is perfectly liberal when it comes to electoral politics and the market economy, and yet, far from peace and stability, the country has suffered from endemic violence. In part, both the competitive electoral system and the liberalisation of markets have contributed to both the widespread societal violence and armed conflict (Richani, 2013; Gutiérrez-Sanín et al., 2007; Thomson, 2011; Voyvodic, 2024). Based largely on the experience of Kosovo, a scholar stated that 'privatisation schemes, whilst failing to transform political economies of violence, (…) have also at times led to new forms of violence in the form of threats and intimidation of individuals and institutions' (Peterson, 2014, p. 125). She goes on to conclude that:

> Privatisation is itself an attempt to depoliticise economic life – the aim being to remove narrow political interests and allow free market forces to guide economic development. It is meant to be apolitical and is largely premised on the assumption that individuals will base their decisions on rational economic considerations. The wealth created by these rational economic choices will supposedly trickle down, leading to broad development based not on political affiliation but on market principles. That such beliefs are valid in relatively peaceful political environments is questionable. In politically unstable situations such beliefs are even more dubious, with empirical evidence challenging these fundamental assumptions. (Ibid., p. 127)

As such, it has been pointed out that very often these policies, which are not neutral but highly political and largely designed to benefit the local and international elites, often create more asymmetries and deepen existing inequalities, exacerbate the marginalisation of the poor, promote dispossession of the subaltern classes, reproduce neo-colonial dynamics and elicit resistance from below (Pugh et al., 2008; Richmond, 2011). All of these effects are to be found among the root causes of many conflicts in the first place, meaning that very often the remedy is as bad as, if not worse than, the disease. Moreover, it has been argued that liberal peacebuilding functions as a myth, a 'discourse [that] overstates the liberalism of contemporary peace interventions, and understates the enduring importance of strategy, states and geopolitics in the making of peace' (Selby, 2013, pp. 58–59). To sum up, liberalism—which is applied in practice both selectively and inconsistently—acts as an ideology (in the Marxian sense of the word) to discursively sugar-coat objectives that are not necessarily liberal-oriented but have more to do with power and the material interests of local and international actors.

That this paradigm has been intrinsically linked to orthodox transitional justice is troubling for the field. In particular, the issue of land—which will be central to the development of the argument of this book—poses particular challenges to an orthodox transitional justice paradigm that seems ill-equipped to deal with structural violence in general, and in particular with colonial legacies (Batisai & Mudimu, 2021), as well as with collective rights over territories or customary land regimes that often these colonial legacies have antagonised and superseded. In the case of Colombia, for instance, it has been acknowledged that ethnic communities' territories should not just be protected from violent dispossession but also from market dynamics that affects them, for despite the system's formal recognition of these communities to their collective territorial rights, the policies that favour extractive industries as a key to national development (and liberal peace) threaten this right in practice (Peña-Huertas et al., 2021).

Despite welcome developments such as initiatives to redress the harm caused to indigenous peoples in Australia and Canada (Nagy, 2012; Balint et al., 2014), transitional justice approaches have been mostly unable to deal with the legacies of colonialism, which cast a long shadow over much of the world with its legacy of structural violence and repression on a number of grounds 'such as the way state power is exercised, ethnic constructs, the arbitrary imposition of land borders, capitalist economic structures, colonial-era land distribution policies, extraction and exploitation of natural resources and slavery arguably form the backbone of numerous conflicts in Africa' (Sehmi, 2024, p. 45. See also Maddison and Shepherd (2014), and elsewhere. What's more, this inability to deal with colonial legacies has been made more evident by the way in which top-down and interventionist approaches replicate neocolonial dynamics, willingly unaware of local sensitivities, priorities or contexts (e.g., Darby, 2009; Sehmi, 2024). As such, cherished institutions of this top-down approach in transitional justice, such as the ICC, have been regarded by disgruntled African leaders and movements as a European court for Africa and as part of a broader network of global interventionist institutions such as the World Bank or the International Monetary Fund (IMF) (McAuliffe & Schwöbel-Patel, 2018), given that the vast majority of cases deal with Africa, while global powers that have arguably far more skeletons in the closet, are simply allowed to get away with illegal occupations and mass atrocities against civilians in other continents.

All of these critiques paved the way, in peacebuilding, to the so-called local turn in peacebuilding, emphasising local agency, bottom-up and participatory approaches and contextualised peacebuilding (Manning, 2003; Pugh et al., 2008; Richmond, 2011, MacGinty & Richmond, 2013). This local turn in peacebuilding had its counterpart in transitional justice in the development of the transformative justice approach.

1.3 The Transformative Turn in Transitional Justice

Partly because of the structural violence blind spot in transitional justice, partly because of the need to factor in gender properly, partly as a reaction against the strict association of transitional justice with a liberal peacebuilding paradigm in crisis and partly because of the need to take seriously social, economic and cultural rights (and now environmental rights too), some have suggested that transitional justice needs to become more 'transformative' by emphasising the needs and priorities of victims and society, and addressing root causes (e.g. Gready & Robins, 2014, 2019; Hoddy & Gready, 2020). Some have also emphasised the role of resistance and mobilisation in contesting orthodox understandings of transitional justice, in favour of more popular articulations of what justice really means (Jones & Bernath, 2017). Earlier, some authors, echoing the local turn in peacebuilding, had advanced a critique to the orthodox top-down approach in transitional justice and called for more local agency and popular participation, calling it transitional justice from below (McEvoy & McGregor, 2008) or from the bottom-up (Lundy & McGovern, 2008). These critiques paved the way for the development of the transformative approach and the notion of transformative justice. Transformative justice can be better understood as the pursuit of 'transformative change that emphasizes local agency and resources, the prioritization of process rather than preconceived outcomes and the challenging of unequal and intersecting power relationships and structures of exclusion at both the local and the global level' (Gready & Robins 2014, p. 340).

This transformative critique has also been associated with the need to explore transformative avenues beyond prosecutions, for, at present, too often transitional justice mechanisms reflect 'the normative priorities of a practice that is grounded in international law and human rights discourse, rather than authentically engaging in meeting the needs of affected populations' (Lambourne, 2014, p. 43). Transformative justice (or the transformative critique of transitional justice) emphasises a bottom-up approach and process as opposed to top-down, legalistic approaches with a preconceived outcome; here the focus is on the need of communities and their right to build a future that fits their own needs and desires. With an emphasis on transforming power relations, challenging them from the local to the global level, transformative justice has contributed to a better understanding of the long-term, structural challenges to peacebuilding and of the importance of the role of social, cultural and economic rights in this process (Gready & Robins, 2020).

For the last decade or so, we have witnessed a veritable explosion of transformative justice critiques to the most narrow and orthodox views on transitional justice (Gready & Robins, 2019; Evans, 2022), to the point that even the above-mentioned UN guidelines (2023) had to emphasise the transformative character of their transitional justice approach. It is not far-fetched to claim that there has been a transformative turn during this time in transitional justice. But while the transformative turn has been very good at diagnoses of the multiple (and too evident) crises of the transitional justice paradigm, it has been slow to be translated into empirical approaches, on the ground, to tackle these issues in practice. However, that the transformative critique of transitional justice has been richer in terms of diagnoses than solutions does not mean that solutions have been absent or have been of no concern to scholars and practitioners engaged in these debates. We have witnessed attempts to operationalise measures in transitional justice that can address structural violence as an important component of the enablers of conflict and as the structures that sustain it (McGill, 2019). More importantly, scholars have identified the areas where the transformative approaches to transitional justice are more likely to have an impact, such as peace processes (Molloy, 2023) or on the issue of reparations, where transformative critiques can go beyond corrective justice to address distributive issues concerning justice (Gready, 2022).

Perhaps one of the most important aspects of the transformative turn in transitional justice is that it allowed to reclaim the very term transition as a site of contestation (cf., Haldemann, 2022) by questioning preconceived goals and by shattering over-normative prescriptions, having thus a more open attitude to people on the ground to lead their own processes of transition. Even before the transformative turn became consolidated among scholars and among an increasing (though still humble) number of practitioners, the question about the nature of transition—a very slippery concept if there ever was one (cf., McAuliffe, 2011)—and the disputes around its real meaning had been raised in the field:

> But what is a 'transition,' and why did it resonate so strongly? The varied instances of political change throughout the world since World War II resist categorization in a neat typology. Many terms might be used: perhaps some countries experienced 'revolutions,' others 'transfers of power,' others 'regime change,' or 'restorations,' or 'independence,' or 'modernization,' or 'political development,' or perhaps 'transitions' of one sort or another. These terms encapsulate changes from capitalism to socialism, military dictatorship to civilian rule, authoritarianism to democracy, communism to liberal democracy, communism to a market economy, and more. The varieties of change are in fact quite staggering (Arthur, 2009, p. 337)

1.4 Why Peasants Matter for Transitional Justice?

While scholars have been busy discussing the potential of transitional and transformative justice to help societies move away from violence, conflict and authoritarian rule into sustainable peace and more equitable social relations, social movements have been busy creating new realities on the ground. It is there where we think that we can find important lessons for the transformative critique of transitional justice, in particular, in the experience of grassroots agrarian movements that have consistently mobilised for change and social justice against dictatorships and prevalent violence (Hoddy, 2021b). Some of these agrarian movements have started, side by side with their mobilisation, to articulate their language, aspirations and visions into a human rights framework, thus creating new sets of rights and new resolutions in international bodies to defend their rights, ways of life or their future (see Chap. 4). The peasant movement, and with them farmers, indigenous groups and rural workers, has been at the forefront of these debates for alternatives and for possible transitions from a present riddled with inequality, repression and violences (direct, structural and systemic).

But although peasants have been at the centre of many of these struggles and have been consistently at the receiving end of much of this violence, with many conflicts having strong agrarian roots (Cramer & Richards, 2011; Villarreal, 2021), transitional justice—to a great extent because of its blind spot for structural violence—is in debt with the peasantry and rural populations. Eric Hoddy argued that although peasants 'have participated in transitional justice mechanisms, and violations against them have been investigated, the peasant status of victims has yet to be fully considered by the field as a major determinant of individual and collective experiences of violence and violations' (2021a, 2021b, pp. 91–92). While peasants and the broader agricultural question have been a blind spot for transitional justice, there are very good reasons why we should, in the field, take seriously peasant rights and agrarian conflict.

> First, direct and indirect non-war violence is pervasive in transition and post-transition settings, where development imperatives, policy decisions past and present, state neglect, and adaptive rural elites have left many violent structures intact. Second, justice interventions may be expected in societies in which there have been largescale protests around agrarian issues, such as in post-uprising Tunisia. Third, conflict and mass violence may be rooted in structures and processes in a rural society and economy. Peaceful rural protest can occasionally turn violent, although peasants are often among the main victims of perpetrators of violence in conflict. And fourth, lingering social and economic issues appear to be playing a key enabling role in the recent rise of authoritarian populism. (Hoddy, 2021a, 2021b, p. 92. See also Gutiérrez et al., 2023)

The intention of this pivot is to bring these discussions into focus through a novel treatment of the rural and agrarian dimensions of conflict and injustice. Its focus is on important questions of agrarian political economy that remain largely unacknowledged and treatment of which can enrichen understandings of post-conflict injustice and the need for new forms of practice for addressing root causes that originated organised violence and repression in the first place. In making these connections, we bring together transitional justice as an interdisciplinary field with a strong legal orientation, with critical agrarian studies and critical development studies, peacebuilding, and peace and conflict studies, thus fulfilling the interdisciplinary promise of the field of transitional justice. This is not merely an academic debate: in particular, ongoing discussions around contemporary peace agreements (like Colombia) that have brought to the fore agrarian issues, the status of peasants and other rural peoples and the environment, make this debate urgent and give it practical importance.

References

Arbour, L. (2007). Economic and social justice for societies in transition. *International Law and Politics, 40*(1), 1–27.

Artaraz, K., Calestani, M., & Trueba, M. (2021). Introduction: Vivir bien/Buen vivir and post-neoliberal development paths in Latin America: Scope, strategies, and the realities of implementation. *Latin American Perspectives, 48*(3), 4–16.

Arthur, P. (2009). How "transitions" reshaped human rights: A conceptual history of transitional justice. *Human Rights Quarterly, 31*(2), 321–367.

Balint, J., Evans, J., & McMillan, N. (2014). Rethinking transitional justice, redressing indigenous harm: A new conceptual approach. *International Journal of Transitional Justice, 8*(2), 194–216.

Batisai, K., & Mudimu, G. (2021). Revisiting the politics of land recovery among white commercial farmers in Zimbabwe: Implications for transitional justice. *International Journal of Transitional Justice, 15*(2), 370–385.

Boutros-Ghali, B. (1992). An agenda for peace: Preventive diplomacy, peacemaking, and peacekeeping. Report of the Secretary-General, UN Doc. A/47/277-S24111, 17 June.

Browne, B. (2023). *Transitional (in)justice and enforcing the peace on Palestine.* Palgrave Macmillan.

Castel-Branco, C., Cramer, C., & Hailu, D. (2001). *'Privatization and economic strategy in Mozambique', WIDER discussion Paper, no. 2001/64.* UNU-WIDER.

Cramer, C., & Richards, P. (2011). Violence and war in agrarian perspective. *Journal of Agrarian Change, 11*(3), 277–297.

Darby, P. (2009). Rolling Back the Frontiers of empire: Practising the postcolonial. *International Peacekeeping, 16*(5), 699–716.

De Greiff, P. (2020). The future of the past: Reflections on the present state and prospects of transitional justice. *International Journal of Transitional Justice, 14*(2), 251–259.

Evans, M. (2019). *Transitional and transformative justice. Critical and international perspectives.* Routledge.

Evans, M. (2022). *Beyond transitional justice: Transformative justice and the state of the field (or non-field).* Routledge.

Gready, P. (2011). *The Era of Transitional Justice.* Routledge.

Gready, P., & Robins, S. (2014). From transitional to transformative justice: A new agenda for practice. *International Journal of Transitional Justice, 8*(3), 339–361.

Gready, P., & Robins, S. (2019). *From transitional to transformative justice.* Cambridge University Press.

Gready, P., & Robins, S. (2020). Transitional justice and theories of change: Towards evaluation as understanding. *International Journal of Transitional Justice, 14*(2), 280–299.

Gready, S. (2022). The case for transformative reparations: In pursuit of structural socio-economic reform in post-conflict societies. *Journal of Intervention and Statebuilding, 16*(2), 182–201.

Gutiérrez, F., Acevedo, T. & Viatela, J. (2007). Violent Liberalism? State, Conflict and Political Regime in Colombia, 1930–2006. Crisis States Research Centre Working Paper No.19. London School of Economics.

Gutiérrez, J., Hoddy, E., McGill, D., del Pilar, R., Peña-Huertas, I. V.-T., & Muriel, D. (2023). *Justicia transformativa y conflicto agrario. Elementos para un debate necesario.* USTA.

Haldemann, F. (2022). *Transitional justice for foxes. Conflict, pluralism and the politics of compromise.* Cambridge University Press.

Hecht, L., & Michalowski, S. (2012). *The economic and social dimensions of transitional justice.* Essex Transitional Justice Network.

Hoddy, E. (2021a). Peasants' rights and agrarian violence in transitional settings: From transitional justice to transformative agrarian justice. *Journal of Human Rights, 20*(1), 91–109.

Hoddy, E. (2021b). Transformative justice in practice: Reflections on the pastoral land commission during Brazil's political transition. *Journal of Human Rights Practice, 13*(2), 339–356.

Hoddy, E., & Gready, P. (2020). From agency to root causes: Addressing structural barriers to transformative justice in transitional and post-conflict settings. *Contemporary Social Science, 15*(5), 561–576.

Jones, B., & Bernath, J. (2017). *Resistance and transitional justice.* Routledge.

Kritz, N. (1995). *Transitional justice: How emerging democracies reckon with former regimes (3 volumes).* United States Institute of Peace Press.

Lambourne, W. (2014). What are the pillars of transitional justice? *The United Nations, civil society and the justice cascade in Burundi', Macquarie Law Journal, 13*, 41–60.

Lucas, K. (2001). *We will not dance on our grandparents' tombs*. LAB.

Lundy, P., & McGovern, M. (2008). Whose justice? Rethinking transitional justice from the bottom up. *Journal of Law and Society, 35*(2), 265–292.

MacGinty, R., & Richmond, O. (2013). The local turn in peace building: A critical agenda for peace. *Third World Quarterly, 34*(5), 763–783.

Maddison, S., & Shepherd, L. (2014). Peacebuilding and the postcolonial politics of transitional justice. *Peacebuilding, 2*(3), 253–269.

Manning, C. (2003). Local level challenges to post-conflict Peacebuilding. *International Peacekeeping, 10*(3), 25–43.

McAuliffe, P. (2011). Transitional justice's expanding empire: Reasserting the value of the paradigmatic transition. *Journal of Conflictology, 2*(2), 32–44.

McAuliffe, P., & Schwöbel-Patel, C. (2018). Disciplinary matchmaking: Critics of international criminal law meet critics of Liberal Peacebuilding. *Journal of International Criminal Justice, 16*(5), 985–1009.

McEvoy, K., & McGregor, L. (2008). *Transitional justice from below. Grassroots activism and the struggle for change*. Bloomsbury.

McGill, D. (2017). Different violence, different justice? Taking structural violence seriously in post conflict and transitional justice processes. *State Crime Journal, 6*(1), 79–101.

McGill, D. (2019). Tackling structural violence through the transformative justice framework. In M. Evans (Ed.), *Transitional and transformative justice, critical and international perspectives* (pp. 36–53). Routledge.

Michalowski, S., Sánchez, N., Marín, D., Jiménez, A., Martínez, H., Domínguez, V., & Arroyave, L. (2018). *Entre coacción y colaboración. Verdad judicial, actores económicos y conflicto armado en Colombia*. Dejusticia.

Molloy, S. (2023). Conceptualising the transformative justice potential of peace processes. *The International Journal of Human Rights, 27*(2), 307–334.

Muvingi, I. (2009). Sitting on powder kegs: Socioeconomic rights in transitional societies. *International Journal of Transitional Justice, 3*(2), 163–182.

Nagy, R. (2012). Centralizing legal pluralism? Traditional justice in transitional settings. In C. Sriram, J. García-Godos, J. Herman, & O. Martin-Ortega (Eds.), *Transitional justice and Peacebuilding on the ground: Victims and ex-combatants* (pp. 81–99). Routledge.

Nagy, R. (2013). The scope and bounds of transitional justice and the Canadian truth and reconciliation commission. *International Journal of Transitional Justice, 7*(1), 52–73.

Olivera, Ó. (2008). *Nosotros Somos la Coordinadora*. Fundación Abril.

Olsen, T., Payne, L., & Reiter, A. (2010). *Transitional justice in balance: Comparing processes, weighing efficacy*. United States Institute of Peace Press.

Paige, J. (2020). *Indigenous revolutions in Ecuador and Bolivia, 1990–2005*. The University of Arizona Press.
Paris, R. (2004). *At war's end: Building peace after civil conflict*. Cambridge University Press.
Peña-Huertas, R., Parada, M., Abril-Bonilla, N., Uribe-Larrota, L., Jiménez-Nicholls, C., & Nieto-Cruz, V. (2021). Collective ownership and land restitution: A new opportunity for afro-Colombian communities. *International Journal of Transitional Justice, 15*(1), 230–241.
Peterson, J. (2014). *Building a peace economy? Liberal Peacebuilding and the development-security industry*. Manchester University Press.
Pugh, M., Cooper, N., & Turner, M. (2008). *Whose peace? Critical perspectives on the political economy of Peacebuilding*. Palgrave Macmillan.
Richmond, O. (2011). *A post-liberal peace*. Routledge.
Richani, N. (2013). *Systems of Violence*. SUNY Press.
Roht-Arriaza, N., & Mariezcurrena, J. (2006). *Transitional justice in the 21st century -beyond truth versus justice*. Cambridge University Press.
Sehmi, A. (2024). Legacies of colonial violence in contemporary transitional justice: Memories of Mau Mau, the "Kapenguria six" and the "Ocampo six" in Kenya. *International Journal of Transitional Justice, 18*(1), 32–48.
Selby, J. (2013). The myth of liberal peace-building. *Conflict, Security & Development, 13*(1), 57–86.
Sharp, D. (2013). Interrogating the peripheries: The preoccupations of fourth generation transitional justice. *Harvard Human Rights Journal, 26*, 149–178.
Simmons, E. (2016). *Meaningful resistance. Market reforms and the roots of social protest in Latin America*. Cambridge University Press.
Teitel, R. (2000). *Transitional justice*. Oxford University Press.
Teitel, R. (2003). Transitional justice genealogy (symposium: Human rights in transition). *Harvard Human Rights Journal, 16*, 69–94.
Thomson, F. (2011). The agrarian question and violence in Colombia: Conflict and development. *Journal of Agrarian Change, 11*(3), 321–356.
UN. (2004). Report of the Secretary-General, 'The rule of law and transitional justice in conflict and post-conflict societies' (S/2004/616).
UN. (2005a). Final report of the Special Rapporteur, Paulo Sérgio Pinheiro, 'Housing and property restitution in the context of the return of refugees and internally displaced persons. Principles on housing and property restitution for refugees and displaced persons' (E/CN.4/Sub.2/2005/17).
UN. (2005b). Basic Principles and Guidelines on the Right to a Remedy and Reparation for Victims of Gross Violations of International Human Rights Law and Serious Violations of International Humanitarian Law (A/RES/60/147).
UN. (2023). Guidance Note of the Secretary General on Transitional Justice: A Strategic Tool for People, Prevention and Peace (OHCHR).

Unruh, J., & Abdul-Jalil, M. (2021). Housing, land and property rights in transitional justice. *International Journal of Transitional Justice, 15*(1), 1–6.
Villarreal, J. (2021). The historical relationship between agrarian reforms and internal armed conflicts: Relevant factors for the Colombian post-conflict scenario. *Land Use Policy, 101*, 105138.
Voyvodic, C. (2024). The fog of war: Development, conflict narratives, and civilian victimisation in Colombia. *Third World Quarterly, 45*(9), 1497–1516.
Wesche, P. (2019). Business actors, paramilitaries and transitional criminal justice in Colombia. *International Journal of Transitional Justice, 13*(3), 478–503.

CHAPTER 2

Peasants, Violence and Transitional Justice

Abstract Peasants are often at the receiving end of most armed conflicts and repressive regimes, and often have been collectively victimised in episodes of mass violence. Agrarian elites have often been active participants in this repression and conflict, shaping states and societies in the process. Yet, agrarian conflict and the specific affectations of the peasantry have been often ignored, and other times their plight not adequately addressed by transitional justice, despite the fact that in many conflicts around the world, some form of agrarian reform, either state-led or market-led, has been promoted in order to build peace. In this scene-setting chapter, I will briefly discuss how rural people have been affected by these legacies of violence and how there is an increasing understanding in the transitional justice field of the importance of understanding these affectations. I will then provide some concrete examples of how transitional justice has engaged with the agrarian question and peasants. It focuses on key relevant cases where truth commission reports have been produced and measures recommended. It considers to what extent such cases attempt to shed light on agrarian dynamics, land and inequality and attempt to address them: Peru, Colombia, Kenya and the Philippines.

Keywords Truth Commissions • Peasants • Agrarian elites • Colombia • Kenya • Peru • The Philippines

J. A. Gutiérrez, *Transitional Justice and Agrarian Conflict*,
https://doi.org/10.1007/978-3-032-25228-9_2

> 'Just what does modernization mean for the peasantry beyond the simple and brutal fact that sooner or later they are its victims?'
> (Moore, 1966, p. 467)

Over the past two centuries, millions of people have migrated from rural areas to urban centres. The scale of this process has been enormous and represents one of the biggest demographic revolutions in human history: while in 1900, a mere 15% of the population was considered to be urban, as we speak, over 50% of the world's population is urban,[1] and in absolute numbers they are more numerous than ever in history (Edelman, 2022). The world's urbanisation, kickstarted by the industrial revolution about two centuries ago, has been one of the defining processes of our age. Over the last decades, this demographic transformation has accelerated, and now (since 2008), for the first time in history, there are more urban dwellers than rural population, the latter being found mostly in the Third World or the Global South (Bernstein, 2010). Yet, despite the many times that the imminent disappearance of the peasantry has been declared by the oracles of social science, the peasantry persists (Edelman, 2000).

This process of mass urbanisation at a global scale has been far from peaceful, and although many would describe this as a logical (and ultimately beneficial) process led by the invisible (and peaceful) hand of the market, the reality is that violence has often been a central feature of this mass rural–urban exodus and of periods of transition (Cramer & Richards, 2011). Violence is not just understood in the physical and direct sense, but also as structural violence as the result of disastrous decision-making by governments and states, which has resulted in massive suffering, pain and death to the rural population of various countries. At the same time that the world's population has become rapidly urbanised, rural inequality and poverty remain acute: three-quarters of the 831 million people living in extreme poverty in the world live in rural areas (World Bank, 2025). Land concentration has exacerbated across the world: it is estimated that 1% of the biggest farms control 70% of the world's arable land, while 84% of the smaller farms, averaging less than two hectares each, control a mere 12% of the world's farmland (IPES-FOOD, 2024). Inequality reflects globally in appalling infrastructure and lack of access to basic services, such as education, sanitation and health, which we find often in rural

[1] Up-to-date information with the numbers can be found in the World Bank data https://data.worldbank.org/. In 2025, there are 3.6 billion people living in rural areas.

settings—reducing the life expectancy of people and increasing child mortality—with children in rural areas accounting for 72% of the deaths of children under five years old in the world (UNICEF, 2024).

Peasants and rural people are largely responsible for feeding the global population: 'While an FAO-led study estimated that small farms feed 35% of the population, civil society organizations have critiqued the definition of small farmers, and the exclusion of artisanal fishers, pastoralists, and urban food producers from the figures. When the limitations are addressed, the figure increases considerably, with peasant food webs estimated to feed at least 70% of the world's population, in terms of food actually consumed, as opposed to total agricultural production' (IPES-Food, 2024, p. 18). But despite the fact that peasants have such an important role in feeding the world, 80% of the people suffering from hunger and malnourishment are to be found in rural areas around the world (Golay, 2022).

Often, segments of the rural population have been subject to various forms of egregious violence, most prominently agricultural workers and the peasantry—the latter a fairly tricky category to conceptualise (Araghi, 1995), having multiple definitions from historical, normative or sociological perspectives (Edelman, 2022). It will suffice here to use an operational definition such as 'small agricultural producers, who, with the help of simple equipment and the labour of their families, produce mostly for their own consumption, direct or indirect, and for the fulfilment of obligations to holders of political and economic power' (Shanin, 1987, p. 3), with 'presumed qualities such as the solidarity, reciprocity and egalitarianism of the village and commitment to the values of a way of life based on household, community, kin and locale' often conflated into the definition (Bernstein, 2010, p. 3; see also Moore, 1966, pp. 475–476, on the issue of solidarity). Within each of these categories, either agricultural workers or peasants, we find an enormous internal differentiation, so we will use the term peasants and other rural people in a very broad sense to account for all of these subaltern sectors that, although affected differentially, still tend to be affected collectively by these processes. Landlords and the rural elites are excluded from this category of people we are concerned with since, as we will discuss later, these sectors are very often the main instigators, perpetrators and beneficiaries of these violent processes.

Yet, agrarian conflict and the specific affectations of the peasantry have often been ignored, and other times their plight not adequately addressed by transitional justice, despite the fact that in many conflicts around the world, some form of agrarian reform, either state-led or market-led, has been promoted in order to build peace (Villarreal, 2021). This is hardly surprising since transitional justice has long been criticised for not factoring in socio-economic and cultural rights, and by an almost exclusive focus on civil and political rights (Arbour, 2007; Muvingi, 2009; Gready & Robins, 2014; Evans, 2019; Boesten & Wilding, 2015). As we will discuss, the violations suffered by peasants and other rural communities, as well as their demands and priorities, often revolve around socio-economic and cultural rights, therefore making them an invisible segment of the population to the more traditional and orthodox approaches of transitional justice. However, this trend has started to change, and the peasantry is starting to become visible to transitional justice, partly because of the critique advanced from some academics and practitioners, but more importantly, because of the push from below from social movements and victims' organisations that have brought these issues to the fore in a number of transitional justice processes, which we will discuss later.

In this scene-setting chapter, I will briefly discuss how peasants and other rural people have been affected by these legacies of violence by providing some concrete examples. It focuses on key relevant cases where Truth Commission reports have been produced and measures recommended. It considers to what extent such cases attempt to shed light on agrarian dynamics, land and inequality and attempts to address them: Peru, Colombia, Kenya and the Philippines.

2.1 Peasants and Violence during Conflict and Repression

Peasants, generally being an impoverished and vulnerable sector of society, have often suffered from—often extreme forms of—violence in most conflicts and during most of the repressive episodes across the world. Wars have regularly been fought in rural settings, and very often, particularly in anti-colonial wars, irregular conflicts and insurgencies, peasants and other rural people have provided the bulk of the fighters but also of the victims in these conflicts (Cramer & Richards, 2011; Villarreal, 2021). This is not a coincidence, but it is intimately linked to the 'ways in which Third World regions were integrated into the global economy as suppliers of raw materials and agricultural goods for the industrial economies of Europe and North America. Adapting to this role required a drastic change in land use and land tenure patters (...) leaving large numbers of peasants devoid of any protections against the ever-present threat of subsistence crisis' (Mason, 2004, pp. 8–9). Land dispossession or land-grabbing and mass displacement have often been mutually reinforcing dynamics in numerous conflicts around the world, with rural populations invariably at the receiving end of it (Grajales, 2011; Edelman et al., 2013; Vargas & Uribe, 2017).

But dispossession does not always take open violent forms. It would be a mistake to believe that land-grabbing only happens at gun point. While the systems of dispossession can be exacerbated by conflict, they often precede conflict (sometimes even by centuries), and they can often operate in parallel or without open physical violence, just resorting through administrative practices and the strong arm of a law that is hopelessly skewed against the peasantry and other subaltern classes (cf. Peña-Huertas et al., 2017). Beyond open armed conflict, force, coercion and repression have often been used against the rural populations to control their labour, through various forms of indentured toil, slavery, *corvée*, while the product of their labour is often appropriated in a similar fashion. These structural and systemic forms of violence, with dispossession and land-grabbing as central elements of it, have been typically worsened during periods of transition from one mode of production into another, such as at the time of the enclosures of the primitive accumulation of capital (Marx, 1999; Bernstein & Byres, 2001), but are a constant in the modern world, and therefore, it is unsurprising that authoritarian and non-authoritarian regimes often resort to violence to subject and to dispossess rural populations (Hilton, 1973; Harvey, 2003; Cramer & Richards, 2011; Thomson, 2011; Hall, 2013; Arango et al., 2025).

Structural and systemic violence always opens the doors to physical forms of violence. Not only peasants have been involved and targeted in conflict situations, but very often the extreme inequality they face, the vulnerability that derives from it, and the large-scale violation of their social and economic rights, while important violations in their own rights, also are at the root of many other forms of violations they face, facilitating physical violence, abuse, displacement, disappearances and even genocide (Verwimp, 2013; Cahill-Ripley, 2014). But far from being passive victims, the peasantry has passively and actively resisted these physical, structural and systemic forms of violence.

While this resistance has been, on a day-to-day basis, predominantly characterised by non-confrontational forms of resistance, such as foot-dragging, sabotage or simply playing dumb (Scott, 1985), on occasions this resistance has manifested in open acts of rebellion in which physical violence has been at the centre of the repertoires utilised by peasants to advance their cause. This has been so the case from the times of slavery, when marronage was a constant threat to the system (Fick, 1990; Tilly, 1987; James, 2001; Cramer & Richards, 2011) to the modern guerrilla movements bent on anti-colonial and liberation struggles that raged from Latin America all the way to Asia, going through Africa, which drew their fighting force predominantly from the peasantry, their basic programmes being largely inspired by rural grievances (Hobsbawm, 1959; Wolf, 1969; Gott, 1973; Davidson, 1981; Kriger, 1991; Wickham-Crowley, 1992). That the bulk of the fighters in these insurgencies is drawn from the peasantry is very telling of the conditions prevalent in most rural settings around the world; but it is also the case that there are, in the peasantry as such, some features and characteristics that make it a likely participant in such acts of rebellion whenever they explode. The peasants' resistance, certainly, has often been underpinned by the tendency towards autonomy, which is typical of most peasants and smallholders across the world (Scott, 2009; Rosset & Pinheiro, 2021), which may be closely linked to the enormous control that peasants have over their labour and their time (Gutiérrez, 2025a). Needless to say, the peasant resistance has, as a rule, been met with vicious and extreme forms of violence from national elites and colonial powers or foreign backers. The devastation and atrocities in rural settings of Vietnam, Korea, Algeria, Angola, Indonesia and Colombia , for example, are well documented.

There was a whole literature on what makes the peasants revolutionary, how this happened and what segments of the peasantry were more prone to revolutionary activity—a discussion that took place from the late 1960 until the 1980s, a period in time that was dominated by guerrillas fighting for agrarian reform and national liberation across those three continents. For Wolf (1969) and Scott (1977), smallholders were more prone to become revolutionary, because of their relative autonomy according to the latter, and because of their material capacity to resist in the case of the former. This argument was also made by McClintock (1984), who adds the crisis of subsistence of smallholders as a decisive element in the revolutionary equation. Paige (1975) introduced a class relational approach to peasant revolutionary mobilisation based on the capacity and structural conditions not just of peasants, but also of the landed elites. Although his conclusions—dismissing the political potential of the peasantry and being over optimistic of the progressive role of the agricultural proletariat—have been critiqued (cf., Skocpol, 1982), his relational approach remains influential.

Migdal (1974), on the other hand, introduced the interactions between the peasantry and other classes (intellectual and disaffected segments of the middle classes or the bourgeoisie) as critical to provide a 'revolutionary' direction to the peasants, a position broadly consistent with most of the Marxist left of the time, who considered that the peasant could not become an agent of revolutionary change without the influence of other classes—either the petty-bourgeoisie or the industrial proletariat (see also Hobsbawm, 1973). This position was fiercely debated by Scott (1977, 2009), who emphasised the autonomous capacity of the peasant struggles. Following Moore's recommendation that 'before looking at the peasantry, it is necessary to look at the whole society' (1966, p. 457), Theda Skocpol (1979, 1982) and others (cf. Jenkins, 1982) advanced more structuralist approaches to understand peasant rebellions: 'Too close a focus on peasants themselves, (…) cannot allow us to understand peasant-based revolutions. A holistic frame of reference is indispensable, one that includes states, class structures, and transnational economic and military relations' (1982, p. 373).

Not only were peasants important in this literature to understand rural conflict, but rural elites were at the centre of this analysis too. Paige (1975) focused on landed elites engaged in the export economy as critical to the development of counter-revolutionary violence; decades later, similarly, Gutiérrez-Sanín and Vargas (2017) focused on the role of cattle-rancher landlords in the development and the promotion and the command of the right-wing paramilitary militias, which brought havoc throughout Colombia and were responsible for massive land-grabbing and forced displacement of mostly peasant populations. In particular, the 'Colombian case shows how the use of violence to achieve certain ends is not confined to repressed, marginalized and poor groups, but is also used by elite classes to maintain and impose a particular development model' (Thomson, 2011, p. 322). The link between political configurations and the agrarian question was explored extensively in an early comparative sociological work written by Barrington Moore, called, quite aptly, *Social Origins of Dictatorship and Democracy: Lord and Peasant in the Making of the Modern World* (1966). There, he argued that depending on the agrarian structure of a country and the predominance of the landed elites vis-à-vis other social forces such as the bourgeoisie or peasants, their respective states would lean more towards a democratic structure or towards authoritarianism. Although much of the conclusions of Moore have been the object of critique and debate (cf., Wiener, 1975), its basic premise that landed elites and agrarian regimes are critical to understand the evolution of societies, regimes and political institutions, being also central to explain later conflict and authoritarian regimes, remains an extremely important contribution, even if the actual ways and mechanisms in which this happens remain contested.

The importance of agrarian structures to understand conflict and authoritarianism was once widely acknowledged by the social sciences. Although there was fierce debate among scholars as to what types of peasant, elites and what mode of agrarian production were more likely to produce conflict or revolutions, all of these schools of thought 'coexisted under a common analytical umbrella: (…) they believed that the proper units of analysis to understand organized violence were classes and states and that agrarian inequality mattered' (Gutiérrez-Sanín, 2015, p. 423). This was the case even with early rational-choice proponents such as Popkin (1979), who, while arguing vigorously against the moral economy perspective of Scott (1976) in relation to peasant mobilisation and contestation, still saw peasantry as a unit of analysis and was concerned with social structures. This was also the case with some later proponents of a rational-choice approach, such as Mason (2004), whose book on how peasants make strategic decisions in relation to rebellion, pondering risks and incentives with the weight of social networks, is an obvious tip of the hat to the work of Samuel Popkin, but also takes peasants as a social category and is concerned with social structures and social processes to understand the rational agency of the peasantry.

However, in the aftermath of the Cold War, a rational-choice and epistemically individualistic literature (which mirrored in academic discourse the neoliberal optimism of the elites) came to dominate the scholarly consensus, and concerns about structural causes, classes and social subjects, and broader social processes were relegated to the background, if not condemned to the dustbin of academic history. Greed became the ultimate explanation of conflict, the appetites of individuals replacing a broader understanding of complex social processes (Collier & Hoeffler, 1998; Collier, 2000), echoing the Thatcherite view that there was no such thing as a society, only individuals. At best, ethnic conflict became as far as you could go, in terms of understanding the social causes behind conflict (Kaldor, 2001). Naturally, peasants and agrarian conflicts became the epistemological victims of this pushback (Buijtenhuijs, 2000).

Despite the pushback and the critique of hardcore rational-choice theory against 'structuralist' views in general, and again this idea that agrarian questions matter in particular, 'by the early 2000s, both the inequality and the rural agenda made a comeback in the study of civil wars. This also occurred hand in hand with new social concerns (climate change, land grab, and state fragility)' (Gutiérrez-Sanín, 2015: 423–424). Even some of the classic so-called criminal conflicts, such as Colombia (the main producer of cocaine in the world), have increasingly come to be understood as a predominantly agrarian conflict, the drug issue reflecting deep-seated patterns of agrarian structural inequality, exclusion and marginalisation (Gutiérrez, 2021). Ultimately, it 'hardly needs to be added that the Latin American "war on drugs" is in effect a war against an agrarian mode of production' (Cramer & Richards, 2011, p. 279).

This comeback was made possible because of the epistemological and methodological shortcomings of the rational and individualist paradigm (Gutiérrez-Sanín, 2015), but most importantly, because a close look at the facts on the ground proved that the paradigm did not hold water. Even the quintessential examples of greedy wars, such as Sierra Leone and Liberia, were proven to have had an important agrarian component at their roots (Munive, 2011; Peters & Richards, 2011). Likewise, the ultimate ethnic conflict of the post–Cold War era, the Rwandan genocide, was also about far more than ethnic politics, with an important dimension provided by rural inequalities, agrarian change and the crisis of rural development against a background of state-sponsored lethal violence against pastoralist Tutsis (Verwimp, 2011, 2013). But as discussed by Gutiérrez-Sanín (2015), this comeback goes hand in hand with new concerns, such as the violence exercised against rural communities through the militarisation of environmental protection in various rural settings across the world (e.g., Ybarra, 2012; Humphreys & Smith, 2014; Lunstrum, 2014; Corredor-García & López, 2024), or new forms of dispossession affecting rural peoples, including the financialisation of land, 'green grabbing' or 'water grabbing' (Edelman et al., 2013).

This renewed emphasis on understanding the agrarian dimensions of conflict and its importance to conflict resolution and peacebuilding (e.g., Unruh, 2010; Thomson, 2011), much of it coming from the Global South, should be welcome by those with an interest in social justice issues and rights in general. Certainly, the agrarian question is something that concerns the bulk of the population and not only peasants or rural people, since it has important implications for urban people as well, as Moore

(1966) reminded us of when exploring the importance of agrarian regimes in the evolution of political regimes and state-building processes. After all, what type of democracy can you build with the current levels of land concentration and with the large-scale dispossession of the livelihoods of millions of people? What type of state can we build when a whole segment of the population is disenfranchised and deprived, in practice, if not legally, of any of the benefits of being a citizen? When one looks at the abyss between the rural and the urban world in most of the globe, one wonders what does the talk of rights, or rules-based order, mean to at least two billion people on our planet.

2.2 Transitional Justice Responses

With an emphasis on civil and political rights, traditional transitional justice has been largely oblivious to the situation of the peasantry and other rural populations and has systematically overlooked the specifics of their situation as a class. When the peasants have been taken into account in transitional justice, it has often been from their condition as individualised victims of torture, disappearance or other violations of their civil and political rights, but not from the perspective of their social, economic and cultural rights and how they relate to the need to change power structures that nurture (physical, systemic and structural) sources of violence. This was the case, for instance, of the Truth Commission of Brazil (Comissão Nacional da Verdade, 2014), which focused exclusively on torture, killings and forced disappearance (Torelly, 2018); despite a working group being created to address violence against peasants and the indigenous, land dispossession was not only not given consideration, but peasants have faced incredible challenges in order to access reparations (Teló et al., 2021). In Timor Leste and South Africa, while there was a recognition in both Truth Commission reports of the massive scale of the violations of social and economic rights, particularly in rural settings (SATRC, 1998; CAVR, 2005), this appears as little more than background information, as contributing factors, or as context for the 'more important' or 'real' violations, and not a primary concern (Cahill-Ripley, 2014). The same author also discusses in a similar light the experiences of Liberia and Sierra Leone). Recently, while talking to transitional justice practitioners in the Gambia, they mentioned there was an important agrarian dimension to the dictatorship of Yahya Jammeh (1996–2017), with rampant land-grabbing, but that this was not even considered in the Truth Commission report, which prioritised civil and political rights.

This is surprising for the reasons already discussed in the previous section, about the levels of violence, marginalisation, exclusion and repression that rural populations have endured as a particular segment of society either in conflict or in authoritarian regimes (as well as in times of 'peace' and 'democracy'), but also because of how critical the agrarian question is for issues related to state-building and social justice, upon which participation, inclusion and equity (all important values for transitional justice goals) depend upon. However, there is a growing tendency to acknowledge the centrality of the agrarian question to peacebuilding, conflict resolution and transitional justice processes. Research has shown that insecure land tenure is rife among peasants globally, and the informality of land tenure also characterises peasant settings and poses formidable challenges to peacebuilding (Unruh, 2010). The transformative critique of transitional justice, without a doubt, has contributed to a growing recognition as well of the importance of social, economic and cultural rights to address issues beyond direct armed conflict or authoritarianism, such as the legacies of colonialism and the structural violence at the root of most wars and dictatorships (Unruh & Abdul-Jalil, 2021). Social and economic grievances, at the same time, are ever more recognised as veritable 'powder kegs' that can blow up attempts at peacebuilding (Muvingi, 2009).

As more and more transitional justice processes around the world have started to look beyond the traditional narrow framework and have started to consider more systematically the impact of structural forms of violence and the violations against socio-economic rights as paramount to deal with past violations and violence (e.g., Sharp, 2014), this has put peasants in the spotlight. We will now discuss four cases (Peru, Colombia, Kenya and the Philippines), where, to various degrees, the agrarian question was at the root of conflict dynamics, and we will discuss how it was factored in (or not) by transitional justice in the multiple mechanisms that were implemented. In some of these cases, there were attempts to engage with this problematic, acknowledging its importance, and even addressing it with concrete proposals. We will devote a larger section of the discussion in this chapter to the Colombian case because this has been—of all the cases—where the most effort was made to address the agrarian dimension of conflict in a transitional justice setting.

2.2.1 *Peru*

Peru suffered throughout the 1980s from a vicious armed conflict, and in the 1990s from the dictatorial regime of Alberto Fujimori. After the fall of Fujimori, and in the context of efforts to foster a democratic transition, the Truth and Reconciliation Commission in Peru (*Comisión de la Verdad y Reconciliación*, CVR) was created as part of the transitional justice mechanisms to support this transition. The CVR worked from 2001 until 2003, covering the period from the launch of the Shining Path (PCP-SL) military campaign in 1980 until the fall of dictator Alberto Fujimori in the year 2000.[2]

During this period, it established nearly 70,000 people had been killed: nearly 80% of the victims were from rural settings, and almost 75% of them were Quechua native speakers, that is, they were indigenous people, and 56% of these victims worked in agriculture (CVR, 2003, vol. 8, p. 316). The vast majority of the victims, 40% of them, were concentrated in the region of Ayacucho, the birthplace of Shining Path and a predominantly peasant region, peasant and indigenous being used as two almost interchangeable categories in Peru (Ibid., p. 315). The main focus of the CVR was to establish the truth around cases of murder and kidnapping, forced disappearance, torture and serious physical harm, although it also focused on the violations of collective rights of indigenous groups. More than 600,000 people had been internally displaced, the vast majority from rural areas, revealing an important agrarian dimension to the conflict, with most violations happening in rural settings. The CVR found out that 'approximately 70% of all internally displaced persons in Peru belonged to peasant communities, native communities, of rural and indigenous origin, ethnic groups that had a special relationship with their lands and territories and that, therefore, saw their way of life radically affected' (CVR, 2003, vol. 6, p. 662).

According to the CVR findings, 'the profile of the victim was somebody who was poor; who lived in rural communities in the poorest and most marginalized departments of the country, located in the Andes or Amazon basin; who was indigenous; and who was illiterate. In sum, it was a picture of the socially and economically excluded' (Guillerot, 2021, p. 12). Poverty is explicitly mentioned as the backdrop [*telón de fondo*] of

[2] The final report of the CVR can be accessed in the following URL: https://www.cverdad.org.pe/ifinal/

violence (CVR, 2003, vol. 8, p. 21). Despite all this evidence, there was no particular focus on the agrarian dynamics of the conflict, but rather, the agrarian context in which these indigenous communities were victimised serves as the background information (as in Cahill-Ripley, 2014), as simply the context that allowed the reproduction and exacerbation of the violence.

But while the rural context is relegated to the background (the mandate of the CVR reflecting the transitional justice priorities of the time), other factors are given more prominence in terms of understanding the differentiated impact of violence. In the CVR report, there are two factors that are considered as having had a differential impact over the violence during these years of conflict: ethnicity and gender (CVR, 2003, vol. 8, Ch. 2). It is these that receive the bulk of the attention—even if terms such as indigenous and peasant in Peru are, to a great degree, and particularly in the Andean regions that concentrated most of the violence, used interchangeably.

The fact that the agrarian dimension was not a mere factor affecting the patterns of violence, but a dynamic at the centre and at the very root of violence itself largely escapes the report. Instead, the report relies on the decision of Shining Path to conduct armed struggle as the ultimate explanation of the armed conflict, although it clearly gives evidence of the appalling conditions of life in most rural communities throughout the country. The Shining Path rebellion is treated, by and large, as an exogenous factor to the peasant and indigenous communities, whereas the full picture was far more complex than that, as will be discussed later. Some authors criticise this as part of a broader narrative constructing an innocent (apolitical) victim, an 'ideological representation of an "ignorant Indian" who does not know about ideologies and who is, therefore, "tricked" by people who do not belong to his world' (Rodríguez, 2010, p. 42). Moreover, the CVR did not considered the extensive violations of social and economic rights as violations in their own right, but again, same as the agrarian context, as the background information which allowed the multiplying effect over the real violations—murders, torture, disappearances, etc. As such, although the report recognises the existence of these deep structural inequalities, it does little to address them in practical terms.

This was reflected in the recommendations of the CVR, which, in spite of very clearly deploring rural poverty and the dismal conditions in which the peasantry and the indigenous lived, left the structural causes of rural poverty and exclusion (including the issue of land) out of the picture when it came to practical recommendations. All of the recommendations were included under four axes: institutional reform and strengthening the rule of law; comprehensive reparations; dealing with the disappeared and the mass graves; and a follow-up mechanism for the recommendations (CVR, 2003, vol. 9). In these recommendations, the issue of land is all but absent other than as background information, save for a vague reference to the need of protecting indigenous communities' lands, without any concrete mechanisms to back this recommendation (Ibid., p. 118). The axis of comprehensive reparations mentions land-grabbing or land loss as a by-product of the conflict and not as a specific dynamic of organised violence, circumscribing its general recommendations to limited land restitution and productive projects, without factoring in the scale of the problem or giving any concrete recommendations as to how this was to proceed (Ibid., p. 198), in stark contrast with the more detailed recommendations on other axes.

The reparation policies that derived from the findings of the CVR have, unsurprisingly, reproduced this agrarian blind spot. In 2005, the Peruvian Parliament approved Law 28,592 of 2005, which created the Normative Framework of the Comprehensive Reparations Plan (*Marco Normativo del Plan Integral de Reparaciones*), to be based on the recommendations of the CVR and to be implemented through the work of the already created High-Level Multisectorial Commission in Charge of the State's Actions and Policies Related to Peace, Collective Reparation and National Reconciliation (*Comisión Multisectorial de Alto Nivel encargada de las Acciones y Políticas del Estado en los Ámbitos de la Paz, la Reparación Colectiva y la Reconciliación Nacional*). At the same time, the Reparations Council (*Consejo de Reparaciones*) was creating a Unified Victims' Registry (*Registro Único de Víctimas*). The comprehensive reparations plan consisted of six programmes, namely a citizens' rights restitution programme, a reparations programme in education, health reparations, collective reparations, symbolic reparations and a programme to promote and facilitate access to housing. The reparations' comprehensive process has been marred by budget constraints, lack of coordination between administrative bodies, bureaucratic issues and so on (Guillerot, 2019; Macher, 2023). According to the ex CVR commissioner Sofía Macher, by 2007, 'only 17%' of the recommendations had had 'satisfactory progress (…) been made and most of the actions carried out refer to the issue of reparations. (…) Of course, there have also been compliances that are only on paper and that have not been translated into practice' (cited in Guillerot,

2021, p. 21). Whatever change has happened since, it has been more the result of bottom-up pressure rather than compliance with the CVR recommendations.

But, as we can see, there is no specific focus on agrarian issues or on the land question, even if the reparations process had gone smoothly. The most relevant form of reparations from the perspective of the peasantry and rural communities was collective forms of reparations, which were mostly limited to productive projects and community infrastructure, with land and all other structural causes of the conflict left untouched. As of 2021, 72% of the collective reparations had been implemented, being one of the areas that is more advanced; in contrast, only 7% of the reparations through education programmes had been implemented (Macher, 2023).

To summarise, we have the paradox of a CVR that exposed 'that the causes of the conflict originated in exclusive social, political and economic structures that must be reversed. (…) However, if the Commission's Final Report was indeed taken into consideration, the country should not continue to be administered as it has been so far. In still having a weak inclusive republic, the social, corruption and political crisis indicate that the past is not far from the surface' (Guillerot, 2019, p. 54). The recent political crisis of 2022 and the subsequent repression that left numerous protesters dead shows that the legacies of authoritarianism and conflict are still, unfortunately, alive and kicking in Peru with its firm oligarchic rule and the widespread institutional violence against most forms of protest (Merino, 2023).

2.2.2 *Colombia*

Colombia suffers from chronic organised violence in one of the most complex and longest ongoing conflicts in the whole world. The main armed actors in this conflict are government forces, guerrillas, right-wing paramilitaries and now also hybrid groups that combine a predominantly criminal objective with grievances and political stances (Leech, 2011; Gutiérrez-Sanín, 2020; Gutiérrez, 2025b). Although Colombia as a country is largely urban, it has a significant rural population. While figures are difficult to obtain because of the challenges of conducting surveys in a country at conflict, in 2011 it was determined that at least 32% of the population was rural (PNUD, 2011). More recent statistics show that out of this rural population, 26% identifies as peasants (DANE, 2024). While a minority, it is a very significant minority if put in the context of global and regional figures. More importantly for the purposes of this book, it is the countryside where the bulk of the armed confrontation is taking place. As such, it is very fitting that Colombia is the case where transitional justice has done some of the most interesting developments to address the specific grievances and harm done to peasants.

2.2.2.1 *Justice and Peace Law (2005)*

The first transitional justice mechanism that had a rather humble impact on the agrarian question to be applied in Colombia was Law 975 of 2005, better known as the Justice and Peace Law (*Ley de Justicia y Paz*). The main goal of this law was not so much reparation, let alone transformation, but to allow the demobilisation of around 30,000 right-wing paramilitaries of the United Self-Defences of Colombia (*Autodefensas Unidas de Colombia*, AUC). After many changes to the original project, the (rather lenient) punitive component became central, which included incentives for telling the truth about the victims and the conflict. This element of truth-telling, allowed for the recording of testimonies, which became the backbone for a titanic task of reconstruction of the reality of the armed conflict and historical memory in later years (Riaño & Uribe, 2016). In particular, this law started a process in which the millions of people who have been victimised in the course of the conflict became undeniable. Not only that, but also even though participation was minimal, it was significant and started a process of victims' direct participations in transitional justice mechanisms, which became very prominent in future processes. In terms of reparations, although it marginally recognised collective reparations, this law emphasised individual reparations, which remains a daunting and altogether impossible task in a country where there were 10.1 million victims officially registered in 2025.[3] In general, the results of the reparations under this process, despite introducing the concept of comprehensive reparations, were disappointing, particularly in cases of land dispossession (Linares, 2021; Ruiz, 2023). After a decade, only 0.1% of the land requested by victims had been restored. But also justice was only piecemeal and many of the demobilised combatants would eventually remobilise in new formations (Daly, 2016), which will be very significant when discussing the next transitional justice landmark in Colombia. In any case, the biggest achievement of this law, from the

[3] According to official records of the Unified Victims' Registry (RUV). See https://www.unidadvictimas.gov.co/registro-unico-de-victimas-ruv/

perspective of the agrarian question, was to place the issue of land dispossession in Colombia at the top of the national agenda.

2.2.2.2 Law of Victims and Land Restitution (2011)

It is therefore unsurprising that, after much mobilisation and given the interest of the government in cleansing the image of Colombia to allow a number of Free Trade Agreements (including with the US and the EU), the Law 1448 of 2011, was enacted (Martínez, 2013). Simply known as Law of Victims and Land Restitution (*Ley de Víctimas y Restitución de Tierras*), it was the first time that the scale of the agrarian question in the country was acknowledged together with the fact that the peasantry, as such, had been affected, and not just a few peasant individuals. The law, despite its name, tried to do more than simple restitution and was aiming at comprehensive reparations, which included services, housing and productive projects to support the livelihoods of the victims, together with symbolic measures. It also used an explicitly transformative language, despite being mostly about restitution. This law also recognised the collective nature of some victimising acts and therefore the need to provide collective forms of reparations, together with a recognition of the differential impacts of the conflict on women ethnic minorities, age groups, etc. The restitution component of the Law was to benefit only people who had suffered from displacement or dispossession since 1991 (Martínez, 2013; Linares, 2021).

The law, foreseeing the difficulty of coordinating the various state structures that would be required to collaborate in this effort, created National System of Attention and Comprehensive Reparation for Victims (*Sistema Nacional de Atención y Reparación Integral a las Víctimas*, SNARIV), with the explicit goal of coordinating the efforts of the various public entities in charge of the attention and the reparation of victims. This system included administrative units created by the law for the purpose of providing reparation to the victims, such as the Administrative Unit for the Comprehensive Care and Reparation of Victims (*Unidad para la Atención y Reparación Integral a las Víctimas*, UARIV, often referred to as Victims' Unit, o *Unidad de Víctimas*) in charge of delivering the assistance and reparations to victims, and the Land Restitution Unit (*Unidad para la Restitución de Tierras*, URT), looking after the specific dimension of land restitution. The UARIV also created the Unified Victims' Registry (*Registro Único de Víctimas*, RUV), a tool to keep a single record of everybody who had been victimised in the context of the armed conflict (Linares, 2021). Another institution created as a result of the law is the National Centre for Historical Memory (*Centro Nacional de Memoria Histórica*, CNMH), which, despite being a state-sponsored historical memory centre, has managed to work side by side with social movements documenting various aspects of their struggles, the realities of the conflict and the ways in which different groups and regions have been victimised and affected by the violence. To this purpose, it has acted as an archive of the data provided by the social movements and victims' organisations, and it has also published various accessible volumes, together with pedagogic tools, to keep the memory of the conflict alive. Among this work, they have conducted an enormous amount of research on how rural populations, and peasants in particular, have been impacted by the conflict, and they have documented extensively the struggles over land and land dispossession in various regions of Colombia (García, 2022; Ríos, 2023).

Under this law, almost 7.5 million people registered in a few years as victims (Pfeiffer, 2015), the vast majority of them as victims of forced displacement, and the vast majority were peasants or people from rural regions. According to official statistics of the RUV, in 2025, there were well over 10 million people registered as victims, which is a staggering 20% of the population. The task was daunting, yet the hopes were high. The results of the land restitution process were underwhelming, nonetheless. Of the 8.3 million hectares of land that had been dispossessed up until that point in time (CNMH, 2013), only 665,000 hectares have been restituted to victims. This is 10% of the original aim of 6.5 million hectares. At the current pace, it will take 109 years to achieve this target (Fundación Paz y Reconciliación, 2024). Most importantly, even if all the land that was meant for restitution was granted, we would still only be back to the situation of 1991, which was far from ideal. This dismal performance has been to a great degree because of the cumbersome judicial processes, with the legal cases being very complex because of the lack of original formal titles and the widespread informality of land tenure in rural Colombia, despite the flexibility of the rules of evidence and the inversion of the burden of proof introduced in restitution cases away from the victims of dispossession (Ruiz et al., 2021). Since these processes have dragged on for many years (well over a decade in most cases), some of the original victims requesting land restitution (often referred to as *reclamantes*) have died and new people have complicated the equation -including different children of dispossessed people and people who moved into the land after the original dispossession, many of them themselves in a situation of vulnerability.

On top of this, the sheer scale of the problem and the enormous number of cases (the law aimed at solving over 360,000 cases) create a real capacity problem for an overstretched judicial system (Restrepo & Bernal, 2014). There are also perennial problems of ineffective or lack of coordination between administrative units and state agencies, and an overcomplicated bureaucracy to deal with the victims, exacerbated by underfunding, lack of capacity and the different priorities between agencies and units when there is a clash between restitution and extractive interests in a particular region (Linares, 2021). Finally, as we will discuss next, the persistence of the conflict and growing insecurity in the territories where land is supposed to be restituted make the scenario very difficult for any meaningful implementation.

In a sinister twist, a law designed to address the grievances of victims has ended up contributing to the creation of new victims and to the re-victimisation of victims. The law created a perverse situation in which the participation of victims in the design and restitution processes made them gain visibility and therefore, turned the leadership into targets for those opposing land restitution. Between 2011 and March 2015, there were 49 homicides and 367 threats against *reclamantes*, but also against human rights defenders and civil servants engaged in land restitution (CINEP, 2015). This trend persists to this day, and the figures are truly alarming: for the last 20 years, the average of rural community leaders assassinated per year is 68, and it is estimated that between 2015 and 2020, at least 15 *reclamante* leaders were assassinated, and these figures do not count others associated with land restitution processes (Gutiérrez-Sanín, 2025). In 2023 alone, 9 *reclamantes* were assassinated (Arango & Cote, 2023). The culprits behind these crimes tend to be the so-called anti-land restitution militias, formed by recycled former right-wing paramilitaries who remobilised after the Justice and Peace Law (Daly, 2016; Gutiérrez-Sanín et al., 2020), being this a problem inherited from the previous transitional justice process. The government did not factor in the enormous opposition land restitution would face from powerful local and national elites, and there were no effective security guarantees provided to those who participated actively in the process, attracting unwanted attention from the 'anti-land restitution militias', resulting in further re-victimisation (Gutiérrez-Sanín et al., 2020). As a result, many victims have become fearful of reclaiming land restitution and of participating in this process.

2.2.2.3 2016 Peace Agreement

Maybe the most important effect of the Victims and Land Restitution Law was to have created a political space for the negotiations between the Revolutionary Armed Forces of Colombia, People's Army (*Fuerzas Armadas Revolucionarias de Colombia, Ejército del Pueblo*, FARC-EP) and the Government of Colombia. The FARC-EP had been for decades fighting for agrarian reform, and the backbone of this group had been traditionally the Colombian peasantry. They had denounced the massive scale of land dispossession in Colombia for decades. As such, the recognition granted to the agrarian problem and to land-grabbing by this law sent a signal to the rebel leadership that some of their agrarian concerns and historical grievances could be addressed through a peace negotiation. Indeed, the agenda of the peace negotiations, which lasted from 2012 until 2016, gave a very prominent position to the agrarian question, turning it into the first issue to be negotiated.

The Final Agreement to End the Armed Conflict and Build a Stable and Lasting Peace (*Acuerdo Final para la Terminación del Conflicto y la Construcción de una Paz Estable y Duradera*) was signed in 2016.[4] Of the many issues that were dealt with in the agreement, the first item was the agrarian question, which was labelled in very grandiloquent terms Comprehensive Rural Reform (*Reforma Rural Integral*). Despite the transformative undertones, the agreement carefully avoided references to an agrarian reform,[5] limiting its provisions to land titling and formalisation, land restitution, the creation of Peasant Reserves Zones (*Zonas de Reserva Campesina, ZRC*)[6] in predominantly smallholding regions, the creation of an agrarian jurisdiction to deal with land issues, an agrarian cadastre for statistical records and developmental measures towards the countryside. The only attempt to do some very limited redistribution was through the creation of a Land Fund (*Fondo de Tierras*) that was aimed at redistributing merely three million hectares to the peasants (which was hardly going to change the patterns of rural inequality), but the fund

[4] The full text of the agreement can be consulted here: https://www.jep.gov.co/Normativa/Paginas/Acuerdo-Final.aspx

[5] Despite this explicit avoidance to use the terminology of agrarian reform, preferring to use that of rural reform or rural development, some scholars still refer to it as such (e.g., Villarreal, 2021).

[6] These are areas to protect and promote the peasant economies, recognised in the Constitution already, and not a creation of the peace agreement, which was only going to boost a legal tool already there. On the ZRC, see Gutiérrez (2016).

found, like almost every other initiative in the agreement, countless problems of implementation. Five years after the creation of the fund, it counted around 1.3 million hectares of land (or around 30% of the original target), obtained through legal proceedings and purchase, but many of the land, for various administrative reasons, simply could not be redistributed; as a result, only 25% of what was in the fund had been redistributed, and of this only a small fraction (around 12,500 hectares) went to the peasantry, the vast majority given to indigenous communities (around 463,000 hectares) and a further 10,000 hectares given to Afro-Colombians (Gutiérrez-Sanín & Parada, 2022).

All of these measures were designed to factor in the differential impact of the conflict over diverse subjects and regions -the premise was to give priority to those regions most affected by the armed conflict. This emphasis was articulated in the Development Programmes with a Territorial Approach (*Programas de Desarrollo con Enfoque Territorial*, PDET), a programme for the rural populations in these conflict-affected areas to get involved in the development of their own territories (Kaplan, 2025; Pinkeviciute, 2025). They were designed to benefit 24% of the rural population, and participation was massive, with over 200,000 people participating in the development of these projects.[7] Almost a decade after, having spent over USD 6.8 billion in nearly 7000 projects, the results have been perceived as insufficient to address the enormous structural inequalities, being also poorly executed, as well as plagued by administrative corruption and deficient institutional capacity (Bonilla, 2025). What is more, the budgets remain directed from the centre, and although communities came with alternative development plans, in practice, these were secondary to the national development plan of the governments, which often privileged an extractive approach at odds with the aspirations of communities (Pinkeviciute, 2025).

The fourth item on the agreement was the issue of illicit drugs, a problem that is closely linked to the land poverty of Colombian peasants and the lack of viable alternatives. This item was going to be linked with the first item (comprehensive rural reform), and it would give support to smallholder families to transition from illicit crops to legal alternatives in a grand programme of substitution. Alas, here again, the implementation problems were massive. While the cultivators overwhelmingly fulfilled their part of the agreement, complying with a 98% of their eradication

[7] See https://centralpdet.renovacionterritorio.gov.co/conoce-los-pdet/

commitments (UNODC, 2020, p. 9), for months many families were left without the economic supports that had been agreed to balance their income loss. Only 34% of the families registered had received the payments the government had committed within 3 years of the 2016 agreement, which were originally promised in full by 2017 (Gutiérrez-Sanín et al., 2019). In the end, many families did not receive any payments at all (Gutiérrez-Sanín et al., 2019; Rubiano et al., 2022), and towards 2020, merely 6.7% of the families registered in the programme had some form of productive projects to support their transition to legal crops (UNODC 2020).

On top of this, the substitution programme, known as Comprehensive National Programme for the Substitution of Illicit Crops (*Programa Nacional Integral de Sustitución de Cultivos de Uso Ilícito*, PNIS), suffered from underfunding -for instance, while in 2020 the programme required COP 2.3 billion to function, it only received COP 1.4 billion (Soto, 2020)-, lack of institutional capacity (Gutiérrez-Sanín et al. 2019), and the above mentioned lack of progress of the first item of the agreement, which contributed to making it a complete failure. More worryingly, in an already familiar pattern, the massive participation in the PDETs and the PNIS, exposed community leaders who were later targeted, with 1770 of them murdered since 2016 (González, 2025).

In the context of the peace agreement, the Comprehensive System for Truth, Justice, Reparation and Non-Repetition (*Sistema Integral de Verdad, Justicia, Reparación y No Repetición*, SIVJRNR) was created as a comprehensive system to coordinate the judicial and extrajudicial mechanisms to address issues related to the victims, truth and non-repetition. This system includes the Special Jurisdiction for Peace (*Jurisdicción Especial para la Paz*, JEP), the Commission for the Clarification of Truth, Coexistence and Non-Repetition (*Comisión para el Esclarecimiento de la Verdad, la Convivencia y la No Repetición*, CEV), and the Search Unit for People Disappeared in the Context of the Armed Conflict (*Unidad de Búsqueda de Personas dadas por Desaparecidas en el Contexto y en Razón del Conflicto Armado*, UBPD). The JEP delivers restorative justice measures, which include reparations in many cases, but, as in the case of most courts, it does not address the structural violence behind many of the violations they prosecute. What's more, the JEP has not identified land issues as the major focus of their prosecution activities, although it has recognised ethnic territories as victims of the conflict, which is an important recognition for indigenous and ethnic groups (Huneeus & Rueda, 2021). But the land question as such remains largely absent of its debates; in fact, none of their macro-cases deals specifically with this issue, and it was only in late 2023 that there was an agreement between the JEP and the URT to exchange information in relation to land-grabbing (JEP, 2023). In any case, business actors, elites and entrepreneurs who sponsored the conflict and profited from it cannot be summoned by the JEP and can testify only on a voluntary basis (Wesche, 2019), which means that in practice they are granted impunity despite their promotion and complicity with egregious abuses. Of all the SIVJRNR mechanisms, it is the CEV that has produced some of the most remarkable insights into the agrarian question in this transitional justice process, alas, with no teeth to implement any of their recommendations.

The Truth Commission, or the CEV, produced a report that tackled some of the core socio-economic problems that underpinned armed conflict in Colombia and stated, in unequivocal terms, the need for deep, structural transformation in order to achieve sustainable peace: 'if profound changes are not made to the country's economic development model, it will be impossible to achieve the non-repetition of the armed conflict, which will be repeated and will evolve in unpredictable ways' (CEV, 2022, p. 34). In this sense, the CEV went beyond the peace agreement, who, despite transformative language, explicitly avoided to touch upon structural changes. After many sessions, which counted on the participation of hundreds of peasants, the CEV, once again, stated the centrality of the agrarian question to the armed conflict and how the peasantry, together with other rural populations, has been the main victimised group in the course of almost seven decades of conflict. It is, according to the CEV report, 'an irrefutable truth', that:

> the Colombian peasantry was the main victim of the internal armed conflict. During the war, peasant farmers were forced off their land, tortured, murdered, kidnapped, extorted, forcibly recruited, made invisible, sexually abused, marginalized, and criminalized. (…) The progress of the peasant farmer struggle for agrarian reform in the 20th century was reversed in a violent agrarian counter-reform at the beginning of the 21st century. The peasantry was persecuted, marginalized, and stigmatized. (CEV, 2022, pp. 28–29)

One remarkable feature of the CEV report is that it does not treat the peasantry merely as victims, but as actors who resisted and fought to shape their own future, giving recognition to the mobilisation of agrarian social movements and to their decades-long struggle:

> Those who did not leave resisted the terror and sieges. (…) Others created «peace communities» or began processes of collective resistance that gave rise to the peasant farmer reserve areas. Many of them persevered by themselves, even when the neighboring farms were left alone: 'We are not going to leave because the only thing we have is a piece of land and we can't take it on our shoulders'. (CEV, 2022, pp. 27–28)

After the diagnosis of the importance of the agrarian question to understand the conflict and after a full recognition of the scale of victimisation of the peasantry, together with the importance of their resistance in order to build a sustainable future, the CEV report goes on to recommend:

> to give peasants farmers the undivided recognition they have for the life of Colombia, to assure them the equal redistribution of land, the prevention and reversal of dispossession, the multimodal cadastral system, the conditions for sustainable production, access to public goods and services - including high quality education relevant to rural areas, security, and justice - and the conditions they need for the care of ecosystems, water, land, and native species. (CEV: 52)

While the Truth Commission gave an important account of the agrarian nature of the conflict and highlighted the need for transformative measures that address the deep-seated land inequality in the country and the generalised marginalisation of the rural populations, in practical terms, it has had limited impact on the political discussion on agrarian reform or on a new land policy, and its impact has been non-existent in the current land restitution policy derived from the transitional justice mechanisms in place. It remains, however, a powerful account of the history of dispossession and land concentration, and the resistance it has elicited among the peasantry and other rural people.

By analysing these transitional justice processes and the, at best, meagre practical results, of both the Law of Victims and Land Restitution and the provisions contained in the 2016 Peace Agreement, one can argue that their crafting 'was more focused on innovation and meeting high standards in terms of guaranteeing the rights of victims than on analyzing what was effectively achievable with a long term and progressive vision' (Linares, 2021, p. 49). Notwithstanding the fact that the experience of transitional justice in Colombia has acknowledged the agrarian dimension of the conflict and the urgency of addressing the pressing rural question, and despite important participation and mobilisation of the peasantry around many of the transitional justice processes, the transformative language and the ambitious goals have not been reflected in practical results:

> the transitional justice processes have not done all that they could have to address and promote the structural social changes that are necessary to resolve the underlying violent dynamics, especially in matters of inequity and discrimination, leaving the door open for future violence. Little progress has been made in addressing economic, social, cultural, and environmental rights violations. Gender and ethnic discrimination have been afforded insufficient attention, in some cases even being reinforced when ethnic groups are completely ignored or when they are taken into account but through a colonialist lens. Where progress has been made in areas such as land restitution and participation, it has been limited by a lack of coordination between the national and local levels, a dearth of political will, and an ensuing failure of implementation, which, given the expectations that were generated around the justice processes, has undermined the trust of victims and of society more generally. (Linares, 2021, p. 4)

2.2.3 Kenya

In the aftermath of the serious political disturbances and widespread violence that took place across Kenya in the context of the 2007 elections—which left 600,000 people displaced and thousands of dead and victims of sexual violence (Ndungú, 2014)—both the government and the opposition reached a power-sharing agreement which led to the creation of the *Truth, Justice and Reconciliation Commission* (TJRC) which was set up to address the multiple violations that took place since Kenya's 1963 independence from the United Kingdom. It is remarkable that despite the fact that the TJRC was responding to the most recent crisis in Kenyan politics, the TJRC took a *long durée* approach to address the underlying issues that led to the recent escalation of violence, revealing a plethora of underlying grievances and generalised malaise (Slye, 2018). The TRJC took off in a difficult context in which transitional justice had come under fire when, in 2010, the prosecutor of the ICC, Luis Moreno Ocampo, indicted six Kenyan political figures for crimes against humanity in relation to the 2007 violence. This led to widespread denunciations in Kenya against the 'anti-African', 'neo-colonial', 'Western' and 'racist' biases of the ICC, indicating the dangers of transitional justice from above processes, and an exclusive emphasis in prosecutions (Sehmi, 2024). The commission itself was also surrounded by controversy from early on, since the appointed chairperson of the TJRC, Bethuel Kiplagat, was accused of having been involved in massacres and land-grabbing (of all things), which led to his resignation in 2010 until being reinstated in 2012 (Ndungú, 2014).[8] This, without a doubt, had an impact on the credibility of the TRJC and, more generally, of transitional justice as such.

While the TJRC's Final Report,[9] published in 2013, emphasised mostly gross violations to civil and political rights, including mass displacement, sexual violence, torture, massacres and assassinations, there was an important component on the violation of socio-economic rights, economic marginalisation, and corruption. Crucially, there was a whole chapter devoted to the land question that highlighted the agrarian dimension of the political violence and authoritarian rule in Kenya. As a matter of fact, the report recognises that 'historical grievances over land constitute the single most important driver of conflicts and ethnic tension in Kenya' (TJRC, 2013, 1: vii). This chapter devoted to land (Chap. 2, Volume 2B), in particular, was subject to much controversy as there was allegedly enormous political pressure from the executive and political elites in order to have parts of this chapter altered for the final version, as discussed in the 'Statement of Dissent' by three of the TJRC commissioners[10] (see also Ndungú, 2014; Slye 2017, 2018).

The chapter recognises the centrality of land for the reproduction of entire communities and as a main means of subsistence for a significant segment of the Kenyan population—as such, it recognises the role played by tensions over land in the ignition of unrest and violence. While the report is mostly concerned with the post-independence period from 1963 to the present, there is a recognition that land dispossession is a phenomenon that took place in large scale from colonial times. However, after independence, resettlement and compensation programmes reproduced these inequalities along ethnic lines, while the problem was exacerbated by the informality of property relations in the countryside. Volume 2C also

[8] See the statement of former commissioners calling for his resignation: https://digitalcommons.law.seattleu.edu/cgi/viewcontent.cgi?article=1019&context=tjrc-kiplagat

[9] The Full Report of the TJRC can be found at a website provided by the School of Law of the Seattle University, https://digitalcommons.law.seattleu.edu/tjrc/

[10] The Statement of Dissent is available here: https://digitalcommons.law.seattleu.edu/cgi/viewcontent.cgi?article=1007&context=tjrc-core (last accessed 04/11/2025).

recognises the link between land and the violations and attacks on women, by stating that the vulnerable position of women derives to a large degree from the fact that

> cultural norms and gendered practices have made women's access to land tenuous. Women own approximately one to five per cent of registered and tilted land. Registration of land acquisition of titles has predominantly been a male preserve thereby increasing women's dependency on men. Furthermore women's exclusion from registration of land titles has also curtailed their rights to resources found on land. Moreover, although statistics shows that women in Africa are responsible for an estimated 70% of total food production throughout the continent, such farming lands are not owned by them. Indeed, more often than not, proceeds flowing from the sale of farm products belong to men. (TJRC, 2013, 2C, p. 48)

While the agrarian question is mostly reduced to the land question throughout most of the TJRC report—this being, without a doubt, the most conspicuous manifestation of this problem—the final document cannot be faulted with ignoring other social and cultural dimensions of the agrarian question. Particularly in volume 2C, where the violations against indigenous groups and pastoralist communities, the report states that:

> To minorities and indigenous groups, land is more than a factor of production. Rather, land is a living space within which a complex range of social-cultural and spiritual relationships subsist and are negotiated. Consequently, displacement from such land causes not merely material deprivation, but may result in the physical destruction of the group. (TJRC, 2013, 2C, p. 248)

Finally, volume 3 also addresses the link between ethnic tensions and land-grabbing. In particular, this link between land and ethnic tensions around election time can lead to widespread violence that is often characterised as ethnic, but which has deep socio-economic roots.

In terms of the recommendations (Volume 4, pp. 54–56), most of the implementation of these was left to the newly created National Land Commission (created the previous year, 2012, with powers to initiate investigations and recommend redress) and the Ministry of Lands. These recommendations included further investigation into land-grabbing, dispossession and irregular/illegal acquisition of land; the implementation of a survey to demarcate and register public land; adjudication and formalisation of land; the creation of a digital inventory of all land; and reparation for historical injustices in relation to land. It is important to note that, addressing the pillar of non-repetition so crucial to transitional justice, as a specific measure to prevent this pattern of land-grabbing and dispossession in the future, the TJRC recommended that 'the National Land Commission formulates and implement strict guidelines in terms of maximum acreage an individual or company can buy hold in respect of private land' (TJRC, 2013, 4, p. 55). Like other recommendations that had specific timelines attached to them, reparations for historical injustices in relation to land were supposed to be implemented 36 months after the publication of the TJRC report in May 2013. The time frame for those historical injustices was very broad: any injustice committed between the 1890s and 2010, that is from the formation of the British East Africa Protectorate and the proclamation of the 2010 Constitution, was to be considered (Bassett, 2017).

In general, we can say that there was much attention paid to the agrarian and land question in the TJRC. Most certainly, the agrarian question was not treated as mere 'background information' in the final report of the TJRC, but as an integral component together with the outbursts of violence that have plagued the country's history, as well as with the broader patterns of exclusion, structural violence and marginalisation that have underpinned it. Despite this recognition, the implementation of the recommendations of the TJRC was made conditional upon their consideration by Kenya's National Assembly, where, as may be expected, many of those who benefitted directly or indirectly from this long history of abuse, are sitting. As a result, the implementation of the recommendations is largely stalled and has encountered numerous problems. The National Land Commission, however, created in 2014 a *Taskforce on the Formulation of Legislation on Investigation and Adjudication of Complaints Arising out of Historical Land Injustices*, and the draft produced by the taskforce was then used by the Ministry of Lands to craft the Land Law Amendment Act (2016), which undermined the National Land Commission and recentralised power on the land question with the Ministry of Lands (Bassett, 2017; Kloop & Lumumba, 2017). The Ministry of Lands has played an obstructionist role in the recommendations of the National Land Commission, which has hampered any possible progress:

> given Kenya's statist land tenure regime and the importance of land to systems of political patronage and the maintenance of power at the centre, the active obstruction of the work of the NLC and undermining of devolved

land institutions could have been foreseen. The pre-devolution administrative apparatus for land allocation and management, while dysfunctional for the majority, has been so lucrative for so long for so few– and those few, a very powerful political and economic elite, do not want to see that change. (Bassett, 2017, p. 559)

As a result, as stated by an ex-commissioner of the TJRC, despite the recognition of the socio-economic rights violations and of the question of land by the commission, it has 'had very little if any impact on efforts to provide redress to those Kenyans who have suffered such violations in the past, and little if any impact on preventing such violations in the future' (Slye, 2017, p. 294).

2.2.4 *The Philippines*

The 2014 peace agreement between the government of the Philippines and the Moro Islamic Liberation Front (MILF), the *Comprehensive Agreement on the Bangsamoro*,[11] as it is called, was an attempt to put an end to a decades-long conflict in the traditionally Muslim regions of Southern Philippines, which up to that point had caused more than 120,000 deaths and over 2 million displaced people (Vellema et al., 2011). Despite widespread recognition of the agrarian dimensions of this conflict, which has been traditionally represented as an ethnoreligious internal war, and although the agrarian question, land dispossession and land-grabbing were at the very heart of the conflict and have a history spanning over five centuries (TJRC, 2017; World Bank, 2017; Vanelli & Ochoa, 2022), the peace agreement, which was divided in two tracks ('political process' and 'normalisation'), did not take the agrarian question as a central issue. The Transitional Justice and Reconciliation Commission (TJRC) was created in the context of the peace agreement, following the recommendations and guidelines contained in the annex on normalisation, to address the legacies of conflict and the historic injustices. The TJRC released a report in 2017 explicitly centred around the issue of land dispossession, entitled 'Dealing with the Past and Land Dispossession', where it was recommended to address this issue (TJRC, 2017), but still the agrarian question

[11] This Peace Agreement can be found at the database Pa-X Analytics (University of Edinburgh and PeaceRep), available at https://www.peaceagreements.org/

was barely addressed in the outcomes of the peace negotiation or the transitional justice mechanisms in place.

The real focus of the agreement was in consolidating the autonomous zone of some 4.5 million Moro people, through the creation of the Bangsamoro Autonomous Region in Muslim Mindanao (BARMM) in southern Philippines, which was an expansion of and replaced the Autonomous Region in Muslim Mindanao (ARMM) created in the context of the previous peace process with the Moro National Liberation Front (MNLF), a peace process that culminated in 1996 (Coronel-Ferrer, 2012). The expectation was that the new autonomous region would create the institutions and the mechanisms to deal with the lingering agrarian question and bring an element of justice after centuries of various forms of dispossession.

In the peace agreement as such, there were, nonetheless, a few mentions of the agrarian question, mostly related to the issue of land formalisation and land registration (Vanelli & Ochoa, 2022), but they are left to the autonomous government to deal with, in accordance with the central government. For instance, in section three of the annex on power-sharing, there is a paragraph on land registration:

> The Bangsamoro Government, in accordance with the land registration system of the Central Government, shall administer land registration in the Bangsamoro territory through an office it shall create for the purpose. The Bangsamoro Government shall furnish copies of the titles, deeds, and other instruments to the relevant Central Government agencies. The Bangsamoro Government can act on *consultas*.
>
> The Bangsamoro Government may institute processes to promote more efficient registration of lands in the Bangsamoro.

This paragraph gave the mandate to the new authorities to deal with this question. As a matter of fact, the brand new BARMM created an Office of the Minister of Agriculture, Fisheries and Land Reform in order to deal with the legacies of the agrarian question and various forms of land-dispossession. Among the powers given to the autonomous authorities were issues related to food production and land uses, the protection of the resources and lands of indigenous peoples and it gave it a specific mandate (in section III.31 and III.32) to organise land management and a cadastral land survey:

> 31. Land management, land distribution, and agricultural land use reclassification – The classification of public lands into alienable and disposable lands shall be initiated and recommended by the Bangsamoro Government to the President for the timely implementation of Bangsamoro development plans and targets.
> 32. Cadastral land survey - The Bangsamoro Government shall have the authority to conduct cadastral surveys, lot surveys, and isolated and special surveys in the Bangsamoro. The Bangsamoro Government shall furnish the results of these surveys to, and coordinate with, relevant Central Government agencies to effect inclusion into the national cadastral survey.

Even if the objectives of this office were far from radical and dealt mostly with issues of land formalisation and surveys, its outcomes, however, have been underwhelming. Only in early 2025, a Transitional Justice and Reconciliation Roadmap between the government and the MILF was created in order 'to address legitimate grievances, correct historical injustices, resolve human rights violations, and remedy marginalization through land dispossession' (OPAPRU, 2025). Land dispossession is a central issue in this roadmap, but it is not yet clear what such a policy will be able to do in practice to correct this problem. The intention is that those properties 'that can be returned, return them; those that cannot be returned, pay for them; those that cannot be paid for, acknowledge and apologize to the owner' (Ibid.). The first action has been the creation of a technical working group to conduct a pilot inventory of statutory and customary claims over land, but it is still too early in this initiative to evaluate its impact.

There are other areas in which the issue of land is indirectly touched upon: for instance, in the normalisation annex, there are mentions of socio-economic programmes to facilitate the reintegration of former combatants, as well as (in rather vague terms) to support impoverished communities and to support internally displaced people, something aligned with the idea of productive projects of the Colombian peace agreement. These programmes were supposed to be community-based and directed towards social cohesion (G.4); since the vast majority of ex combatants would be reintegrating in rural areas, many of these projects were to be agrarian in nature, including some dealing with the construction of farm-to-market roads, pre and post-harvest facilities and livelihood programmes; these projects have been left to be funded mostly to aid agencies. For example, the Spanish Agency for International Development cooperation destined €35.5 million for an agricultural cooperative and related infrastructure projects (Andaya, 2021).

While these interventions are welcome and represent a relief in a very depressed and economically marginalised region, its impact and results are rather limited and insufficient as issues of underfunding and other implementation challenges are widespread (Garcia, 2021; Ali, 2022; ICG, 2023), and in the absence of adequate redistributive measures that address head on these historic patterns of dispossession; more importantly, the emphasis in socio-economic programmes for ex combatants can risk alienating indigenous and other rural poor who are not necessarily prioritised as targets for these interventions but who, nonetheless, have suffered from this history of marginalisation. In this scenario of poor implementation and lack of engagement with root causes such as land, the risk of a descent into full-scale violence remains a real possibility (ICG, 2023).

References

Ali, J. (2022). *Philippines' Bangsamoro peace process normalization track hits some bumps, United States Institute of Peace*, 6 September. Retrieved December 01, 2025,fromhttps://www.usip.org/publications/2022/09/philippines-bangsamoro-peace-process-normalization-track-hits-some-bumps

Andaya, R. (2021). Transformation through normalization: Delineating justice in the Bangsamoro peace process. *Hiroshima Peace Research Journal, 8*, 133–157.

Araghi, F. (1995). Global Depeasantization, 1945–1990. *The Sociological Quarterly, 36*(2), 337–368.

Arango, V., & Cote, J. (2023). Morir acribillado buscando la restitución de la tierra: los nueve casos de 2023, El Espectador, 28 December.

Arango, L., Arias, J., Borras, S., Coronado, S., Díaz, I., Fajardo, D., Ojeda, D., Peña-Huertas, R., Rojas, I., & Serrano, A. (2025). Land grabbing, land dispossession, land rush: What can we learn from Colombia? *The Journal of Peasant Studies, 52*(7), 1632–1665.

Arbour, L. (2007). Economic and social justice for societies in transition. *International Law and Politics, 40*(1), 1–27.

Bassett, E. (2017). The challenge of reforming land governance in Kenya under the 2010 constitution. *The Journal of Modern African Studies, 55*(4), 537–566.

Bernstein, H. (2010). *Class dynamics of agrarian change*. Fernwood Publishing.

Bernstein, H., & Byres, T. (2001). From peasant studies to agrarian change. *Journal of Agrarian Change, 1*(1), 1–56.

Boesten, J., & Wilding, P. (2015). Transformative gender justice: Setting an agenda. *Women's Studies International Forum, 51*, 75–80.

Bonilla, L. (2025). Contra los PDET, la promesa monumental del Acuerdo de Paz que nunca aterrizó. *El Espectador,* 1st May.

Buijtenhuijs, R. (2000). Peasant wars in Africa: Gone with the wind? In D. Bryceson, C. Kay, & J. Mooij (Eds.), *Disappearing peasantries? Rural labour in Africa, Asia and Latin America* (pp. 112–122). ITDG.

Cahill-Ripley, A. (2014). Foregrounding socioeconomic rights in transitional justice: Realising justice for violations of economic and social rights. *Netherlands Quarterly of Human Rights, 32*(2), 183–213.

CAVR (2005). Chega! The Report of the Commission for Reception, Truth and Reconciliation in Timor-Leste. Commission for Reception, Truth and Reconciliation.

CEV. (2022). *There is future if there is truth. Call for great peace (final report). Declaration of the Commission for the Clarification of truth, coexistence and non-repetition.* CEV.

CINEP. (2015). La política de restitución de tierras. Una oportunidad para acercar al Estado y la sociedad civil en una meta común: la dignidad de las víctimas del despojo y el abandono de tierras', *Programa por la Paz* (October).

CNMH. (2013). *¡Basta Ya! Colombia: Memorias de Guerra y Dignidad.* CNMH.

Collier, P. (2000). Rebellion as a quasi-criminal activity. *Journal of Conflict Resolution, 44*(6), 839–853.

Collier, P., & Hoeffler, A. (1998). On economic causes of civil wars. *Oxford Economic Papers, 50*(4), 563–573.

Comissão Nacional da Verdade. (2014). *Relatorio da CNV: Volume II—Textos Tematicos.* Comissão Nacional da Verdade.

Coronel-Ferrer, M. (2012). To share or divide power? Minorities in autonomous regions, the case of the autonomous region in Muslim Mindanao. *Ethnic and Racial Studies, 35*(12), 2097–2115.

Corredor-García, J., & López, F. (2024). The logic of "war on deforestation": A military response to climate change in the Colombian Amazon. *Alternatives: Global Local, Political, 49*(4), 325–343.

Cramer, C., & Richards, P. (2011). Violence and war in agrarian perspective. *Journal of Agrarian Change, 11*(3), 277–297.

CVR. (2003). *Comisión de la Verdad y Reconciliación. Informe Final.* CVR.

Daly, S. (2016). *Organized violence after civil war.* Cambridge University Press.

DANE. (2024). *Resultados para población campesina. Encuesta Nacional de Calidad de Vida (ECV) 2023. Boletín Técnico.* DANE.

Davidson, B. (1981). *The people's cause.* Longman.

Edelman, M. (2000). The persistence of the peasantry. *NACLA Report on the Americas, 33*(5), 14–19.

Edelman, M. (2022). ¿Qué es un campesino? ¿Qué son los campesinados? Un breve documento sobre cuestiones de definición. *Revista Colombiana de Antropología, 58*(1), 153–173.

Edelman, M., Oya, C., & Borras, S. (2013). Global land grabs: Historical processes, theoretical and methodological implications and current trajectories. *Third World Quarterly, 34*(9), 1517–1531.
Evans, M. (2019). Transitional and Transformative Justice. *Critical and International Perspectives.* Routledge.
Fick, C. (1990). *The making of Haiti: The saint Domingue revolution from below.* The University of Tennessee Press.
Fundación Paz y Reconciliación. (2024). *Los Decepcionantes Números de la Restitución de Tierras en Tiempos de Petro,* 22nd April. Retrieved July 22, 2024, from https://www.pares.com.co/post/los-decepcionantes-n%C3%BAmeros-de-la-restituci%C3%B3n-de-tierras-en-tiempos-de-petro
Garcia, R. (2021). *Disrupting cycles of discontent. Transitional justice and prevention in The Philippines.* International Center for Transitional Justice.
García, R. (2022). La política de memoria en Colombia. El relato histórico del Centro nacional de Memoria. *Pasado y Memoria, 25,* 375–398.
Golay, C. (2022). The rights to food and food sovereignty in the UNDROP. In M. Alabrese, A. Bessa, M. Brunori, & P. F. Giuggioli (Eds.), *The United Nations' declaration on peasants' rights* (pp. 134–147). Routledge.
González, L. (2025). *Entre la Impunidad y la Resistencia: Tendencias Recientes en el Asesinato de Líderes Sociales en Colombia.* Indepaz.
Gott, R. (1973). *Rural guerrillas in Latin America.* Penguin.
Grajales, J. (2011). The rifle and the title: Paramilitary violence, land grab and land control in Colombia. *The Journal of Peasant Studies, 38*(4), 771–792.
Gready, P., & Robins, S. (2014). From transitional to transformative justice: A new agenda for practice. *International Journal of Transitional Justice, 8*(3), 339–361.
Guillerot, J. (2019). *Reparations in Peru: 15 years of delivering redress.* Queens University Belfast.
Guillerot, J. (2021). *Alive in the demand for change. Transitional justice and prevention in Peru.* ICTJ.
Gutiérrez, J. (2016). Participatory action research (PAR) and the Colombian peasant reserve zones: The legacy of Orlando Fals Borda. *Policy & Practice, 22,* 59–76.
Gutiérrez, J. (2021). "Whatever we have, we owe it to coca" insights on armed conflict and the coca economy from Argelia, Colombia. *International Journal of Drug Policy, 89,* 103068.
Gutiérrez, J. (2025a). Rebel governance: A matter of time. *Civil Wars, 5,* 1–26.
Gutiérrez, J. (2025b). Greedy peace-makers. Post-FARC-EP trajectories from political crime to politicised common crime. In J. Gutiérrez & F. Gutiérrez-Sanín (Eds.), *Criminality, political power and conflict. Critical perspectives* (pp. 177–204). Manchester University Press.

Gutiérrez-Sanín, F., & Vargas, J. (2017). Agrarian elite participation in Colombia's civil war. *Journal of Agrarian Change, 17*(4), 739–748.

Gutiérrez-Sanín, F. (2015). Agrarian inequality and civil war revisited. *Geography Compass, 9*(8), 423–431.

Gutiérrez-Sanín, F. (2020). *¿Un nuevo ciclo de la guerra en Colombia?* Debate.

Gutiérrez-Sanín, F. (2025). *Tierra, Guerra, Política.* Debate.

Gutiérrez-Sanín, F., Machuca, D., & Cristancho, S. (2019). ¿Obsolescencia programada? La implementación de la sustitución y sus inconsistencias. *Análisis Político, 97*, 136–160.

Gutiérrez-Sanín, F., Marín, M., Machuca, D., Parada, M., & Rojas, H. (2020). Paz sin garantías: el asesinato de líderes de restitución y sustitución de cultivos de uso ilícito en Colombia. *Estudios Socio-Jurídicos, 22*(2), 361–418.

Gutiérrez-Sanín, F., & Parada, M. (2022). *Las Deudas de la Paz.* Observatorio de Tierras.

Hall, D. (2013). Primitive accumulation, accumulation by dispossession and the global land grab. *Third World Quarterly, 34*(9), 1582–1604.

Harvey, D. (2003). *The new imperialism.* Oxford University Press.

Hilton, R. (1973). *Bond men made free. Medieval peasant movements and the English rising of 1381.* M. Temple Smith Ltd..

Hobsbawm, E. (1959). *Primitive Rebels.* Norton &.

Hobsbawm, E. (1973). Peasants and politics. *The Journal of Peasant Studies, 1*(1), 3–22.

Humphreys, J., & Smith, M. L. R. (2014). The "rhinofication" of south African security. *International Affairs, 90*(4), 795–818.

Huneeus, A., & Rueda, P. (2021). Territory as a victim of armed conflict. *International Journal of Transitional Justice, 15*(1), 210–229.

ICG. (2023). *Southern Philippines: Making peace stick in the Bangsamoro.* International Crisis Group.

IPES-Food. (2024). *Land Squeeze: What is driving unprecedented pressures on global farmland and what can be done to achieve equitable access to land?* Retrieved February 27, 2026, from https://ipes-food.org/wp-content/uploads/2024/05/LandSqueeze.pdf

James, C. L. R. (2001). *Black Jacobins.* Penguin.

Jenkins, C. (1982). Why do peasants rebel? Structural and historical theories of modern peasant rebellions. *American Journal of Sociology, 88*(3), 487–514.

JEP. (2023). *JEP firma convenio con la URT para luchar contra la impunidad en cuanto al despojo de tierras durante el conflicto armado (Comunicado 146)*, 11 December. Retrieved January 21, 2026, from https://www.jep.gov.co/Sala-de-Prensa/Paginas/-jep-firma-convenio-con-la-urt-para-luchar-contra-la-impunidad-en-cuanto-al-despojo-de-tierras-durante-el-conflicto-armado.aspx

Kaldor, M. (2001). *New & old wars.* Polity.

Kaplan, O. (2025). Development for peace in Colombia: Experiences with PDETs in El Carmen and Cartagena del Chairá. *Journal of Peacebuilding & Development, 20*(3), 439–448.

Kloop, J., & Lumumba, O. (2017). Reform and counter-reform in Kenya's land governance. *Review of African Political Economy, 44*(154), 577–594.

Kriger, N. (1991). Zimbabwe's guerrilla war: peasant voices. *Cambridge University Press.*

Leech, G. (2011). *The FARC. The longest insurgency.* ZED Books.

Linares, M. (2021). *Setting an agenda for sustainable peace. Transitional justice and prevention in Colombia.* ICTJ.

Lunstrum, E. (2014). Green militarization: Anti-poaching efforts and the spatial contours of Kruger National Park. *Annals of the Association of American Geographers, 104*(4), 816–832.

Macher, S. (2023). *Las Recomendaciones de la CVR 20 Años Después.* CNDDHH.

Martínez, P. (2013). *The victims and land restitution law in Colombia in context. An analysis of the contradictions between the agrarian model and compensation for the victims.* FDCL.

Marx, K. (1999). *Capital.* Oxford University Press.

Mason, D. (2004). *Caught in the crossfire. Revolutions, repression, and the rational peasant.* Rowman & Littlefield.

McClintock, C. (1984). Why peasants rebel: The case of Peru's Sendero Luminoso. *World Politics, 37*(1), 48–84.

Merino, R. (2023). Lost in transition: Explaining authoritarianism in Peru. *International Journal of Transitional Justice, 17*(3), 480–488.

Migdal, J. (1974). *Peasants, politics, and revolution. Pressures toward political and social change in the third world.* Princeton University Press.

Moore, B. (1966). *Social origins of dictatorship and democracy. Lord and peasant in the making of the modern world.* Beacon Press.

Munive, J. (2011). A political economic history of the Liberian state, forced labour and armed mobilization. *Journal of Agrarian Change, 11*(3), 357–376.

Muvingi, I. (2009). Sitting on powder kegs: Socioeconomic rights in transitional societies. *International Journal of Transitional Justice, 3*(2), 163–182.

Ndungú, C. (2014). *Lessons to be learned: An analysis of the final report of Kenya's Truth, Justice and Reconciliation Commission.* ICTJ Briefing, Retrieved November 10, 2025, from https://www.ictj.org/sites/default/files/ICTJ-Briefing-Kenya-TJRC-2014.pdf

OPAPRU. (2025). *GPH, MILF launch Transitional Justice Roadmap to address historical grievances in Bangsamoro*, Office of the Presidential Adviser on Peace, Reconciliation and Unity (OPAPRU), 9 December, Retrieved February 27, 2026, from https://peace.gov.ph/2025/12/gph-milf-launch-transitional-justice-roadmap-to-address-historical-grievances-in-bangsamoro/

Paige, J. (1975). *Agrarian revolution. Social movements and export agriculture in the underdeveloped world*. The Free Press.

Peña-Huertas, R., Ruiz, E., Parada, M., Zuleta, S., & Álvarez, R. (2017). Legal dispossession and civil war in Colombia. *Journal of Agrarian Change, 17*(4), 759–769.

Peters, K., & Richards, P. (2011). Rebellion and agrarian tensions in Sierra Leone. *Journal of Agrarian Change, 11*(3), 377–395.

Pfeiffer, S. (2015). Building up a peace infrastructure for Colombia: lessons from implementing the Victims Law. Norwegian Peacebuilding Resource Centre. NOREF Report October 2015.

Pinkeviciute, J. (2025). The limits of participation without economic justice in Peacebuilding: A study of Colombia. *Journal of Peacebuilding & Development, 21*, 52–69.

PNUD. (2011). *Colombia Rural: Razones para la esperanza. Informe Nacional de Desarrollo Humano 2011*. PNUD.

Popkin, S. (1979). *The rational peasant: The political economy of rural Society in Vietnam*. University of California Press.

Restrepo, J., & Bernal, A. (2014). *La Cuestión Agraria: Tierra y Posconflicto en Colombia*. Debate.

Riaño, P., & Uribe, M. V. (2016). Constructing memory amidst war: The historical memory Group of Colombia. *International Journal of Transitional Justice, 10*(1), 6–24.

Ríos, S. (2023). The fragmentation of historical memory in Colombia. In A. Bazin, E. Hébert, V. Rosoux, & E. Sangar (Eds.), *Memory fragmentation from below and beyond the state. Uses of the past in conflict and post-conflict settings*. Routledge.

Rodríguez, S. (2010). Política del testimonio y reconocimiento en las comisiones de la verdad guatemalteca y peruana: En torno a la figura del "indio subversivo". *Revista Crítica de Ciências Sociais, 88*, 23–55.

Rosset, P., & Pinheiro, L. (2021). Peasant Autonomy: The Necessary Debate in Latin America. *Interface, 13*(1), 46–80.

Rubiano, M., Vélez, M. A., & Arenas, P. (2022). *¿Cómo va la implementación del PNIS en las Zonas de Manejo Especial?* CESED, Universidad de los Andes.

Ruiz, E., Peña-Huertas, R., Parada-Hernández, M., Lozano, A., Triana, B., & Valencia-Herrera, M. (2021). Who owns what in Macondo? The Flexibilization of the rules of evidence in land restitution in Colombia. *International Journal of Transitional Justice, 15*(1), 26–46.

Ruiz, M. (2023). *El cascarón y la semilla. Lecciones de la negociación con las Autodefensas Unidas de Colombia*. ICTJ.

SATRC (1998). Truth and Reconciliation Commission of South Africa Report. South African Truth and Reconciliation Commission.

Scott, J. C. (1976). *The moral economy of the peasant*. Yale University Press.

Scott, J. C. (1977). Hegemony and the peasantry. *Politics and Society, 7*(3), 267–296.

Scott, J. C. (1985). *Weapons of the weak. Everyday forms of peasant resistance*. Yale University Press.

Scott, J. C. (2009). *The art of not being governed. An anarchist history of upland Southeast Asia*. Yale University Press.

Sehmi, A. (2024). Legacies of colonial violence in contemporary transitional justice: Memories of Mau Mau, the "Kapenguria six" and the "Ocampo six" in Kenya. *International Journal of Transitional Justice, 18*(1), 32–48.

Shanin, T. (1987). *Peasants & peasant societies*. Basil Blackwell.

Sharp, D. (2014). *Justice and economic violence in transition*. Springer.

Skocpol, T. (1979). *States and social revolutions*. Cambridge University Press.

Skocpol, T. (1982). What makes peasants revolutionary? *Comparative Politics, 14*(3), 351–375.

Slye, R. (2017). Putting the J into the TRC: Kenya's truth justice and reconciliation commission. In M. Swart & K. van Marle (Eds.), *The limits of transition: The south African truth and reconciliation commission 20 years on* (pp. 282–307). Brill.

Slye, R. (2018). *The Kenyan TJRC. An outsider's view from the inside*. Cambridge University Press.

Soto, L. (2020). En medio de la incredulidad, Duque apuesta por nueva estrategia de sustitución de coca, La Silla Vacía, 17 July. Retrieved March 23, 2025, from https://www.lasillavacia.com/silla-nacional/en-medio-de-la-incredulidad-duque-apuesta-por-nueva-estrategia-de-sustitucion-de-coca/

Teló, F., Gasparotto, A., de Medeiros, L., & Fernandes, R. (2021). Land and transitional justice in Brazil. *International Journal of Transitional Justice, 15*(1), 190–209.

Thomson, F. (2011). The agrarian question and violence in Colombia: Conflict and development. *Journal of Agrarian Change, 11*(3), 321–356.

Tilly, C. (1987). Conflict, resistance and collective action versus capitalization and Statemaking. In T. Shanin (Ed.), *Peasants & peasant societies* (pp. 340–342). Basil Blackwell.

TJRC (2013). Report of the Truth, Justice, and Reconciliation Commission (4 volumes). TJRC, Kenya.

TJRC. (2017). *TJRC Land Report: Dealing with the Past and Land Dispossession*. Retrieved December 01, 2025, from https://cdn.viiworksdemo.com/pdf/snrz-TJRC%20Land%20Report%20PPT.pdf

Torelly, M. (2018). Assessing a late truth commission: Challenges and achievements of the Brazilian National Truth Commission. *International Journal of Transitional Justice, 12*(2), 194–215.

UNICEF. (2024). *Levels & trends in child mortality. Report 2023*. UNICEF.

UNODC. (2020). *PNIS, Monitoreo a la implementación del Plan de Atención Inmediata -componente familiar, Informe No. 23.* UNODC.

Unruh, J. (2010). Land rights and peacebuilding: Challenges and responses for the international community. *International Journal of Peace Studies, 15*(2), 89–125.

Unruh, J., & Abdul-Jalil, M. (2021). Housing, land and property rights in transitional justice. *International Journal of Transitional Justice, 15*(1), 1–6.

Vanelli, F., & Ochoa, D. (2022). Territorial peace: Land governance and sustainable peacebuilding. *International Journal of Urban Sustainable Development, 14*(1), 368–387.

Vargas, J., & Uribe, S. (2017). State, war, and land dispossession: The multiple paths to land concentration. *Journal of Agrarian Change, 17*(4), 749–758.

Vellema, S., Borras, S., & Lara, F. (2011). The agrarian roots of contemporary violent conflict in Mindanao, southern Philippines. *Journal of Agrarian Change, 11*(3), 298–320.

Verwimp, P. (2011). The 1990–92 massacres in Rwanda: A case of spatial and social engineering? *Journal of Agrarian Change, 11*(3), 396–419.

Verwimp, P. (2013). *Peasants in power. The political economy of development and genocide in Rwanda.* Springer.

Villarreal, J. (2021). The historical relationship between agrarian reforms and internal armed conflicts: Relevant factors for the Colombian post-conflict scenario. *Land Use Policy, 101*, 105138.

Wesche, P. (2019). Business actors, paramilitaries and transitional criminal justice in Colombia. *International Journal of Transitional Justice, 13*(3), 478–503.

Wickham-Crowley, T. (1992). *Guerrillas & revolution in Latin America.* Princeton University Press.

Wiener, J. (1975). The Barrington Moore thesis and its critics. *Theory and Society, 2*, 301–330.

Wolf, E. (1969). *Peasant wars of the twentieth century.* Harper and Row.

World Bank. (2017). *Land: territory, domain, and identity. A report submitted by the WB-IOM technical team to the Transitional Justice and Reconciliation Commission (TJRC).* Retrieved November 29, 2025, from https://openknowledge.worldbank.org/server/api/core/bitstreams/124f3544-3e59-5992-8347-828324797e51/content

World Bank. (2025). Poverty & inequality update. October 2025.

Ybarra, M. (2012). Taming the jungle, saving the Maya Forest: Sedimented counterinsurgency practices in contemporary Guatemalan conservation. *The Journal of Peasant Studies, 39*(2), 479–502.

CHAPTER 3

The 'Peasant Wars' of the Late Twentieth Century: Colonialism, Agrarian Change and the Long Durée

Abstract Despite the growing recognition of structural causes of conflict and the institutions of repression, transitional justice has been ill-equipped to deal with the agrarian dimensions of conflict and authoritarianism and/or to bring about redress to the rural populations. Armed conflict in rural settings often has to do with processes of agrarian change and of rural development that pre-exist, exacerbate and often outlive open conflict. The agrarian dimensions of armed conflict are usually obscured by privileging other prisms, such as ethnic perspectives or criminalising narratives (war on drugs, war on terror, etc.), owing much to the 'new wars' paradigm. We will discuss four cases (Peru, Colombia, Kenya and the Philippines) which are representative of mobilisation and contestation rooted in agrarian conflict and patterns of extremely unequal access to land. This chapter contextualises agrarian dynamics in relation to contemporary and historic conflict and repression to further underscore the centrality of these to many contexts and to provide a more grounded understanding of why transitional justice should make more efforts in order to address them.

Keywords Peasants • Agrarian reform • Land-grabbing • Agrarian change • Colombia • Kenya • Peru • The Philippines

J. A. Gutiérrez, *Transitional Justice and Agrarian Conflict*,
https://doi.org/10.1007/978-3-032-25228-9_3

Despite the growing recognition of the importance of structural causes of conflict and the institutions of repression (including colonial legacies), as we have seen, transitional justice has been ill-equipped to deal with the agrarian dimensions of conflict and authoritarianism, and/or to bring about redress to the rural populations, and in particular, to peasants who have suffered greatly from both scourges. Armed conflict in rural settings often has to do with processes of agrarian change and of rural development that pre-exist, exacerbate and often outlive open armed conflagration (Mason, 2004; Thomson, 2011; Betancur-Alarcón & Krause, 2020). In fact, in Third World or Global South setting, agrarian reform has often been considered by incumbents as a means to prevent or to address conflict, not always successfully (Mason, 2004; Villarreal, 2021). It is, therefore, all the more surprising that transitional justice, given its blind spots, has failed to engage extensively with issues of land or agrarian reform.

Often, the agrarian dimensions of armed conflict, or even the participation of peasants in war, has been obscured by privileging other prisms to look at these conflicts, such as ethnic perspectives or criminalising narratives (war on drugs, war on terror, etc.) (Cramer & Richards, 2011), owing much to the 'new wars' paradigm (as in Kaldor, 2001). But if we scratch the surface, even some of the most stereotypical cases of these 'new wars' have an important and almost completely overlooked agrarian question at their very heart (Verwimp, 2013; Gutiérrez-Sanín, 2025). As a result, transitional justice has been particularly disappointing when trying to address questions related to peasants or to agrarian conflict, even in those cases such as Colombia or Kenya, where there was an explicit acknowledgment of this issue and where, in the case of the former, a real effort was made to address it through a number of policies over the last decade and a half.

This chapter contextualises agrarian dynamics in relation to contemporary and historic conflict and repression to further underscore the centrality of these to many cases and to provide a more grounded understanding of why transitional justice should make more efforts in order to address them.

3.1 Extended Cases

In this sub-section, we will discuss four cases (Peru, Colombia, Kenya and the Philippines) in which transitional justice played, to various degrees, a role in addressing some of the underlying agrarian causes of conflict. While we already discussed in Sect. 1.2 the ways in which transitional justice addressed these issues 'from above', in this section we will discuss in more detail the agrarian nature of these conflicts, and this will help us to set the scene for a better understanding of attempts by peasant and agrarian movements to mobilise from below to demand justice, rights and transformation. The four cases discussed are representative of mobilisation and contestation deeply rooted in agrarian conflict and patterns of extremely unequal access to land. In some of these cases, agrarian conflict was also mixed with ethnic grievances. These cases are drawn from three continents (Latin America, Asia and Africa), demonstrating that these issues are prevalent in a significant chunk of the world.

3.1.1 Peru

Peru has a long history of rural and agrarian unrest, with large-scale agrarian revolt throughout much of its history, including the legendary rebellion of Tupac Amaru in the eighteenth century (Stern, 1987). The peasant question in the case of Peru has been intrinsically linked to the indigenous question, since most of the peasants are indigenous, concentrated mostly in the Andean highlands of the country, and the use of either term highlights the complexities of class and race in Peruvian society (Cadena, 2000). During the 1960s, inequality in the countryside was extreme: 80% of the land was controlled by less than 1% of the population, with 0.1% of the population owning 60% of the arable land, which prompted peasant organisations' struggles for land and widespread rural agitation (Handelman, 1975; Milton, 2007). Around this time, and on the back of this unrest, small guerrilla groups like the National Liberation Army (*Ejército de Liberación Nacional*, ELN) and the Movement of Revolutionary Left (*Movimiento de Izquierda Revolucionaria*, MIR), inspired by the focus guerrilla theory and the Cuban experience, were formed in Peru, and although they failed to grow, to attract the peasantry, being ultimately defeated (Wickham-Crowley, 1992), the need for reform was felt acute among vast sectors of society. Since the start of that decade, hundreds of occupations were the practical response of the peasantry to the growing demand for the breakup of the *haciendas*; these occupations were often violent, with the police routinely using lethal force against the protesters whose deaths, being mostly indigenous and peasants, did not cause an uproar among the educated elites of the cities (Handelman, 1975).

In 1968, sectors of the army launched a military coup d'etat that put in power general Juan Velasco Alvarado, who led the so-called *Gobierno Revolucionario de la Fuerza Armada* (Revolutionary Government of the Armed Forces). The dictatorship, unlike other conservative and openly right-wing military coups like those in Guatemala in 1954, in Paraguay on the same year, or in Brazil in 1964 (or like those that would later take place in Chile in 1973, in Uruguay the same year, or in Argentina in 1976), was a reformist and nationalist attempt, closer to the Argentinian *peronismo*, which brought about important progressive change for Peru, such as granting official status to Quechua and Aymara, the majority indigenous languages in the country (a measure of inclusion to an important part of the population traditionally marginalised) and promoting the organisation of workers' unions, cooperatives and workers' self-management in the economy. In this process, it faced numerous contradictions, being authoritarian but not repressive, promoting people's participation (and creating its own social movement, SINAMOS), while at the same time being centralist and hierarchical (Knight, 1975; Gorman, 1982; Aguirre & Drinot, 2017).

One of the most important aspects of his government was a serious attempt to implement an agrarian reform. Although there had been serious pressure from below for decades over the agrarian question, the government decided instead to conduct a revolution from above with minimal decision-making participation of the peasantry in the direction of the process. The land was expropriated and only exceptionally handed to individual peasants or indigenous communities. By and large, the land was given to cooperatives organised from above by the government (Knight, 1975; McClintock, 1984).

This experience kept going formally even after Velasco Alvarado was toppled in 1975 by another coup, led this time by less progressive generals that gradually rolled back most reforms (Aguirre & Drinot, 2017). Without attacking the reform frontally, in the coming years its pace would decelerate until the whole process petered out in 1979 (Olivari, 2015). Still, by then, some 370,000 peasants became beneficiaries of this agrarian reform that redistributed some nine million hectares, most of them in the period up to 1975 (Matos & Mejía, 1980). Although the numbers are impressive, and this process undermined the landed elites and serfdom relations that had plagued the Peruvian countryside since colonial times (Olivari, 2015), it benefitted around a meagre 20% of the Peruvian peasantry, most of them ex *hacienda* workers, and its impact was very uneven across the country, with some areas, such as Ayacucho, barely touched by the reform. The majority of the peasantry, in any case, remained by and large as precarious smallholders (Knight, 1976; McClintock, 1984; Eguren, 1990; Mason, 2004).

Since this was a process from above, and the lands were given to the peasants only nominally through the figure of state-led cooperatives, there was dissatisfaction, and many (though not all) among the peasantry viewed the state (with its managers and bureaucrats) as the new landlord (Caballero, 1986). As such, the mobilisation continued in the form of land-squatting, including some big cooperatives where, sometimes, the squatters were no other than the beneficiaries themselves and often were the vast majority of smallholders with less than three hectares that were completely ignored by the agrarian reform:

> The reform did not stop the unrest. Many haciendas were not divided, and new cooperatives proved inefficient. The state failed to provide money for loans or technical assistance even as official rhetoric during the early Velasco years of equality and campesino pride further radicalized many peasants. (...) Campesinos now invaded not only undivided haciendas, but also the cooperatives. Agrarian leagues first formed by the Velasco government became independent, and by the late 1970s a mosaic of militant regional stretched across the highlands. (Starn, 1991, p. 76)

This process of radicalisation, which would later be critical to the support initially found by the Shining Path insurgency (Degregori, 1990), was nurtured by this top-down reform that although it changed the power balance in rural Peru, failed to benefit the majority of the peasantry and, most importantly, excluded them from any form of ownership, decision-making or direction of the process (Caballero, 1986). With the fall of Velasco Alvarado in 1975 and the lack of enthusiasm of successive governments in this reform, the process had little time to consolidate: the cooperatives became increasingly de-funded, and mismanagement crippled them eventually; as a result, since the 1980s, there has been a tendency towards the extreme fragmentation of land in ever smaller smallholdings (Olivari, 2015).

Ayacucho, in the centre of Andean region, was chosen by the fanatical Maoist Communist Party of Peru, Shining Path (*Partido Comunista del Perú -Sendero Luminoso*, PCP-SL), as the launching point for their campaign, since they had a base there mostly of youths with extensive links to their original indigenous rural communities (McClintock, 1984; Degregori, 1990; Starn, 1991).[1] This was a region of mostly Quechua-speaking indigenous peasants, smallholders, who had been largely unaffected by the agrarian reform; only one property was expropriated, and a mere 54 families were beneficiaries (Palmer, 1986). At the end of the 1960s, 85% of the local population were peasants, but 37 landlords owned more than 50,000 hectares of land, while 18% of the peasants did not even have two hectares (Díaz, 1969). Not only was the region barely touched by the agrarian reform, but peasants had actually become poorer after it because the soil was less productive and the population was growing fast (McClintock, 1984). Life expectancy in Ayacucho was 44 years, and only 7% of the population had access to drinkable water (Palmer, 1986).

Despite all the red flags (figuratively and literally), for the vast majority of the many anthropologists working in the region, the depth of discontent, the official violence and resentment of the peasants went unnoticed, because their symbolic and idealistic paradigms made issues related to class and the deep changes in the socio-economic conditions, invisible: 'They gave us detailed pictures of ceremonial exchanges, Saint's Day rituals, weddings, baptisms, and work parties. Another kind of scene, just as common in the Andes, almost never appeared: the girl with an abscess and no doctor, the woman bleeding to death in childbirth, a couple in their dark adobe house crying over an infant's sudden death' (Starn, 1991, p. 79).

It was in these areas of scarce implementation of the agrarian reform where the expansion of Shining Path was more dramatic (CVR, vol. I, 2003). It is notable that their campaign was launched after the return of democracy in 1980, and during a time when the government was introducing US- and IMF-sponsored measures that hurt the peasantry—slashing subsidies for fertilisers, higher interest rates for agricultural loans, reduction on tariffs for agricultural imports and counter-narcotics operations against coca farmers in areas like the Upper Huallaga Valley (McClintock, 1984; see also Mason, 2004). While the cadres of the Shining Path were mostly young students from a rural background, their campaign involved mostly smallholders amidst a serious crisis of subsistence (Ibid.). This campaign was launched with destructive ferocity against

[1] There was another rival guerrilla around this time, the MRTA (Revolutionary Movement Túpac Amaru), with a stronghold in the northeast of Peru, in the regions of San Martín, Huánuco, Ucayali and Junín. It was smaller and did not have the same prominence as Shining Path.

the 'people's enemies'—policemen, rustlers, local authorities, deviants, even small shop owners and cooperatives created during the agrarian reform:

> They arrived preaching the overthrow of the government and often redistributing land and animals from state-administered cooperatives. The call for radical change appealed to many villagers. The young guerrillas, who sometimes had relatives in the communities where they went to organize, had the knowledge of Quechua and mountain life that enabled them to bear the revolutionary doctrine effectively. Executions of corrupt bureaucrats and cattle rustlers were generally greeted with enthusiasm. They bolstered the Shining Path's popularity. Torture and massacres by the security scare off support. (Starn, 1991, p. 76)

The government response was brutal, decreeing in 1982 an emergency and giving the military special powers in the Andean regions of Ayacucho, Huancavelica and Apurímac, considered to be strongholds of Shining Path. Support, at least during the first years of the insurrection, seemed to have been quite high, with the funeral of the dead guerrilla Edith Lagos attracting 30,000 mourners in 1982, despite official repression. However, after the initial counter-insurgent operations of 1983–1984, which left an estimated 3500 dead, 1500 disappeared and 4000 arrested, support became more costly, particularly since Shining Path seemed unable or unwilling to protect their own base of support (McClintock, 1984; see also Starn, 1998; Schubiger, 2021).

As part of the counter-insurgent efforts, the army promoted the creation of paramilitary forces among the peasants—the *rondas contrasubversivas*, which were modelled on *rondas campesinas*, anti-criminal organisations formed in the 1970s by the peasants themselves—to assist them in the containment and destruction of Shining Path. Many peasants joined the *rondas* (which had various names until being known as self-defence committees or CAD) either coerced or to avoid being targeted by the brutal counter-insurgent tactics of the army, but then they were expected not just to prevent Shining Path to get a foothold in their village but to actively fight them throughout the region (Degregori, 1998; Starn, 1998; Tapia, 1997). The intrinsically problematic nature of these civilian–military counter-insurgent strategies, which turned peasants against peasants in a war of proximity (cf., Theidon, 2006), was made evident in the massacre of Uchuraccay, where eight journalists were killed by indigenous people, under pressure of the army, in 1983 because they were mistaken with guerrillas (Rodríguez, 2010). Atrocities like this were common (Starn, 1998).

In turn, the *ronderos* were targeted in kind by Shining Path, and this led to a brutal spiralling of violence, with Shining Path's attacks becoming ever more brutal and wanton, being 'clear by the end of 1980s that the tactics of terror often backfired' (Starn, 1991, p. 76). By 1986, the massive support that Shining Path have had started to wane, partly because of their brutality, but also because of their authoritarianism and intrusiveness in villagers' lives; by 1992, there were 50,000 *ronderos* who played a crucial role in the eventual defeat of this guerrilla (Tapia, 1997. See also McClintock, 1989; del Pino, 1996; Mason, 2004; Schubiger, 2021). That year, the leader of Shining Path, Abimael Guzmán, was arrested, and the organisation and its 'people's war', which had been structured around his figure in an almost mystical cult of personality, was largely diminished (Degregori, 2012).

Peasants were critical in both the rise and the fall of Shining Path. Today, there are heirs and remnants of Shining Path in the valleys of Mantaro, Huallaga and Apurímac-Ene. It is in the latter valley where they are the strongest, but although they are largely a local phenomenon, they still seem to have some capacity and enjoy support from the local peasantry. This was the result of their shifting politically and ideologically away from their past authoritarianism, 'having eschewed its earlier ideological rigidity (…) It has turned instead to building constructive relationships with those local populations where it has a presence (…) Members now work the fields with peasants there, pay for needed supplies, and visit peasant communities to acknowledge past errors and to promise not to repeat them' (Palmer and Bolívar, 2011, p. 4).

At the time of Shining Path's campaign defeat in 1992, the president Alberto Fujimori staged a self-coup and started a period of authoritarianism, aided by the militarisation of much of the country. Fujimori's regime was marked by gross human rights violations, until he was toppled in 2000. Among the worst abuses was the widespread forced sterilisation of up to 300,000 indigenous women for purposes of racist eugenics (Theidon, 2022). The peasants, at the same time, saw inequality and poverty rise with a number of neoliberal reforms that open the markets to agricultural imports and lowered the prices of their agricultural produce (Crabtree, 2002), while the extractivist industry sparked many environmental conflicts with rural communities (Vila, 2022, 2025), who have also mobilised massively for their cultural, economic and social rights over the decades (Guillerot, 2021). In the Amazon region, indigenous peoples had obtained recognition at the time of Velasco Alvarado, which allowed them to obtain collective titling of their lands, which then, from the 1990s, put them in course of conflict with the extractive industries in their territories (Merino, 2021).

The legacies of this turbulent history of frustrated reform, conflict and authoritarianism are many. Peru has been unable to have any form of stability for over two decades, and the rural world remains trapped in structures of violence, with any form of protest of civil disobedience being labelled with counter-insurgent language and monikers as in the past decades (Meléndez, 2007): 'a discourse, supported by leaders of opinion and the national media, that disqualifies and delegitimizes protesters—which is to say, anyone who is against the development model—as criminals, antiestablishment, and, in the most radical case, terrorists' (Guillerot, 2021, p. 42). The political crisis of 2022 and the subsequent protests that left around 70 dead, where overwhelmingly peasant and indigenous protesters were targeted (Merino, 2023), are nothing but the latest example of the systematic repression against the rural populations and the generalised indifference among urban elites about the lives of the indigenous peasants.

3.1.2 Colombia

The recognition of the agrarian nature of the Colombian conflict during the 2012–2016 peace negotiations did not come out of the blue or was a sudden realisation of political elites. The agrarian nature of the actual armed actors involved in the conflict has been extensively discussed (Gutiérrez-Sanín, 2025). The most prominent guerrilla movement in Colombia, the FARC-EP, is a remarkable case of agrarian guerrilla that grew organically from the peasant self-defence groups of the 1940s and whose political backbone rested upon the Agrarian Programme of Marquetalia, its foundational document (Pizarro, 1991; Ferro & Uribe, 2002). Unlike authors who have claimed that peasants always require an external leadership in their struggles (cf., Hobsbawm, 1973; Migdal, 1974), the FARC-EP was not only composed primarily of peasants, but their leadership was historically drawn from the smallholding peasantry, something that Hobsbawm (1986) recognised as a reason why most political actors in Colombia, particularly middle class intellectuals, tended to be dismissive of this guerrilla movement.

After their demobilisation in 2016, a survey found that only 19% of the guerrillas had an urban background (UNAL, 2017). Their irregular counterpart, the AUC, the right-wing paramilitaries that fought the dirty war against the FARC-EP, often in collusion with the army and the political establishment, came largely from the landowning class, and many of them came specifically from prominent cattle-rancher families who provided the bulk of the political and financial support for their expansion. But also, this class provided the leadership cadres for the counter-insurgent movement (Gutiérrez-Sanín & Vargas, 2017). The agrarian roots of this conflict, despite systematic attempts to portray it as purely criminal and narcotised violence, are undeniable: '[a]t the very heart of the violence in Colombia lies the struggle to dispossess the peasantry of its land and resources in favour of a caste of rentier great property owners, who, in turn, control the electoral trading machine and the regional bureaucracies' (Reyes, 2009, p. 27).

This recognition of the importance of the agrarian nature of the conflict was, as well, the acknowledgment of over a century of mass peasant mobilisation for the right to land. While sometimes localised, and not always organised, the struggle for land has been one of the most extended social rights movements in this country. The Colombian countryside was shaped by 300 years of colonial rule that systematically dispossessed the indigenous population, which was pushed to the margins, while creating a rich landlord class of European origin, and a racially mixed labouring force of *mestizos* who toiled in the *haciendas* for the landlords. The modern struggle for land started at the end of the nineteenth century, when Colombia found a way to insert itself in the global markets, thanks to the international demand for tropical products, such as tobacco, quinine and coffee (the demand for coca, a century later, follows exactly the same pattern, despite the illegal nature of the crop). The Liberal Party laid the foundation for an export-oriented economy by freeing the slaves in 1851, breaking up the indigenous reservations and promoting colonisation of public lands to foster productivity and access to markets, thus increasing the State revenues. Two laws, one in 1874 and another in 1882, tied property to economic exploitation and imposed limits on land concentration. Peasants started to abandon the Andean highlands, where the old *haciendas* had been established and where they were still the dominant force of social life, looking for land to colonise in order to become independent producers who benefitted from this international demand, thus reproducing their own peasant way of life as smallholders. This created a very different type of peasantry than in Peru, one which was fairly individualistic when it came to property, more family than community oriented, although with collective practices and organisations that guaranteed local order and survival in this fast-expanding agrarian frontier (LeGrand, 1986; Palacios, 2011).

In 1850, 75% of the land was in public ownership (*baldío*), meaning that it was not claimed by any particular owner and was therefore up for grabs by these peasants bent on colonising these *baldíos*. Behind these settlers (*colonos*), after they had cleared the jungle and prepared the land, came entrepreneurs and landlords who, having friends in public office and armies of lawyers on their side, claimed property rights to the land fraudulently (often through a mix of violence and deception), trying to turn the peasants into tenants or face eviction. Often, the peasants, in order to preserve their independence, went deeper into the jungle to clear new land, only to be followed again by this cycle of dispossession. This has led to a historical tendency, which remains up to the present, characterised by the constant expulsion of the peasantry from central lands to marginal regions, uphill or deeper into the jungle, thus pushing the 'agrarian question' to the ever-expanding agrarian frontier (Gilhodes, 1970; Bergquist, 1986; LeGrand, 1986; Molano, 1994; Palacios, 2011; Fajardo, 2015).

Sometimes these peasants resisted, often in the context of the frequent civil wars between Liberals and Conservatives that plagued most of the nineteenth and early twentieth centuries. Their resistance included forms of violent opposition with far more frequent forms of passive resistance and active squatting of lands nominally claimed by landlords. With the advent of trade unionist ideas, their resistance became more and more organised and autonomous. An indigenous uprising in 1914 was the start of a cycle of fierce agrarian struggles that lasted until 1935. This was a period of unprecedented economic growth, partly because of a boom of the coffee economy, partly by the development of capitalist enclaves in the oil, sugar and banana industries (Gilhodes, 1970; Gaitán, 1984; Fajardo et al., 1999). The peasants formed agrarian unions, the *Ligas Campesinas*, in the 1920s to agitate for the right to land, but also to defend the rights of peasants and to stop the pattern of expulsion of the peasantry (Sánchez, 1977). In 1928, during a workers' strike in a banana plantation of United Fruit Co. in Magdalena, over 1000 workers were killed, a bloodbath later to be immortalised by García Márquez in *A Hundred Years of Solitude* (Archila & Torres, 2009; Caro & Vidal, 2012).

Haciendas, in the meantime, were bypassed by this economic dynamism, and most, by the twentieth century, were bankrupt and highly unproductive. From 1926, there were increasing attempts to reform the agrarian structure, including breaking up unproductive and bankrupt *haciendas* to be sold as smallholdings, which accelerated when the Liberals came to power in 1931. The first attempt at Agrarian Reform, in 1936, was an attempt to make sure that land had a primarily economic function, but this came to nothing as the reform was delayed and obstructed, then mostly reverted by another law in 1944, and finally this process was stopped in its tracks by the outbreak of *La Violencia*, as the civil war from 1946–1958 is known[2] (Palacios, 2011). This war, which left around 200,000 dead, was mostly fought in the countryside, where pressure for land (spurred by rising coffee prices) was intense and the bipartisan conflict gave a cover to much bloodshed by Conservative gangs, which was about land-grabbing. Liberals and then Communists formed peasant self-defence groups, which laid the foundations for the future guerrillas in Colombia and marked a departure point in which the peasantry gained autonomy from the tutelage of the traditional parties. While Liberal guerrillas received an amnesty in 1953, the Communist guerrillas did not; they were miniscule in any case, and they retreated to agrarian enclaves in a process known as armed colonisation, undisturbed for years, even after *La Violencia* formally ended with the bipartisan power-sharing agreement between Liberals and Conservatives (Fajardo, 1985; Ortiz, 1985; Christie, 1986; Vega & Rodríguez, 1990).

The 1960s brought the Cold War to Colombia. Growing US concern about the existence of armed Communist colonies in discrete pockets of southern Colombia led the government to conduct major counter-insurgent operations between 1964 and 1965: these operations were the birth of the modern guerrilla movement and, in particular, of the communist detachment that then would be just known as FARC in 1966[3] (Pizarro, 1991). On the other hand, the counter-insurgent policies also had a devel-

[2] There is much debate around the periodisation of *La Violencia*. Some authors place it from 1948 to 1953. I take as the starting date the electoral victory of the Conservative party, which was followed by widespread rural violence, and the fall of the Rojas Pinilla dictatorship in 1958, which inaugurated a period of Liberal-Conservative power-sharing.

[3] Originally called the FARC, they expanded their name to FARC-EP in 1982.

opmentalist dimension based on Kennedy's *Alliance for Progress*, which promoted agrarian reforms to prevent socialist revolutions. In 1966, the Liberal president Lleras Restrepo promoted agrarian reform and, to have some leverage against sectors bitterly opposed to any prospect of agrarian modernisation, formed a peasant union, the ANUC, which was supposed to support the government's initiatives. However, frustrated by the government's lack of ability to deliver, the peasant movement became more independent and radicalised, resorting to direct action in the form of land squatting and occupations. This panicked the elites, who quickly reverted their policies, frustrated once again the attempted agrarian reform and turned to repression against the peasantry. Thus, the peasantry continued being uprooted by successive waves of violence, and the guerrilla movement provided smallholders both sanctuary from this cycle of dispossession and political direction with their agrarian programme (Zamosc, 1986, 2001; Fajardo, 2015). The coca boom in the 1980s also provided material conditions for the reproduction of the land-poor peasantry. In this context, the FARC became the People's Army, the FARC-EP in 1982 and their movement grew to become the biggest of the guerrillas in Colombia (CNMH, 2014; Gutiérrez, 2018).[4]

From the 1980s, counter-insurgency received a boost in the form of counter-narcotics operations, combining counter-insurgent actions with fierce attacks against smallholders in coca-producing regions. At the same time, an alliance of military officers, state officials, landlords, drug barons and cattle-ranchers formed death-squads known as paramilitary forces (who would eventually unite in 1996 as the AUC), who spearheaded a massive process of land-grabbing and dispossession against the smallholder peasantry in the name of counter-insurgency (Reyes, 2009; Grajales, 2011; Fajardo, 2014; Gutiérrez-Sanín, 2019). This process, which displaced millions and was conducted with extreme violence (murders, disappearances, arson, sexual violence, mutilations, torture and everything imaginable were used in this crusade), led to extreme forms of land-grabbing and land concentration in Colombia: until 2012, over 8 million

[4] There have been many other guerrilla movements in Colombia, most notably the EPL (a Maoist fraction which split from the FARC in 1966 and which had important presence among the peasantry) and the ELN (a Cuban-inspired guerrilla formed in 1964 that brought together popular sectors and the middle classes. Although far less peasant than the FARC-EP, it still has peasant support in some discrete regions, and some authors have done an agrarian reading of this organisation too, see Gutiérrez-Sanín, 2015). For the purposes of this book, the FARC-EP is the main actor among the guerrillas.

hectares of land had been dispossessed in this process (CNMH, 2013). In the end, 0.1% of the total of estates control 58.72% of the arable land, while 81% of the total landholdings (with an average of merely two hectares each) control a meagre 4.92% of the arable land (Oxfam, 2017). This shocking pattern of land distribution is one of the worst in the whole world, and it is indissociable from legal and illegal counter-insurgent violence (escalating in the late 1990s both with the AUC and US intervention through Plan Colombia; see Lindsay-Poland, 2018), which often combined legal and administrative methods to enhance dispossession and cover it with a varnish of legality (Grajales, 2011, 2015). Thus, 'paramilitary groups were able to promote broad networks of dispossession firmly grounded in the legal system under the umbrella of anti-insurgent alliances' (Peña-Huertas et al., 2017, p. 767. See also Vargas & Uribe, 2017; Navarrete-Cruz et al., 2023). At the same time, from the 1990s, the agrarian crisis propelled by the neoliberal opening of the economy and the breakdown of the International Coffee Agreement (Rettberg, 2010; Thomson, 2011; Fajardo, 2014), only worsened the situation of the peasantry.

With this background, it is therefore no surprise that for the 2012–2016 peace process as well as for previous transitional justice mechanisms, land became a key issue. Yet, the treatment, as we discussed previously, has been insufficient. In particular, the Comprehensive Rural Reform, as defined in the peace agreement, 'does not question historical problems about access and use of land. The transfer of the rural land stipulated in the CRR [ed. Comprehensive Rural Reform] is insignificant for reducing the high levels of land concentration in the country' (Villarreal, 2021, p. 9). Even with the mass demobilisation of FARC-EP combatants after the 2016 peace agreement, other groups (notably the rival guerrillas of the ELN and groups coming from the paramilitary tradition such as the EGC) have remained on arms, some FARC-EP units have never demobilised (and indeed have managed to grow considerably in the space of a decade) and new armed groups have also emerged (Gutiérrez, 2020; Gutiérrez-Sanín, 2020). The army remains a force perceived as hostile in many rural regions, where they have colluded with criminal groups for counter-insurgent purposes (Gutiérrez, 2025) and engaged in extensive violence against the rural population in the name of counter-narcotics operations, while the failure to properly implement any of the agreements in relation to land or to the closely related illicit crops substitution question is behind much of the continuation of the conflict dynamics (Gutiérrez, 2020;

Gutiérrez-Sanín, 2020). Although much of this persistence of conflict dynamics (and their evolution into new dynamics in some cases) is portrayed, just like in previous decades, as a purely criminal problem, the fact is that land (which remains as concentrated as ever), and the agrarian problem, is now, as it was before, at the heart of it. The unresolved agrarian question will remain the real question to deal with in order to build that elusive, sustainable and lasting peace:

> The intense mobilisation of the peasants, and in general, of the rural poor in Colombia, their legendary struggle for land, for resources, and for their political autonomy persists up to the present. Their resistance creates a power opposed to the expansion of the latifundia and to the onslaught of the institutional order. As long as the (...) agrarian problem is not solved, the social and armed conflict will remain an option. (Anrup, 2011, p. 161)

3.1.3 Kenya

Conflicts over land in Kenya have a long history that spans for the best part of four centuries. For this section, we will rely heavily on the work of the TJRC, mostly because a great deal of the agrarian dimension of violence and conflict in Kenya depends on testimonies and public hearings that were organised directly by the TJRC, which made a reconstruction of land conflicts based on these (Slye, 2017). While the report is mostly concerned with the post-independence period from 1963 to the present, there is a recognition that land dispossession is a phenomenon that took place on a large scale from colonial times. There is a recognition, in the TJRC report, that the conflicts over land go back to the colonial history of Kenya, in which entire communities were made landless, first by the Arabs (under the Omanis and the Sultanate of Zanzibar), who took over the coast in the 1600s and who were heavily involved in the slave-trade, forcing entire communities to flee, and then by the British, who claimed a protectorate over all of the territory of Kenya and grabbed enormous amounts of land, turning it into 'Crown Land' in the 1890s (Lonsdale & Berman, 1979; Jackson, 2016; Kloop & Lumumba, 2017):

> Protectorate officials saw as their task to provide the land and the labor. Land for the Europeans had to be removed from its traditional availability to Africans. Between 1895 and 1930, officials acquired land for Europeans through military pressure, occasionally by the physical movement of whole

> tribes, and by the eventual assignment of nearly all Africans to strictly limited reserved areas. British courts declared all Protectorate land to be the property of the Crown and all Africans, therefore tenants-at-will, subject to legal eviction. Most Europeans settled in the central highlands where temperature, rainfall, and soil conditions were among the best in the Protectorate. Negligible rents and 999-year leases were granted to support the settlers. (Wolff, 1970, pp. 275–276)

According to the Truth Commission, 'Kenyans displaced from their land by the colonial government were concentrated in reserves, something that considerably restricted their socio-economic life. Those who did not prefer to live in the reserves remained in European farms either as squatters or as labourers, or sought employment in urban areas' (TJRC, 2013, p. 25). The links between ethnic tensions and land-grabbing can be traced back to the 'divide and rule' colonial policies reinforced by arbitrary administrative borders, negative cultural stereotypes and development policies that privileged only those areas of interest for the extractive colonial project while marginalising other regions (TJRC, 2013, vol. 3). The Nandi rebellion during that period, mostly led by the Kalejin people, was the best coordinated resistance to the expansion of the British empire, but they were defeated in 1905 after some 15 years of resistance and guerrilla warfare (Gold, 1978).

The Mau Mau rebellion (1952–1956) represented a decisive moment in the struggle against British settler colonialism, but it was also a movement that sprang from deep agrarian problems derived from the pattern of colonisation of central Kenya. This rebellion was led and fought mostly by the Kikuyu people, who organised the Kenya Land and Freedom Army (KLFA), although the rebellion as such seems to have been the work of a loose network resulting from various processes of contestation and mobilisation by mostly the landless and the rural poor against both the colonisers and the Kikuyu landed elites, who benefitted from colonialism (Kershaw, 1997). The events leading to the Mau Mau rebellion can be traced back to the early twentieth century large-scale land-grabbing in the so-called White Highlands of Kenya, a region around the Rift Valley comprising extremely productive lands at a certain altitude that made settlement for Europeans placid, affecting mostly the pastoralist Maasai, who were the main inhabitants of this region. Not only millions of hectares of land were stolen by the British colonial administration and the settlers, but the native population—forcefully dispossessed—was coerced into working for the settlers in conditions that very often resembled slavery, with physical punishment and flogging being common occurrences (Kanogo, 1987; Throup, 1987).

Kikuyu peasants were brought to the region as labourers, without much coercion: 'the thousands of unexploited acres under speculative ownership provided (…) the means to attract a permanent labour force on to the settler manor by letting land to Africans under various forms of tenancy. (…) Maasailand was being turned inside out, as African cultivators, the majority of them Kikuyu, now invaded the choicest areas of the pastoral plain, under the protection of its new overlords' (Lonsdale & Berman, 1979, p. 500). It is in this context that the Mau Mau rebellion needs to be understood: the Kikuyu, resenting the dispossession they had suffered in central Kenya, and eager to access land that was in the hands of extremely racist white settlers, organised in secret oaths and conducted a guerrilla campaign attacking, often under the cover of darkness in the night, settlers, cattle and collaborators, in particular, the Home Guards, the paramilitary force of Kikuyu people formed during the declared state of emergency to confront the insurgency. This was a complex movement in which anti-colonial struggle co-existed with the settling of private scores, some of them related to land (Kanogo, 1987; Throup, 1987; Kershaw, 1997).

The savagery and brutality of the British counter-insurgency operations was frightful; dozens of thousands were killed; over a thousand people hanged, thousands tortured, mutilated and castrated; hundreds of thousands were displaced and suffered from collective punishment measures such as food deprivation; and tens of thousands were interned into concentration camps, where thousands perished because of mistreatment and neglect (Davidson, 1981; Furedi, 1989; Anderson, 2005; Elkins 2005). In fact, after much pressure and a demand by the Kenya Human Rights Commission in the British Courts, the British Government had to compensate over 5000 survivors of the Mau Mau repression, who received, in total, nearly £20 million as compensation in 2011, and a public apology in 2013 (Sehmi, 2024, footnote 26), which gave some recognition to the British colonial atrocities. Although the movement was ultimately defeated, they managed to precipitate the crisis of the British Empire in East Africa, paving the way for independence. Most importantly for the purposes of this book, the British Government, knowing too well the agrarian causes of the unrest, was forced to start the Million Acre scheme to transfer (through favourable sales) 1 million acres of land from settlers to a wide range of differentiated African (mostly Kikuyu) peasants, which started in practice the process of decolonisation before independence (Leys, 1971). However, this process would leave behind one of the most enduring colonial legacies that shape out to this day the agrarian roots of Kenyan ethnic conflict: the land was prioritised for the Kikuyu, the ethnic group that was regarded as a threat because of the Mau Mau rebellion, as a way to pacify them, but not to the native groups of that region, such as the Maasai or the Kalenjin (Leo, 1981, 1984; Boone, 2011). According to the Truth Commission: 'The Mau Mau rebellion to colonial rule (...) forced the colonial government to rethink and reformulate its discriminatory policies', provoking reforms 'designed to alleviate the grievances of those Africans who had not yet chosen to resort to violence, and to stem support for those who had. While these policies were aimed at minimizing rebellion and dissent, they further divided Kenyans along ethnic lines' (TJRC, 2013, pp. 25–26).

After independence in 1963, instead of addressing these colonial legacies of ethnic division, the new elites built their power by utilising them to their advantage, which 'enhanced, rather than reduced, the balkanization of the country along ethnic lines' (TJRC, 2013, vol. 3: 21). The Jomo Kenyatta regime started a series of resettlement and compensation programmes that, following the pattern established by the British, benefitted some communities along ethnic lines, particularly the Kikuyu, to which he belonged, at the expense of others, leading to long-term ethnic resentment. The government, representing Kikuyu elites, and with a deep antipathy against the memory of the Mau Mau- supported mostly Kikuyu farmers to purchase land in very favourable terms in the White Highlands, while the majority of the original settlers, mostly the Maasai and Kalenjin, remained landless and dispossessed (Leo, 1981, 1984; Barkan, 2008; Boone, 2011; Kloop & Lumumba, 2017). In fact, while the Kikuyu represented less than 20% of the population, they were allocated more than 45% of the land through the resettlement programme (Vianni, 2016), which saw 2.5 million acres of land (out of a total of 3.4 million) pass into African hands (Leys, 1971). This imbalance had been exacerbated by the settlement of agricultural communities in the lands of pastoralist communities, such as the Kalenjin. These forms of resettlement, in the face of an almost total lack of titles, official deeds or proper surveys about land tenure and ownership, made land-grabbing all the more problematic and prevalent. According to the report, '[c]entral to many of the ethnic tensions in post-independence Kenya is the issue of redistribution of the land formerly occupied by white settlers. Due to the skewed post-colonial land redistribution policy that was deliberately designed to favour the ruling class and not the landless masses, it is now estimated that more than half of the arable land in the country is in the hands of only 20% of the population. Politicians in successive governments used land to induce patronage and build political alliances. Much of the most valuable and productive land has ended up in the hands of the political class, members of their families, and friends (often of the same ethnicity) rather than being returned to the communities from which the colonialists had taken it. (TJRC, 2013, volume 3: 26)

In the post-colonial context, instead of agrarian justice, the Kenyatta regime (and its successor) used the colonial architecture to consolidate an agrarian clientelistic state (Barkan, 1987), where politicians used offers of access to land as part of power consolidation strategies, to reward friends and punish foes. Whenever there were electoral campaigns, to mobilise voters often along ethnic lines, land rights were used as an incentive (denying them against opponents), as a powerful weapon against a land-hungry population with genuine land grievances (Miguel, 2004; Boone, 2011; Dercon & Gutiérrez-Romero, 2011; Kloop & Lumumba, 2017). This link between land and ethnic tensions has been exploited around election time, turning the struggle for scarce fertile land, particularly that of the Rift Valley, in election-time violence (Boone, 2011). This widespread violence, often characterised as ethnic, has deep socio-economic roots.

It is against this backdrop that we need to make sense of the post-electoral violence in 2007, in which the ruling Party of National Unity (PNU) and the opposition Orange Democratic Movement (ODM) were confronted. Violence broke out in the aftermath of a flawed, dubious and non-transparent election, in which the PNU was declared the victor, while the ODM. contested the results. Finally, a power-sharing agreement was reached with the intervention of the UN in February 2008, over the corpses of around 1000 people killed, while hundreds of thousands had been displaced by the violence, which assumed largely ethnic lines, confronting mostly the Luo, Kikuyu and Kalenjin (Barkan, 2008). This was not a one-off incident, but part of a longer pattern, being estimated that at least 4000 people had been killed and a further 600,000 displaced by state-sponsored violence, with the Rift Valley being a central setting for this violence (Kenyan Human Rights Commission, 2001). Electoral violence had been a regular staple in the three previous elections since the reintroduction of electoral democracy in 1992 by President Daniel arap Moi, who continued to rule until the elections of 2002. Often, this violence was linked to the ways in which state officials and politicians had allocated land to particular constituencies (often along ethnic lines), with research demonstrating that electoral violence was most intense wherever the state had been allocating land rights: 'The property regime centered on state-allocated land rights structured the geographic pattern of land-related grievances, defined rival constituencies of land claimants, and created opportunities and incentives for ruling elites to manipulate existing land grievances and land-tenure relationships for electoral gain'. (Boone, 2011, p. 1313).

Ethnic factors came to the fore in this turmoil. President Mwai Kibaki, who was running for re-election after his first electoral victory in 2002, was largely perceived to benefit the Kikuyu and close ethnic groups, such as the Meru and the Embu, in what was called the Mount Kenya mafia, since these ethnic groups are all originally from central Kenya, around Mount Kenya. But while the ethnic factor was strategically used to mobilise people, land had a long history of being the real bounty: it is no coincidence that, once again, the most serious violence happened in the Rift Valley, a region with a long history of contention over land, which had been the scene of the Mau Mau rebellion, but also of colonisation by Kikuyus and the resettlement programmes of the Kenyatta government (Barkan, 2008). The link between ethnic tensions and land, land disputes being in the background of much of the violence, was very clear:

> The media frequently mentioned land disputes as one of the components of electoral violence. According to our survey 5% of respondents "Had land disputes over the year ahead of the election" and these disputes occurred with the same frequency in urban and rural areas. Similarly 5.3% accepted to be "Settled in an irregular land scheme." Among those who reported having a land dispute before the election 57% were victims of post-electoral violence, a statistically significant higher figure compared to those who did not have land disputes before the election among which 18% were victims of post-electoral violence. (Dercon & Gutiérrez-Romero, 2011, p. 737)

Elections, since then, have been largely peaceful, although the issue of land remains a haunting presence in political debate, its disruptive potential simmering beneath the surface. Since then, all attempts at agrarian reform or to address the issue of land injustice have met fierce resistance from elites and from powerful sectors within the state apparatus, very often landlords themselves. Indeed, every attempt at reform has led to a counter-reform, with the newly formed National Land Commission facing stiff resistance:

> The cumulative effect of Kenya's post-colonial land governance system is more contention and dispute over land. The strong link between land and power, especially Presidential power, and the opaqueness of land transactions, produce politicisation of land. Despite the clear class dimensions of land grabbing and accumulation, the political class most often ethnicises land disputes. This diverts attention away from the need for institutional reform of a system benefiting politicians who often strive to gain access to it via the ballot box or political appointment. (Kloop & Lumumba, 2017, p. 583)

3.1.4 The Philippines

The Moro people, the name given to a variety of ethnic groups in the Southern Philippines united by their common Muslim faith, have a long history of rebellion that dates back all the way to the sixteenth century when they put fierce resistance to the Spanish colonisation of the Philippines, then to the US invasion and occupation in 1898, and later to the creation of the new independent republic, with a full-scale insurgency developing largely under the dictatorship of Ferdinand Marcos (1965–1986) (Montiel et al., 2012; Garcia, 2021). After serious violence in the late 1960s, including the Jabidah massacre of 1968, Moro secessionism gained momentum with the creation of the Moro National Liberation Front (MNLF), formed in 1972 and inspired by the national liberation movements of the time. The MNLF sustained an insurgent campaign until they largely demobilised after a peace agreement in 1996 led to the creation of an autonomous region for the Moro people. An important splinter of this group, the MILF (officially named as such in 1984), was created after the initial discussions for such an autonomous region in 1977, claiming that nothing short of full independence in order to preserve the integrity of Muslim culture and traditions would be acceptable and taking an ideological stance more akin to political Islam than traditional national liberation movements (Molloy, 1985; Buendia, 2006). They kept fighting until they signed their own peace agreement in

2014—one of the peace agreements, together with the Colombian one, with the highest participation of women (Jopson, 2023)—which expanded the autonomous region, the *Bagsamoro*, or the Nation of the Moro (Vanelli & Ochoa, 2022).

While this conflict has largely been explored through the prism of ethno-religious conflict, given the fact that Moros are a Muslim people in a largely Christian country and this tension has been very evidently pushed to the fore, the conflict clearly has an agrarian dimension as well (Tan, 1995; World Bank, 2017). Since the early twentieth century, migration of landless poor[5] from the Catholic north to the Muslim south, particularly to the Moro region of Mindanao, was stimulated through a series of laws, policies and decrees as part of a state-led process to reclaim the 'frontier' into the process of state-building and capital accumulation through increasingly market-oriented agricultural production in agrarian colonies, a process that counted on the explicit support of the Muslim local elites who operated as brokers (Vellema et al., 2011). Together with the rural poor looking for opportunities to break the chains of poverty, came entrepreneurs, as well as agribusiness (mostly rubber, coconut, pineapple and banana plantations) and logging corporations with timber concessions, a process that intensified since the 1960s. To this day, the wealthiest families in the south of the Philippines are the descendants of businessmen and entrepreneurs who settled and increased their fortunes astronomically amidst this land-grabbing rush (Gutierrez & Borras, 2004). Then, the (largely Christian) settlers in the countryside were given individual titles to the land, while the whole property structure was organised in a way that undermined the traditional, pre-colonial and communal structures of the native Moro people and other indigenous groups (known as Lumads):

> The institutionalization of the state's Torrens titling system,[6] which recognizes individual land ownership, contradicted the traditional concept of communal ownership observed and practised by Muslim and other indige-

[5] Many of these poor settlers came from other areas of the country, and the state tried to diffuse pressure and unrest, which was feeding communist-inspired insurgencies in other parts of the country, by moving landless peasants from one area and creating new landless peasants in another (World Bank, 2017).

[6] The Torrens system is a land registration system introduced at the time of the US occupation of the Philippines, in which titles given by the state, which keeps a register of land holdings, are the decisive proof of land ownership, as opposed to deeds or customary methods. This system was developed in Mindanao, Sulu and the Muslim regions of southern Philippines

nous communities. The state's recognition of individual land ownership, evidenced by an individual's possession of a Torrens Land Title, thus tended to favour Christian settlers who were more literate and adept at using the law to their advantage than Muslims and non-Christians/non-Muslims, who were ignorant of the laws and incapable of using the legal processes involved in land titling, let alone able to afford the exorbitant fees required. Moreover, it is an anathema to the culture of such people to have a collectively owned ancestral land parcelled out with individual titles given to members of the tribe. (Buendia, 2006, p. 17)

The impact of these policies was far-reaching: the demographics changed dramatically in the region, with the native Muslims and Lumads becoming a minority—extremely impoverished—population in some localities with their traditions, customs and ways of life completely dislocated, becoming effectively landless or in a chronic state of land poverty (Rodil, 1994; World Bank, 2017). The vast majority of Christian settlers who moved to the southern region also were eventually marginalised, as a few prominent landlords and agribusiness/timber corporations emerged as the clear winners in this scramble. The winners of this scramble resorted to all available means to this end: government favouritism, skewed laws, the power of money and the resort to 'violence entrepreneurs', who through violence and intimidation favoured their powerful patrons (Gutierrez & Borras, 2004). It is in this context of dispossession, poverty (the Muslim provinces of the south are the poorest in the whole country), marginalisation, exclusion and extreme inequality that the movement for the self-determination of the Moro people emerged. After the violent response of the dictatorship of Marcos and the ongoing violence of local elites, all the ingredients were in place for this aspiration of self-determination to be channelled through armed contestation. Once armed conflict took hold of the region, violence produced displacement, some of it with land-grabbing as the goal (World Bank, 2017; Garcia, 2021).

This agrarian dimension has not been totally ignored by the state: after the return to democracy in 1986, this question was addressed by the Comprehensive Agrarian Reform Program (CARP) of 1988, aimed at redistributive (but market-assisted) land policies to favour four million landless or land-poor peasants, and the Indigenous Peoples' Rights Act (IPRA) of 1995, designed to protect the ancestral lands of indigenous

as a mechanism to advance the process of dispossession to develop agricultural capitalism in the region in order to incorporate it into the US economy orbit (World Bank, 2017).

peoples, including the Moros (Gutierrez & Borras, 2004). CARP performance has been deemed a disappointment despite some limited successes to provide access to land from agribusiness to peasants; the results have been particularly disappointing in Mindanao and the Muslim south when compared to the rest of the country, because of lack of reliable data, its lack of sensitivity about the customary land tenure patterns and the prioritisation of people who are already working on the land, leaving the landless and the dispossessed (groups that should have been prioritised), apart from the ubiquitous issue of implementation challenges. In fact, in some cases it has been argued that CARP has institutionalised dispossession of the Muslim landless peasants by prioritising the claims of landed farmers—some of them linked to landlords (Gutierrez & Borras, 2004). In Mindanao, large agribusiness corporations like Dole or Del Monte managed to use CARP to their advantage during the 1990s by creating cooperatives of their own employees and using productive alliances to operate in ways which ran directly contrary to the spirit of this policy. Although whenever Muslim leaders had the capacity to act as effective brokers, their religious paternalist approach could put on occasion clear limits to exploitation and promote a more equitable form of development (Vellema et al., 2011), more often than not the advancement of agribusiness happened to the detriment of the peasantry (Larsen et al., 2019).

IPRA introduced important elements that could correct some of the limitations of the CARP by bringing into the debate customary forms of land tenure and the need to protect ancestral lands of ethnic and indigenous groups; however, implementation has been slow and marred by institutional problems and capacity issues (Vellema et al., 2011). But other policy developments put in question some of the effects that IPRA could have had on the dispute over land in this region: the passing of the Mining Act in 1995 effectively gave priority to mining investments over indigenous rights over land and territory, a particularly worrying fact, given that the bulk of mineral reserves are underground in indigenous territories (World Bank, 2017). Even more worryingly, in the Muslim south, there had been conflicts and tensions between the claims of landless Muslim peasants and the claims of the indigenous Lumads, leaving the Muslim peasants, who represented the main social base of armed insurgency, in an impossible situation:

> It is possible that landless Muslims are caught in a multiple squeeze: CARP has been encroaching onto their ancestral lands; non-Muslim indigenous

> communities have been claiming part of the Muslim ancestral lands (...); some Muslim elites may have appropriated their land for personal private use; and, finally, other non-Muslim elites, domestic and transnational, have appropriated portions of the Muslim ancestral domain. (Gutierrez & Borras, 2004, p. 41)

In a damning indictment, a report stated that 'these well-intentioned initiatives contributed to the contemporary legal and policy confusion that has often been exploited for land grabbing, further complicating the task of finding solutions to land dispossession' (World Bank, 2017, p. 50). Despite the fact that for the MILF agrarian issues were never a top priority in their agenda, the agrarian question, as we discussed, was touched upon in various components of the peace negotiations' agenda, and the peace agreement needed to address aspects of the agrarian question in Mindanao that were not addressed by either of these policies. However, the results are underwhelming, despite the issue of land being raised on various occasions and in some key reports (see Andaya, 2021). This is so because of lack of implementation (mostly because of budgetary constraint and lack of institutional capacity), lack of representation of indigenous and Muslims non-aligned with the MILF, opposition by landed elites and the fact that the priority remained the issue of regional autonomy, of which the agrarian question was merely understood as one of the aspects that it was up to the autonomous authorities to deal with. An Office of the Minister of Agriculture, Fisheries and Land Reform was created in the autonomous region, but its role was largely limited to title formalisation, and this in insufficient numbers (Andaya, 2021).

Since the agrarian question was not the priority of the MILF or their supporters back during wartime, it is not hard to see why it was not their priority after the peace settlement. Therefore, the pre-conflict agrarian dynamics remain unchallenged, risking the emergence of new forms of violence (c.f., Vanelli & Ochoa, 2022). As in many other conflicts, the solution of the agrarian question underlying the dynamics of organised violence will depend on the capacity and ability of the peasants and rural peoples themselves to push for their own agenda, as it has become increasingly clear with the emergence of a new wave of peasant and agrarian movements that have contested the terms of agrarian change.

References

Aguirre, C., & Drinot, P. (2017). *The peculiar revolution. Rethinking the Peruvian experiment under military rule*. University of Texas Press.

Andaya, R. (2021). Transformation through normalization: Delineating justice in the Bangsamoro peace process. *Hiroshima Peace Research Journal, 8*, 133–157.

Anderson, D. (2005). *Histories of the hanged: The dirty war in Kenya and the end of empire*. Weidenfeld & Nicolson.

Anrup, R. (2011). *Antígona y Creonte. Rebeldía y Estado en Colombia*. Ediciones B.

Archila, M., & Torres, J. (2009). *Bananeras. Huelga y Masacre, 80 años*. UNAL.

Barkan, J. (1987). The electoral process and peasant-state relations in Kenya. In F. Hayward (Ed.), *Elections in independent Africa* (pp. 213–237). Westview Press.

Barkan, J. (2008). Will the Kenyan settlement hold? *Current History, 107*(708), 147–153.

Bergquist, C. (1986). *Coffee and conflict in Colombia, 1886–1910*. Duke University Press.

Betancur-Alarcón, L., & Krause, T. (2020). Reaching for the mountains at the end of a Rebelocracy: Changes in land and water access in Colombia's highlands during the post-peace agreement phase. *Frontiers in Environmental Science, 8*, 546821.

Boone, C. (2011). Politically allocated land rights and the geography of electoral violence: The case of Kenya in the 1990s. *Comparative Political Studies, 44*(10), 1311–1342.

Buendia, R. (2006). Mindanao conflict in The Philippines: Ethno-religious war or economic conflict? In A. Croissant, M. Beite, & S. Kneip (Eds.), *The politics of death: Political violence in Southeast Asia* (pp. 147–187). Lit Verlag Berlin.

Caballero, V. (1986). La Crisis de las Empresas Asociativas en el Agro Puneño. In V. Gómez, B. Revesz, E. Grillo, & R. Montoya (Eds.), *Perú: El Problema Agrario en Debate* (pp. 123–151). SEPIA.

Caro, J., & Vidal, A. (2012). The worker's massacre of 1928 in the Magdalena Zona Bananera-Colombia. An unfinished story. *Memorias: Revista Digital de Historia y Arqueología desde el Caribe, 9*(18), 22–54.

Christie, K. (1986). *Oligarcas, Campesinos y Política en Colombia*. Universidad Nacional.

CNMH. (2013). *¡Basta Ya! Colombia: Memorias de Guerra y Dignidad*. CNMH.

CNMH. (2014). *Guerrilla y Población Civil*. CNMH.

Crabtree, J. (2002). The impact of neo-liberal economics on Peruvian peasant agriculture in the 1990s. *Journal of Peasant Studies, 29*(3–4), 131–161.

Cramer, C., & Richards, P. (2011). Violence and war in agrarian perspective. *Journal of Agrarian Change, 11*(3), 277–297.

Davidson, B. (1981). *The people's cause*. Longman.

de la Cadena, M. (2000). *Indigenous mestizos: The politics of race and culture in Cuzco, Peru, 1919–1991*. Duke University Press.

Degregori, C. (1990). *Ayacucho 1969–1979. El surgimiento de Sendero Luminoso*. IEP.

Degregori, C. (1998). Harvesting storms: Peasant Rondas and the defeat of Sendero Luminoso in Ayacucho. In S. Stern (Ed.), *Shining and other paths. War and Society in Peru, 1980–1995* (pp. 128–157). Duke University Press.

Degregori, C. (2012). *How difficult it is to be god. Shining path's politics of war in Peru, 1980–1999*. University of Wisconsin Press.

del Pino, P. (1996). Tiempos de Guerra y de Dioses: Ronderos, Evangélicos y Senderistas en el Valle del Rio Apurímac. In C. Iván, J. de Gregori, P. Coronel, & d. P. y. O. Starn (Eds.), *Las Rondas Campesinas y la Derrota de Sendero Luminoso* (pp. 117–188). IEP.

Dercon, S., & Gutiérrez-Romero, R. (2011). Triggers and characteristics of the 2007 Kenyan electoral violence. *World Development, 40*(4), 731–744.

Díaz, A. (1969). *Ayacucho: Hambre y Esperanza*. Waman Puma.

Eguren, F. (1990). La Reforma agraria y el nuevo orden en el campo peruano. In Á. Fernández & A. Gonzalés (Eds.), *La Reforma Agraria Peruana, 20 años después*. Centro de Estudios Sociales Solidaridad.

Elkins, C. (2005). *Britain's gulag: The brutal end of empire in Kenya*. Jonathan Cape.

Fajardo, D. (1985). La Violencia 1946-1964: Su Desarrollo y su Impacto. In *Once Ensayos sobre la Violencia*. CEREC.

Fajardo, D. (2014). *Las Guerras de la Agricultura Colombiana, 1980–2010*. ILSA.

Fajardo, D. (2015). Estudio sobre los Orígenes del Conflicto Social Armado, Razones de su Persistencia y sus Efectos más Profundos en la Sociedad Colombiana. In C. H. d. C. y. s. Víctimas (Ed.), *Contribución al Entendimiento del Conflicto Armado en Colombia* (pp. 361–419). Desde Abajo.

Fajardo, L., Gamboa, J. C., & Villanueva, O. (1999). *Manuel Quintín Lame y los Guerreros de Juan Tama*. Nossa y Jara.

Ferro, J. G., & Uribe, G. (2002). *El Orden de la Guerra*. CEJA.

Furedi, F. (1989). *The Mau Mau war in perspective*. Ohio University Press.

Gaitán, G. (1984). *La lucha por la tierra en la década del 30*. El Ancora.

Garcia, R. (2021). *Disrupting cycles of discontent. Transitional justice and prevention in The Philippines*. International Center for Transitional Justice.

Gilhodes, P. (1970). Agrarian struggles in Colombia. In R. Stavenhagen (Ed.), *Agrarian problems and peasant movements in Latin America* (pp. 407–452). Anchor Books.

Gold, A. (1978). The Nandi in transition: Background to Nandi resistance to the British 1895-1906. *Kenya Historical Review, 6*(1–2), 84–104.

Gorman, S. (1982). *Post-revolutionary Peru. The politics of transformation*. Westview Press.

Grajales, J. (2011). The rifle and the title: Paramilitary violence, land grab and land control in Colombia. *The Journal of Peasant Studies, 38*(4), 771–792.
Grajales, J. (2015). Land grabbing, legal contention and institutional change in Colombia. *Journal of Peasant Studies, 42*(3–4), 541–560.
Guillerot, J. (2021). *Alive in the demand for change. Transitional justice and prevention in Peru*. ICTJ.
Gutierrez, E., & Borras, S. (2004). *The Moro conflict: Landlessness and misdirected state policies*. East-West Center.
Gutiérrez, J. (2018). Insurgent Institutions: Refractory communities, armed insurgency and institution-building in the Colombian conflict (PhD Dissertation: University College Dublin).
Gutiérrez, J. (2020). Toward a new phase of guerrilla warfare in Colombia? The reconstitution of the FARC-EP in perspective. *Latin American Perspectives, 47*(5), 227–244.
Gutiérrez, J. (2025). Greedy peace-makers. Post-FARC-EP trajectories from political crime to politicised common crime. In J. Gutiérrez & F. Gutiérrez-Sanín (Eds.), *Criminality, political power and conflict. Critical perspectives* (pp. 177–204). Manchester University Press.
Gutiérrez-Sanín, F., & Vargas, J. (2017). Agrarian elite participation in Colombia's civil war. *Journal of Agrarian Change, 17*(4), 739–748.
Gutiérrez-Sanín, F. (2015). Agrarian inequality and civil war revisited. *Geography Compass, 9*(8), 423–431.
Gutiérrez-Sanín, F. (2019). *Clientelistic warfare*. Peter Lang.
Gutiérrez-Sanín, F. (2020). *¿Un nuevo ciclo de la guerra en Colombia?* Debate.
Gutiérrez-Sanín, F. (2025). *Tierra, Guerra, Política*. Debate.
Handelman, H. (1975) Struggle in the Andes: Peasant Political Mobilization in Peru. University of Texas Press.
Hobsbawm, E. (1973). Peasants and politics. *The Journal of Peasant Studies, 1*(1), 3–22.
Hobsbawm, E. (1986). Murderous Colombia. *New York Review of Books*, 20 November.
Jackson, W. (2016). Settler colonialism in Kenya, 1880–1963. In E. Cavanagh & L. Veracini (Eds.), *The Routledge handbook of the history of settler colonialism* (pp. 231–246). Routledge.
Jopson, T. (2023). Moro women's participation and legitimation in the Bangsamoro peace process. *Journal of Current Southeast Asian Affairs, 42*(2), 143–167.
Kaldor, M. (2001). *New & old wars*. Polity.
Kanogo, T. (1987). *Squatters and the roots of Mau Mau*. Ohio University Press.
Kenyan Human Rights Commission. (2001). *The right to return: The internally displaced persons and the culture of impunity in Kenya*. KHRC.
Kershaw, G. (1997). *Mau Mau from below*. James Currey.

Kloop, J., & Lumumba, O. (2017). Reform and counter-reform in Kenya's land governance. *Review of African Political Economy, 44*(154), 577–594.

Knight, P. (1975). New forms of economic Organization in Peru: Towards workers' self-management. In A. Lowenthal (Ed.), *The Peruvian experiment* (pp. 350–401). Princeton University Press.

Knight, P. (1976). Social property in Peru: The political economy of predominance. *Economic Analysis and Workers' Management, 10*(3–4), 167–195.

Larsen, R., Dimaano, F., & Pido, M. (2019). Can the wrongs be righted? Prospects for remedy in the Philippine oil palm agro-industry. *Development and Change, 50*(5), 1373–1397.

LeGrand, C. (1986). *Frontier expansion and peasant protest in Colombia, 1830–1936.* University of New Mexico Press.

Leo, C. (1981). Who benefited from the million-acre scheme? Toward a class analysis of Kenya's transition to independence. *Canadian Journal of African Studies/Revue Canadienne des Études Africaines, 15*(2), 201–222.

Leo, C. (1984). *Land and class in Kenya.* University of Toronto Press.

Leys, C. (1971). Politics in Kenya: The development of peasant society. *British Journal of Political Science, 1*(3), 307–337.

Lindsay-Poland, J. (2018). *Plan Colombia: U.S. ally atrocities and community activism.* Duke University Press.

Lonsdale, J., & Berman, B. (1979). Coping with the contradictions: The development of the colonial state in Kenya, 1895–1914. *The Journal of African History, 20*(4), 487–505.

Mason, D. (2004). *Caught in the crossfire. Revolutions, repression, and the rational peasant.* Rowman & Littlefield.

Matos, J., & Mejía, J. (1980). *La reforma agraria en el Perú.* IEP.

McClintock, C. (1984). Why peasants rebel: The case of Peru's Sendero Luminoso. *World Politics, 37*(1), 48–84.

McClintock, C. (1989). Peru's Sendero Luminoso rebellion: Origins and trajectory. In S. Eckstein (Ed.), *Power and popular protest. Latin American social movements* (pp. 61–101). University of California Press.

Meléndez, C. (2007). Los conflictos después del conflicto. Desestructuración del sistema político y conflictos sociales después de la violencia. In F. Reátegui (Ed.), *Conflictos sociales y respuestas del Estado: del orden interno a la protección de los derechos* (pp. 47–54). IDEHPUPC.

Merino, R. (2021). Buen vivir and the making of indigenous territories in the Peruvian Amazon. *Latin American Perspectives, 48*(3), 136–151.

Merino, R. (2023). Lost in transition: Explaining authoritarianism in Peru. *International Journal of Transitional Justice, 17*(3), 480–488.

Migdal, J. (1974). *Peasants, politics, and revolution. Pressures toward political and social change in the third world.* Princeton University Press.

Miguel, E. (2004). Tribe or nation? National building and public goods in Kenya and Tanzania. *World Politics, 56*(3), 327–362.

Milton, C. (2007). At the edge of the Peruvian truth commission: Alternative paths to recounting the past. *Radical History Review, 98*, 3–33.

Molano, A. (1994). Algunas Consideraciones sobre Colonización y Violencia. In A. Machado (Ed.), *El Agro y la Cuestión Social* (pp. 27–41). Tercer Mundo.

Molloy, I. (1985). Revolution in The Philippines: The question of an alliance between Islam and communism. *Asian Survey, 25*(8), 822–833.

Montiel, C., Rodil, R., & de Guzman, J. (2012). The Moro struggle and the challenge to peace building in Mindanao, southern Philippines. In D. Landis & R. Albert (Eds.), *Handbook of ethnic conflict* (pp. 71–89). Springer.

Navarrete-Cruz, Á., Birkenberg, A., & Birner, R. (2023). Agrarian change and land dispossession linked to the armed conflict in Colombia - a review. *Third World Quarterly, 44*(7), 1526–1545.

Olivari, W. (2015). El problema de la tierra. El caso peruano: un análisis comparativo. *Cultura Latinoamericana, 22*(2), 19–40.

Ortiz, C. (1985). *Estado y Subversión en Colombia*. CEREC.

Oxfam. (2017). *Snapshots of inequality*. Oxfam.

Palacios, M. (2011). *¿De Quién es la Tierra?* Fondo de Cultura Económica.

Palmer, D. (1986). Rebellion in rural Peru: The origins and evolution of Sendero Luminoso. *Comparative Politics, 18*(2), 127–146.

Palmer, D., & Bolívar, A. (2011). *Peru's shining path: Recent dynamics and future prospects*. WHEMSAC/Florida International University.

Peña-Huertas, R., Ruiz, E., Parada, M., Zuleta, S., & Álvarez, R. (2017). Legal dispossession and civil war in Colombia. *Journal of Agrarian Change, 17*(4), 759–769.

Pizarro, E. (1991). *Las FARC (1949–1966) de la Autodefensa a la Combinación de Todas las Formas de Lucha*. IEPRI/Tercer Mundo.

Rettberg, A. (2010). Global markets, local conflict: Violence in the Colombian coffee region after the breakdown of the international coffee agreement. *Latin American Perspectives, 37*(2), 111–132.

Reyes, A. (2009). *Guerreros y Campesinos*. Norma.

Rodil, R. (1994). *The Minoritization of the indigenous communities of Mindanao and the Sulu archipelago*. Philippine Edition.

Rodríguez, S. (2010). Política del testimonio y reconocimiento en las comisiones de la verdad guatemalteca y peruana: En torno a la figura del "indio subversivo". *Revista Crítica de Ciências Sociais, 88*, 23–55.

Sánchez, G. (1977). *Las Ligas Campesinas en Colombia*. Tiempo Presente.

Schubiger, L. (2021). State violence and wartime civilian agency: Evidence from Peru. *The Journal of Politics, 83*(4), 1383–1398.

Sehmi, A. (2024). Legacies of colonial violence in contemporary transitional justice: Memories of Mau Mau, the "Kapenguria six" and the "Ocampo six" in Kenya. *International Journal of Transitional Justice, 18*(1), 32–48.

Slye, R. (2017). Putting the J into the TRC: Kenya's truth justice and reconciliation commission. In M. Swart & K. van Marle (Eds.), *The limits of transition: The south African truth and reconciliation commission 20 years on* (pp. 282–307). Brill.

Starn, O. (1991). Missing the revolution: Anthropologists and the war in Peru. *Cultural Anthropology, 6*(1), 63–91.

Starn, O. (1998). Villagers at arms: War and counterrevolution in the central-South Andes. In S. Stern (Ed.), *Shining and other paths. War and Society in Peru, 1980–1995* (pp. 224–257). Duke University Press.

Stern, S. (1987). *Resistance, rebellion, and consciousness in the Andean peasant world, eighteenth to twentieth centuries.* University of Wisconsin Press.

Tan, S. (1995). *The socioeconomic dimension of Moro secessionism.* University of the Philippines Center for Integrative and Development Studies.

Tapia, C. (1997). *Las Fuerzas Armadas y Sendero Luminoso. Dos Estrategias y un Final.* IEP.

Theidon, K. (2006). Justice in transition: The micropolitics of reconciliation in Postwar Peru. *Journal of Conflict Resolution, 50*(3), 433–457.

Theidon, K. (2022). Reproductive warfare: Enforced sterilizations in Peru. In N. Hirschmann & D. Thomas (Eds.), *Citizenship on the edge: Sex/gender/race. Democracy, citizenship, and constitutionalism* (pp. 228–240). University of Pennsylvania Press.

Thomson, F. (2011). The agrarian question and violence in Colombia: Conflict and development. *Journal of Agrarian Change, 11*(3), 321–356.

Throup, D. (1987). *Economic & Social Origins of Mau Mau.* Ohio University Press.

TJRC (2013) Report of the Truth Justice and Reconciliation Commission (4 volumes) TJRC Kenya

UNAL. (2017). *Caracterización Comunidad FARC-EP. Resultados Generales.* Universidad Nacional de Colombia.

Vanelli, F., & Ochoa, D. (2022). Territorial peace: Land governance and sustainable peacebuilding. *International Journal of Urban Sustainable Development, 14*(1), 368–387.

Vargas, J., & Uribe, S. (2017). State, war, and land dispossession: The multiple paths to land concentration. *Journal of Agrarian Change, 17*(4), 749–758.

Vega, R., & Rodríguez, E. (1990). *Economía y Violencia.* Universidad Distrital Francisco José de Caldas.

Vellema, S., Borras, S., & Lara, F. (2011). The agrarian roots of contemporary violent conflict in Mindanao, southern Philippines. *Journal of Agrarian Change, 11*(3), 298–320.

Verwimp, P. (2013). *Peasants in power. The political economy of development and genocide in Rwanda*. Springer.

Vianni, W. (2016). Jomo Kenyatta: War, land, and politics in Kenya. In E. Obadare & W. Adebanwi (Eds.), *Governance and the crisis of rule in contemporary Africa* (pp. 97–117). Palgrave Macmillan.

Vila, G. (2022). Natures of concern: The criminalization of artisanal and small-scale mining in Colombia and Peru. *The Extractive Industries and Society, 13*, 101105.

Vila, G. (2025). From minería comunitaria to illegal mining: Indigenous territories and mining formalization in Peruvian Amazonia. In J. A. Gutiérrez & F. Gutiérrez-Sanín (Eds.), *Criminality, political power and conflict. Critical perspectives*. Manchester University Press.

Villarreal, J. (2021). The historical relationship between agrarian reforms and internal armed conflicts: Relevant factors for the Colombian post-conflict scenario. *Land Use Policy, 101*, 105138.

Wickham-Crowley, T. (1992). *Guerrillas & revolution in Latin America*. Princeton University Press.

Wolff, R. (1970). Economic aspects of British colonialism in Kenya, 1895 to 1930. *The Journal of Economic History, 30*(1), 273–277.

World Bank. (2017). *Land: territory, domain, and identity. A report submitted by the WB-IOM technical team to the Transitional Justice and Reconciliation Commission (TJRC)*. Retrieved November 29, 2025, from https://openknowledge.worldbank.org/server/api/core/bitstreams/124f3544-3e59-5992-8347-828324797e51/content

Zamosc, L. (1986). *The agrarian question and the peasant movement in Colombia*. Cambridge University Press.

Zamosc, L. (2001). Peasant struggles of the 1970s in Colombia. In S. Eckstein (Ed.), *Power and popular protest* (pp. 102–131). University of California Press.

CHAPTER 4

Understanding Agrarian Change

Abstract Peasants and agrarian struggles often reflect broader social processes. These processes of agrarian change, affecting labour relations, social relations of production, property structures, massive concentration of power and new technologies of production, have brought to the fore new forms of violence against the peasantry. This chapter's central contention is that transitional justice does not respond to agrarian conditions and circumstances in which violence occurs, placing an excessive emphasis on direct, physical violence, while much of the violence that the rural populations endure is structural and systemic in character. In the scholarly literature, meanwhile, discussions of the nexus between transitional justice and development are, at best, weak or ambiguous in their treatment of 'development' and change and, at their worst, uncritical and accommodating to neoliberal economics, which has had disastrous consequences for rural communities. This chapter introduces the political economy of agrarian change and its concepts and tools, drawing strongly on contemporary critical agrarian studies, as a field that has embraced and drawn on traditions of Marxism, critical development studies, postcolonial studies, interpretivist epistemologies and methodological pluralism.

Keywords Agrarian change • Structural adjustments • Globalisation • De-peasantisation • Re-peasantisation • Class • Intersectionality • Gender • Poverty • Inequality • Environment

J. A. Gutiérrez, *Transitional Justice and Agrarian Conflict*,
https://doi.org/10.1007/978-3-032-25228-9_4

More than half a century ago, reflecting on the peasant rebellions of the twentieth century, Eric Wolf observed that they

> are no longer simple responses to local problems, if indeed they ever were. They are but the parochial reactions to major social dislocations, set in motion by overwhelming social change. The spread of the market has torn men up by their roots, and shaken them loose from the social relationships into which they were born. Industrialization and expanded communication have given rise to new social clusters, as yet unsure of their own social positions and interests, but forced by the imbalance of their lives to seek a new adjustment. Traditional political authority has eroded or collapsed; new contenders for power are seeking new constituencies for entry into the vacant public sphere. Thus when the peasant protagonist lights the torch of rebellion, the edifice of society is already smouldering and ready to take fire. (1969, p. 295)

Peasants and agrarian struggles often reflect broader social processes, and their impact is hardly ever limited to the confines of the rural world. These processes of agrarian change, affecting labour relations, social relations of production, property structures, concentration of power and new technologies of production, have brought to the fore new forms of violence against the peasantry. The recent decades have witnessed massive changes in

> the deregulation of financial markets; shifts in the production, sourcing and sales strategies and technologies of transnational manufacturing and agribusiness corporations; the massive new possibilities attendant on information technologies, not least for mass communications, and how they are exploited by the corporate capital that controls them; the demise of the Soviet Union and finally of any plausible socialist model of development; and the ideological and political ascendancy of neoliberalism in a highly selective rolling back of the state, including the structural adjustment programmes, economic liberalisation, and state reform/good governance agendas imposed on the countries of the South and, more recently, the former Soviet bloc. (Bernstein, 2008, p. 247)

This chapter's central contention is that transitional justice does not respond to agrarian conditions and circumstances in which violence occurs. Usually, this literature's treatment of violent pasts is limited and incomplete, while often its practice fits all too comfortably with a liberal state-building project that sees market economies as its endpoint. Furthermore transitional justice have placed an excessive emphasis in direct, physical violence (Gready & Robins, 2014; Boesten & Wilding, 2015), but a lot of the violence that the peasantry and rural populations endure is structural in character. As we have discussed, transitional justice's traditional toolbox seems often inadequate to deal with these challenges that are nonetheless paramount to build a sustainable peace or real guarantees of non-repetition. In the scholarly literature, meanwhile, discussions of the nexus between transitional justice and development are, at best, weak or ambiguous in their treatment of 'development' and change and, at their worst, uncritical and accommodating to neoliberal economics, which has had disastrous consequences for rural communities. This chapter introduces the political economy of agrarian change and its concepts and tools, drawing strongly on contemporary critical agrarian studies (cf., Borras, 2023).

4.1 Defining Agrarian Change

Agrarian change refers to the processes of transformation of rural societies by the development and changes in social relations of production, technologies and productive methods, circulation and exchange patterns and power structures, among others. In a nutshell, we can say that agrarian change refers to the 'social relations and dynamics of production and reproduction, property and power in agrarian formations and their processes of change, both historical and contemporary' (Bernstein, 2010, p. 1). Today, this refers mostly to the penetration of capitalist relations in the agrarian society and its articulation to processes of globalisation, but we are also talking about *long durée* processes, such as the transitions between modes of production, the impact of colonialism on agrarian systems and rural modernisation and development projects, all of which have been at the heart of agrarian change and peasant studies for decades (Bernstein & Byres, 2001).

How can we understand this process of change? The political economy of agrarian change is better understood by using the four classic questions of political economy as analytical tools:

- Who owns what?
- Who does what?
- Who gets what?

- What do they do with it?

These four questions deal, respectively, with different aspects of the social relations, production methods, power structures, labour processes, gender relations, forms of distribution, consumption and reproduction, etc., that we need to grasp in order to analyse processes of agrarian change in any given concrete context. 'The first question concerns the social relations of different "property" regimes: how the means of production and reproduction are distributed. (…) The second question is about social divisions of labour. (…) The third question is about the social division of the "fruits of labour," which is often termed the distribution of "income"', which does not necessarily or exclusively take the form of monetary compensation, salary or wages. 'The fourth question', finally, 'is about social relations of consumption, reproduction and accumulation' (Bernstein, 2010, pp. 22–23).

More recently, Ian Scoones, in his work on rural development and livelihoods, has added two more questions to better capture the social and environmental challenges of the world in which we live now. These questions are the following:

- How do social classes and groups in society and within the state interact with each other?
- How do changes in politics get shaped by dynamic ecologies and vice versa?

The first of these two questions 'focuses on the social relations, institutions and forms of domination in society and between citizens and the state as they affect livelihoods', while the second one 'relates to questions of political ecology, and to how environmental dynamics influence livelihoods. These in turn are shaped by livelihood activities through patterns of resource access and entitlement' (2015, pp. 82–83). While his description of these four questions is related to livelihoods (the main subject of his book), these two questions can further be applied to any of the problems related to agrarian change, be factoring the state in as a massive force shaping agrarian change, and be shaping in the environment, which, as we will discuss, is a major question at present, partly because of the impact of agrarian systems on nature and the impact that then the environmental crisis and climate change are having on agrarian systems and on rural populations in general. These six general questions can help us better understand and investigate some of the case studies of agrarian conflict that we have discussed, but also the cross-cutting themes that we will explore next.

4.1.1 Poverty and Inequality

In 2022, more than three-quarters of the world's extreme poor lived in rural areas, with rural Sub-Saharan Africa concentrating a great amount of this population; if we focus on the poor, and not the extreme poor, 66% of them live in the rural areas of the world, despite the majority of the population living in urban areas. Multidimensional approaches to measure poverty show that rural populations tend to be well at the bottom on most indicators (malnourishment, health, education, livelihoods, living standards, access to safe drinking water, exposure to natural hazards, etc.); the evident gaps with the urban population show important patterns of inequality between the urban and the rural territories; in particular with education, the gap widened enormously because of the infrastructural problems of the rural world and the closure of schools (World Bank, 2024). Within the rural world, inequality is also most striking when looking at the massive imbalance in access and ownership to land across the globe, which has been worsening steadily over the last decades. South Asia and Latin America rank as the most unequal places in the world when it comes to land concentration: 75% of the land is owned by 10% of landowners, while the poorest 50% of landowners control merely a 2% of the land, and this without taking into account the masses of landless peasants (Bauluz et al., 2020).

The patterns of inequality and the gap we see between the rural and the urban population can also be identified with the gap between rural men and women. Women are far more likely to be deprived of food security—a gap of 4.3% and growing—, while there is an enormous gap in terms of landownership between men and women (FAO, 2023). In fact, as agrifood systems go, 'women's roles tend to be marginalized and their working conditions are likely to be worse than men's – irregular, informal, part-time, low-skilled, labour intensive and thus vulnerable. Women also have higher burdens of unpaid care, limiting their opportunities for education and employment' (FAO, 2023, p. xviii). This, despite the fact that the participation of women in agricultural or agrifood labour is very high and sometimes bigger than that of men—66% against a 60% participation in Sub-Saharan Africa, and a 71% against a 47% in Asia, with women earning, on an average, 18.4% less than men doing the same agricultural work. Precarity is also higher; after the COVID-19 pandemic, 22% of women working in the agricultural sector lost their jobs, compared to a 2% of the men (Ibid.). This pattern of systematic marginalization and discrimination is hardly a peculiarity of the rural world, but because poverty is experienced more acutely here, the effects of this precarity and vulnerability are also felt much stronger.

These figures aren't, of course, the result of extreme bad luck, and they aren't coincidental in any way. They reflect a global trend by which rural areas are spaces where there is a chronic lack of investment in basic infrastructure, where development projects fail to even consider the needs and/or views of the rural population and are territories regarded more often than not as mere places where extraction takes place. And even within the rural population, it shows a worrying tendency for women to be at the bottom of the equation in most indicators. Thus, these appalling conditions, which have been consistent throughout the decades, amount to a systemic violation of the basic economic, social and cultural rights of the rural population.

4.1.2 Class and Intersectionality

While Shanin's definition of peasant (1987) provided in Chap. 1, based around the family orientation of their economic activity and with the primary purpose of the reproduction of their force, will suffice for our purposes here, it is important to keep in mind that there are processes of class differentiation among small farmers and peasants, terms often used interchangeably, linked to their degrees of capitalist penetration and articulation, access to other forms of income, technology and/or credit, environmental conditions, labour relations, etc. making generalisations often challenging (Bernstein, 2010). Classes, as Scoones reminds us, are 'not unitary, naturalized, or static' (Scoones, 2015, p. 78), and they are constantly evolving. In rural settings, these processes of social division of labour and differential access to resources, livelihoods and means of production that underpin the definition of social classes are often gendered and in some cases would have ethnic components that relate us to the massive reorganisation of international labour by colonialism.

Regardless of the difficulties of defining what a peasant is in terms of class and accepting a great degree of internal differentiation, the actual status of that 'awkward class', as Shanin called it (1972), as a particular *subject* with specific grievances and voice, has been, in any case, largely elusive to transitional justice. This is probably the case because, on the one hand, classes have become an invisibilised category in social sciences in general and in transitional justice scholarship in particular (where other categories such as race or gender have taken priority); on the other hand, class is a term directly linked to socio-economic conditions, and as we have discussed, transitional justice has been focused primarily on civil and political rights and conditions, therefore rendering classes as such further invisibilised.

Over the last decade, however, other groups have been gaining increased recognition in transitional justice, after being initially invisibilised. There is, for instance, a growing focus on the specific affectations and impacts experienced in the course of conflict, dictatorships and transitional contexts by ethnic or indigenous groups (Chapman, 2011; Rodríguez-Garavito & Lam, 2011; Littlechild & Stamatopoulou, 2014; Young, 2014). More recently, there was a whole ethnic chapter in the 2016 Colombian peace agreement, which, like much of the rest of the agreement, remains an unfulfilled promise and faces serious challenges in its implementation (Góngora-Mera, 2019). Likewise, the Truth Commission in Colombia faced the challenge of incorporating the marginalised voices of ethnic and gendered groups into its narrative (González & Bueno-Hansen, 2021).

There has also been an increased feminist reflection on the specific problematic of women in conflict and in transitional settings (Ní Aoláin, 2009; Ní Aoláin & O'Rourke 2010; Boesten & Wilding, 2015; O'Rourke, 2015). More recently, some authors have expanded the reflections on gender to also incorporate the LGTBI+ community (Bueno-Hansen, 2018; Schulz, 2020; Haastrup & Hagen, 2021; Biddolph, 2024). At first, the interest on women in transitional justice was largely limited to cases of sexual violence, which, as some feminist scholars have argued, can be problematic on a number of grounds, including the fact that the 'fetishisation' of sexual violence can sideline other issues affecting women (Autesserre, 2010; Eriksson-Baaz & Stern, 2013; Meger, 2016), and that a reductionist focus on women as mere victims can be depoliticising and infantilising, with women, children and 'other vulnerable groups' often collapsed into a single category (Carpenter, 2005).

However, feminist reflections on transitional justice have moved beyond the sole focus on sexual violence, to incorporate other forms of gendered violence and systematic discrimination against women, but also demonstrating that violence suffered by women during conflict is firmly rooted in patterns of exclusion, discrimination, marginalisation and violence pre-dating conflict (Boesten, 2014; Meger, 2016). Still, drawing from the intersectional perspective, it is wrong to assume that the experience of all women is the same, and Acosta et al. (2018), for instance, discuss how the experience of indigenous women amidst the Colombian conflict was peculiar and therefore required particular approaches in order to redress the harms they suffered. And even at this point, one may also point that the experience of indigenous women can be disaggregated into the dozens of indigenous groups, each one of them distinctive.

This last point is not a recent realisation. Some feminist authors had realised, decades ago, that class, gender, sex and race were interconnected in an interlocking system of oppression, resulting in different experiences of oppression by different members in various emancipatory social movements, noticing that the experience of working-class black women was not the same as the experience of upper-class white males or females (Carastathis, 2016). This was later developed as intersectionality, the paradigm that seeks to understand how different forms of oppression overlap, intersect and reinforce one another (Crenshaw, 1989, 1991; Collins, 2019). Hill Collins describes it as 'the critical insight that race, class, gender, sexuality, ethnicity, nation, ability, and age operate not as unitary, mutually exclusive entities, but as reciprocally constructing phenomena that in turn shape complex social inequalities' (Collins, 2015, p. 2). In that sense, both the field of transitional justice and that of agrarian studies have been paying much more attention to the gendered dimensions of the agrarian populations, and the historic forms of exclusion, marginalisation and oppression that women have endured precisely because of their class and gender (Meertens, 2015, 2016; Rodríguez et al., 2016), but also because of their ethnicity (González & Bueno-Hansen, 2021; Presta, 2024).[1]

As it is often the case, much of this reflection was prompted from below. The transnational peasant organisation *La Vía Campesina* (see Chap. 5), recognised the importance and the particularities of peasant women (Desmarais, 2003), a stance that they pushed in their advocacy work and

[1] Again, in this case, a significant proportion of the recent literature is coming from Colombia, a country which has become not only an important transitional justice case-study but also one with a vibrant peasant movement that is well connected to international organisations.

their mobilisation for the expansion of rights to peasants and for the creation of a new normative framework in international human rights law (see 5.3.2). In 2008, they declared: 'We recognize the central role of women in agriculture for food self-sufficiency, and the special relationship of women with the land, with life and with seeds. (…) If we do not eradicate violence towards women within our movement, we will not advance in our struggles, and if we do not create new gender relations, we will not be able to build a new society' (Martínez-Torres & Rosset, 2010, p. 167). This statement reflects a growing understanding of the nuances of the peasant struggles; apart from the class differentiation inherent to the concept of peasantry, there is gender, race, age, global inequalities, etc., affecting differentially the peasantry which needs to be addressed in order to produce sound and contextualised responses.

4.1.3 Globalisation and De-Peasantisation/re-Peasantisation

The process that we describe as globalisation—that is, the processes 'transforming our present social condition of conventional nationality into one of globality' (Steger, 2020, p. 2)—has been in the making for centuries, clearly since the start of modernity 500 years ago, accelerating in more recent decades with the advent of neoliberalism that pushed for a return to orthodox free market capitalism and the dismantling of whatever was left of the welfare state (Wallerstein, 2000). This process of neoliberal globalisation had very dramatic impacts over agriculture due to trade liberalisation and the proliferation of free trade agreements; financialisation processes that foster speculation with agricultural commodities; structural adjustment, austerity and the pressure on Global South countries to remove subsidies; the emergence of large agri-business and land-grabbing; the global food market represented in large supermarkets and long food supply chains; the rise of biopiracy and the hoarding of intellectual property rights on genetic plant material by oligopolies; and the massive expansion of monoculture, cash crops, biofuels and genetically modified organisms (GMOs). This process has had devastating effects over ecosystems, the environment, biodiversity, climate and human health (Bernstein, 2010, pp. 82–84; Margulis et al., 2023).

These factors already mentioned, but in particular the expansion of agri-business, large-scale land-grabbing and free trade policies, led to the rapid deterioration of the conditions of life for multiple rural populations and threatened the livelihoods and access to food of millions; this process has rapidly accelerated since the end of the Cold War (Desmarais, 2007). At the same time that the process of globalisation has accelerated, exercising pressure 'from above' over the peasantry, there has also been another process taking place 'from below', that of political de-centralisation, as well as privatisation 'from the side' of the state, dismantling all the traditional supports of agrarian systems (Borras et al., 2008). This long process of globalisation, accelerated over the neoliberal decades, provides the backdrop needed to make sense of the concept of de-peasantisation, which describes the progressive disappearance of the peasantry, either through displacement or their transformation into wage-labourers -often by a combination of both (Araghi, 1995; Vanhaute, 2012). As one of the opening quotes in this book mentioned, (capitalist) modernisation means little more to the peasant other than the fact that 'sooner or later they are its victims' (Barrington Moore, 1966, p. 467).

However, the peasantry is persistent. It has been argued by some that this persistence 'is tolerated, and even encouraged, by capital as long as peasant or family farming can continue to produce "cheap" food commodities that lower the costs of labour power (wages) to capitalists, and indeed itself produces "cheap" labour power. That is, peasants and small farmers who also sell their labour power can be paid less because their wage does not have to cover the full costs of household reproduction, which are partly met through its farming -sometimes seen as a "subsidy" to the capitals that employ rural labour migrants' (Bernstein, 2010, pp. 94–95). That is, the persistence of small-scale agriculture and family farming has more to do with the fact that they still play a role in the capitalist mode of production, and pockets of peasant economy can be useful to agri-business as cheap labour or for the production of food (e.g., Mudimu et al., 2022).

But we also need to factor in the role played by peasant resistance who actively have fought for their right to exist as a mode of production and as a distinct social subject: as we have discussed earlier, peasants have mobilised and struggled for centuries for their right to land and autonomy, they have taken up arms against dispossession, mobilised in alliance with urban sectors for agrarian reform and escaped the enclosures, as well as practised foot-dragging and other day-to-day forms of resistance, what James C. Scott (1985, 1990, 2009) calls the 'weapons of the weak'. As we will discuss later (Chap. 5, this active resistance led to the emergence of new transnational movements that have contested the terms of agrarian change and re-imagined the place of the peasantry in alternative social projects.

There is, indeed, a process of re-peasantisation taking place over the last decades, by which people are going back to the land, becoming peasants or small-scale farmers as their primary occupation again, intensifying and diversifying their production and reclaiming their autonomy as producers (Singh & Sharma, 2013; van der Ploeg, 2018; Jansen et al., 2022). While some experiences of re-peasantisation have been top-down and state-led (for the cases of Venezuela and Cuba see Page, 2010), the vast majority of them of them have happened through direct struggles and through spontaneous action from below, either because of broader struggles for land and rights (Mançano Fernandes, 2013; Rosset & Ule Muñoz, 2025), or because of a desire of autonomy and a better life (Philip, 2023). In any case, re-peasantisation remains a contested process, one in which the forces of de-peasantisation and the risk of ending articulated to agribusiness as an enclave of cheap labour are always present.

4.1.4 Environmental Crisis and Agrarian Dynamics

The environmental crisis and climate change are one of the most era-defining challenges at present. Biodiversity in the world is declining rapidly as a result of human activity, with the rate of species' extinction skyrocketing over the last hundred years to a staggering rate 1000 times more than the background extinction rate, leading some to talk of a sixth mass extinction in the world (Pimm et al., 2014; Cowie et al., 2022). Climate change, on the other hand, primarily caused by greenhouse gas emissions, has been reflected in unequivocal global warming of 1.1 °C above 1850–1900 levels in the period 2011–2020, a tendency which is accelerating (IPCC, 2023; Pielke, 2004). Some authors have even gone to propose a new categorisation for the current epoch as the Anthropocene, a period in which human activity and its impact on pollution, biodiversity loss, mass extinction, destruction of ecosystems and climate change have become dominant features (Crutzen, 2002; Lewis & Maslin, 2015).

People across the globe are affected differentially by climate change, with the Global South and specifically the rural poor among them as a sector particularly affected in exceedingly intense ways by rising tempera tures, droughts and climate chaos, despite contributing the least to climate change (Margulis et al., 2023). Approximately 3.3 to 3.6 billion people and their livelihoods, together with the ecosystems in which they live, are highly vulnerable to climate change (IPCC, 2023), forcing millions, particularly rural poor, into mass displacement with extremely destabilising consequences (Balsari et al., 2020). In Sub-Saharan Africa alone, over 2.5 million have already been displaced and 7 million more have been made food insecure (Adepoju, 2019). This, of course, is not a fact of nature but something completely caused by power structures (economic, social, political) entrenched in our current system (Dietz et al., 2020), which is characterised by the scramble for the control of resources. And while some voices focus purely on adaptating to these changes and building resilience, the challenge ahead—-given the massive threat posed on to life itself by these power structures—requires nothing short of large-scale structural transformations (Scoones, 2015; Borras et al., 2023).

In this context, extractivism (sometimes referred to as neo-extractivism, to stress the continuity with the original colonial practices) or the 'production of value through physically extractive processes (mining, oil extraction, certain kinds of agriculture, etc.) where value generation is necessarily temporary and generally followed by barrenness and an inability to sustainably reproduce livelihoods in the affected habitat' (Ye et al., 2020, p. 155) poses a particular threat to peasant livelihoods and modes of production because of its particularly destructive nature, in which resources are used without reproducing them, representing a classical example of 'accumulation by dispossession' (Harvey, 2003).[2] In this process, it 'drain(s) off considerable tranches of wealth. This is facilitated since no substantive and ongoing investments in the reproduction of resources are needed and because financialization is now the main mechanism for funding: the required capital is obtained on the capital markets (banks and stock markets). This means that costs are lower and, due to leverage, the rates of return are higher' (Ye et al., 2020, p. 162). Extractivism

> implies (if not requires) monopoly control over specific natural resources (minerals, oil, gas, fertile land, aquifers, woodlands, etc.) and it results in their ruthless exploitation. After the resource in question has been extracted, only "negative externalities" remain: pollution, impoverished populations, exhausted resources, etc. The value entailed in the particular resources is mined – leaving a void. The mined products are exported and the value obtained transferred to other places. (Ye et al., 2020, p. 155)

[2] This threat is real even in models where there has been a certain co-existence between extractivist practices and agricultural peasant production (McKay, 2020).

While traditionally extractivism has been associated with mineral resources or fossil fuels, the concept has now been expanded to imply a certain pattern of extractive production, dominant in contemporary capitalism across various industries (Chagnon et al., 2022). Among the various industries contributing actively to environmental damage and climate change, unsustainable agri-business, large-scale cattle ranching and industrial monoculture of cash crops such as sugar-cane, soybeans, palm oil and others have been major forces behind the destruction of the ecosystems and biodiversity, large-scale emissions, mechanisation, dependence on unsustainable global markets and use of chemical inputs (Martínez-Alier, 2011; Wolford, 2021; Yaşın, 2023). This large-scale, industrial, corporate monoculture industry, because of its continuity with extractivist practices linked to forms of accumulation by dispossession, intensifying the struggle over land and the degradation of livelihoods and of soil, has been labelled agro-extractivism (Veltmeyer & Ezquerro-Cañete, 2023). The global expansion of extractivist industries, threatening the livelihoods and right to land of peasantries all over the world with its neo-colonial grip, has led to the agrarian question becoming firmly entrenched within the broader environmental question (Yaşın, 2023), because:

> The rural world is the site where forests are both protected and exploited; where huge mining interests compete with small-scale miners and where rural industrial activity pollutes the air and destroys the land (…). Yet industrial capitalism has often treated nature as inexhaustible and rural inhabitants as disposable through the extraction of vast quantities of resources, from crops to oil, natural gas, minerals and more (…). Neoliberal, state socialist and populist governments alike have thus predicated national development on cheap natural resources and this tendency is likely to be aggravated in the context of climate change. (Borras et al., 2023, p. 5)

Apart from these impacts caused by the extractivist economy, climate chaos and the environmental crisis, rural populations have been, paradoxically, affected by top-down and coercive attempts at conservation, in what has been labelled as 'green militarisation', or the use of military methods for the protection of the environment and conservation purposes (Lunstrum, 2014). In the process, 'Culprits are created—slash-and-burn cultivators, backward pastoralists, wood fuel collectors, charcoal burners, hunters and gatherers, for example—and demonized in policy narratives, often with little substantive evidence. The culprits are often the poor, the marginalized (…) livelihoods are criminalized and outlawed and people are denied access to the resources on which they have long depended' (Scoones, 2015, p. 65). The militarisation of conservation in Africa has not only contributed to exacerbating the marginalisation of already impoverished rural communities (traditionally excluded from wild-life management), but also, by tackling the symptoms rather than the root causes of environmentally detrimental activities such as poaching, it has entrenched conflict dynamics, military-styled authoritarianism and colonial legacies (Humphreys & Smith, 2014; Massé et al., 2018; Duffy et al., 2019; Jones, 2021; Luoma, 2023; Ashaba & Marijnen, 2025).

In Latin America, a similar green militaristic approach has been taken, usually criminalising small artisanal miners in places like Peru who often supplement through mining activities their agricultural income,[3] orpeasant smallholders in the national parks of Colombia, who are redefined as criminal, and in the context of well-seated counter-insurgent practices and institutions in the region, as terrorists and therefore as military targets (Vila, 2022, 2025; Corredor-García & López, 2024; Samper et al., 2024). This is most clear in Guatemala and in Colombia, where rural populations living in forested areas and jungles have been for decades the object of scorched-earth counter-insurgent practices and have been constructed as an internal enemy by the army and counter-insurgent institutions, with recent large-scale military operations subjecting these same populations to unspeakable violence and to current patterns of violent exclusion, only now with a green façade and often with the full collusion of conservation agencies (Ybarra, 2012; Corredor-García & López, 2024). As rural movements worldwide keep contesting their rights to social justice and to live, as they have done traditionally, in forested areas (Kashwan, 2017) and since this militarised variant of conservationism as an extension of colonial legacies against indigenous peoples remains firmly in place, this violence is unlikely to decrease in the coming years and has called the attention of transitional justice scholars and practitioners (Luoma, 2023).

Of course, all of these processes of extraction and militarisation, with the multiple environmental dislocations they produce, have elicited resistance. Some of it has been based around this non-articulated but pervasive form of resistance to militarised conservation in Africa, which often

[3] Although the impact of neoliberal economics and the assault over the livelihoods of peasants is pushing an increasing number of peasants and farmers into small-scale extractive activities (Lahiri-Dutt, 2018).

assumes the form of 'social banditry' (Humphreys & Smith, 2014), a phenomenon observed in other rural contexts marred by violence. In Latin America, extractivism has generated important resistance from powerful social movements (Palmisano & Wahren, 2023), becoming even a bridge to articulate a wide range of social movements, including peasants and environmentalists (Dietz, 2019). Among these, ethnic and indigenous groups have been identified as being at the forefront of this resistance, according to some authors, because of their cultural and spiritual relationship with their territory and nature (Pastor & Santamaría, 2021). Still, while recognising the important role played by rural people in protecting nature and placing limits through their resistance to its destruction, we would do good to avoid the post-modern romanticisation and idealisation of whole categories of complex and contradictory subjects (e.g., women, indigenous and peasants) as if they were quintessential and mystical guardians of nature or as if they could have a special and metaphysical relationship with nature that is somehow (and inexplicably) vetoed to other categories of people:

> Such narratives of local people as saviours are just as problematic as their casting as culprits and villains. A much more nuanced, differentiated analysis is required. Some people may be exploiters of nature, others guardians. How they ultimately behave has more to do with their social relations and local political positioning than their identification as local or indigenous people or as women *per se*. (Scoones, 2015, p. 67)

The shift of the environmental movement to discourses that demand not just the protection of nature but climate justice (Dietz et al., 2020) creates opportunities to expand the framework of transitional justice in order to address environmental harm and environmental impacts:

> This ecocentric turn is driving increasing traction for a move to criminalize mass damage and destruction of ecosystems ('ecocide') at a global level, along with growing support for recognizing the rights of nature, with potentially disruptive implications for property regimes. The enshrining of legal and constitutional rights for nature and its localized systems such as rivers is an emerging transnational legal framework fast gaining international traction as a new tool to combat extractivism and environmental destruction. (Viaene et al., 2023, p. 2)

Critical to these developments have been the processes of transitional justice in Colombia that have been deeply influenced by the pressure of rural peoples, of the indigenous, peasants and Afro-Colombians, even as (and maybe precisely because) some forms of environmental damage have been exacerbated after the 2016 peace agreement (Betancur-Alarcón & Krause, 2020; Corredor-García & López, 2024; Samper et al., 2024). This should not come as a surprise, since the conflict has been historically fuelled by land-grabbing, which is underpinned now by the new extractivist fever; therefore, various social movements and civil society organisations have made enormous efforts for the recognition of nature as a victim of conflict, thus moving away from a purely anthropocentric notion of justice (Ariza-Buitrago & Gómez-Betancur, 2023). The JEP, in response to this mobilisation, 'has issued five resolutions which accredit the territories of indigenous peoples and Black communities as victims of the armed conflict. Thus, the Katsa Su, the Cxhab Wala Kile and the Eperera Euja—the territories of the Awá, the Nasa and the Sia people, respectively—as well as the territories of the Black communities of Tumaco, have been transformed into legal subjects with rights to justice, truth and reparation, and the right to participate in each stage of the legal process' (Huneeus & Rueda, 2021, p. 210), demonstrating the potential opened up in rural contexts for the intersections between climate and transitional justice.

References

Acosta, M., Castañeda, Á., García, D., Hernández, F., Muelas, D., & Santamaría, Á. (2018). The Colombian transitional process: Comparative perspectives on violence against indigenous women. *International Journal of Transitional Justice, 12*(1), 108–125.

Adepoju, A. (2019). Migrants and refugees in Africa', in Erin Hannah (ed.), *Oxford Research Encyclopedia of Politics*. Oxford University Press. Retrieved February 15, 2026, from https://doi.org/10.1093/acrefore/9780190228637.013.723

Araghi, F. (1995). Global Depeasantization, 1945–1990. *The Sociological Quarterly, 36*(2), 337–368.

Ariza-Buitrago, I., & Gómez-Betancur, L. (2023). Nature in focus: The invisibility and re-emergence of Rivers, land and animals in Colombia's transitional justice system. *International Journal of Transitional Justice, 17*(1), 71–88.

Ashaba, I., & Marijnen, E. (2025). "We are soldiers now": Green militarism and (foreign-assisted) military training in conservation. *International Affairs, 101*(2), 565–582.

Autesserre, S. (2010). Dangerous tales: Dominant narratives on The Congo and their unintended consequences. *African Affairs, 111*, 202–222.
Balsari, S., Dresser, C., & Leaning, J. (2020). Climate change, migration and civil strife, current environmental. *Health Reports, 7*, 404–414.
Bauluz, L., Yajna, G., & Filip, N. (2020). *Global land inequality* (WID.world WORKING PAPER No. 2020/10).
Bernstein, H. (2008). Agrarian questions from transition to globalisation. In H. A. Lodhi & C. Kay (Eds.), *Peasants and globalisation: Political economy, rural transformation and the agrarian question* (pp. 239–261). Routledge.
Bernstein, H. (2010). *Class dynamics of agrarian change*. Fernwood Publishing.
Bernstein, H., & Byres, T. (2001). From peasant studies to agrarian change. *Journal of Agrarian Change, 1*(1), 1–56.
Betancur-Alarcón, L., & Krause, T. (2020). Reaching for the mountains at the end of a Rebelocracy: Changes in land and water access in Colombia's highlands during the post-peace agreement phase. *Frontiers in Environmental Science, 8*, 546821.
Biddolph, C. (2024). Queering the global governance of transitional justice: Tensions and (Im)possibilities. *International Journal of Transitional Justice, 18*(2), 281–298.
Boesten, J. (2014). *Sexual violence during war and peace. Gender, power, and post-conflict justice in Peru*. Palgrave Macmillan.
Boesten, J., & Wilding, P. (2015). Transformative gender justice: Setting an agenda. *Women's Studies International Forum, 51*, 75–80.
Borras, S. (2023). Politically engaged, pluralist and internationalist: Critical agrarian studies today. *The Journal of Peasant Studies, 50*(2), 449–489.
Borras, S., Edelman, M., & Kay, C. (2008). Transnational agrarian movements: Origins and politics, campaigns and impact. *Journal of Agrarian Change, 8*(2–3), 169–204.
Borras, S., Scoones, I., Baviskar, A., Edelman, M., Peluso, N. L., & Wolford, W. (2023). Climate change and agrarian struggles. In I. Scoones, S. Borras, A. Baviskar, M. Edelman, N. L. Peluso, & W. Wolford (Eds.), *Climate change and critical agrarian studies* (pp. 1–28). Routledge.
Bueno-Hansen, P. (2018). The emerging LGBTI rights challenge to transitional justice in Latin America. *International Journal of Transitional Justice, 12*(1), 126–145.
Carastathis, A. (2016). Interlocking Systems of Oppression. In N. Rodríguez, W. Martino, J. Ingrey, & E. Brockenbrough (Eds.), *Critical concepts in queer studies and education. An international guide for the twenty-first century*. Palgrave Macmillan.
Carpenter, C. (2005). "Women, children and other vulnerable groups": Gender, strategic frames and the protection of civilians as a transnational issue. *International Studies Quarterly, 49*(2), 295–334.

Chagnon, C., Durante, F., Gills, B., Hagolani-Albov, S., Hokkanen, S., Kangasluoma, S., Konttinen, H., Kröger, M., LaFleur, W., Ollinaho, O., & Vuola, M. (2022). From Extractivism to global Extractivism: The evolution of an organizing concept. *The Journal of Peasant Studies, 49*(4), 760–792.
Chapman, C. (2011). Transitional justice and the rights of minorities and indigenous peoples. In P. Arthur (Ed.), *Identities in transition: Challenges for transitional justice in divided societies* (pp. 251–270). Cambridge University Press.
Collins, P. H. (2015). Intersectionality's definitional dilemmas. *Annual Review of Sociology, 41*, 1–20.
Collins, P. H. (2019). *Intersectionality as critical social theory.* Duke University Press.
Corredor-García, J., & López, F. (2024). The logic of "war on deforestation": A military response to climate change in the Colombian Amazon. *Alternatives: Global Local, Political, 49*(4), 325–343.
Cowie, R., Bouchet, P., & Fontaine, B. (2022). The sixth mass extinction: Fact, fiction or speculation? *Biological Reviews, 97*, 640–663.
Crenshaw, K. (1989). Demarginalizing the intersection of race and sex: A black feminist critique of antidiscrimination doctrine, feminist theory and antiracist politics. *University of Chicago Legal Forum, 1*, 139–167.
Crenshaw, K. (1991). Mapping the margins: Intersectionality, identity politics, and violence against women of color. *Stanford Law Review, 43*(6), 1241–1299.
Crutzen, P. (2002). Geology of mankind - the Anthropocene. *Nature, 415*, 23.
Desmarais, A. (2003). The Vía Campesina: Peasant women on the frontiers of food sovereignty. *Canadian Woman Studies/les cahiers de la femme, 23*(1), 140–145.
Desmarais, A. (2007). *La Vía Campesina. Globalisation and the power of peasants.* Fernwood Publishing.
Dietz, K. (2019). Direct democracy in mining conflicts in Latin America: Mobilising against the La Colosa project in Colombia. *Canadian Journal of Development Studies/Revue canadienne d'études du développement, 40*(2), 145–162.
Dietz, T., Shwom, R., & Whitley, C. (2020). Climate change and society. *Annual Review of Sociology, 46*, 135–158.
Duffy, R., Massé, F., Smidt, E., Marijnen, E., Büscher, B., Verweijen, J., Ramutsindela, M., Simlai, T., Joanny, L., & Lunstrum, E. (2019). Why we must question the militarisation of conservation. *Biological Conservation, 232*, 66–73.
Eriksson-Baaz, M., & Stern, M. (2013). *Sexual violence as a weapon of war? Perceptions, prescriptions, problems in The Congo and beyond.* Zed.
FAO. (2023). *The status of women in Agrifood systems.* FAO.
Góngora-Mera, M. (2019). The ethnic chapter of the 2016 Colombian peace agreement and the afro-descendants' right to prior consultation: A story of

unfulfilled promises. *The International Journal of Human Rights, 23*(6), 938–956.

González, J., & Bueno-Hansen, P. (2021). The promise and perils of mainstreaming Intersectionality in the Colombian peace process. *International Journal of Transitional Justice, 15*(3), 553–575.

Gready, P., & Robins, S. (2014). From transitional to transformative justice: A new agenda for practice. *International Journal of Transitional Justice, 8*(3), 339–361.

Haastrup, T., & Hagen, J. (2021). Racial hierarchies of knowledge production in the women, peace and security agenda. *Critical Studies on Security, 9*(1), 27–30.

Harvey, D. (2003). *The new imperialism*. Oxford University Press.

Humphreys, J., & Smith, M. L. R. (2014). The "rhinofication" of south African security. *International Affairs, 90*(4), 795–818.

Huneeus, A., & Rueda, P. (2021). Territory as a victim of armed conflict. *International Journal of Transitional Justice, 15*(1), 210–229.

IPCC. (2023). *Climate change 2023 synthesis report. Summary for policymakers. A report of the intergovernmental panel on climate change*. IPCC.

Jansen, K., Vicol, M., & Nikol, L. (2022). Autonomy and repeasantization: Conceptual, analytical, and methodological problems. *Journal of Agrarian Change, 22*(3), 489–505.

Jones, E. (2021). Capital and control: Neocolonialism through the militarization of African wildlife conservation. *Flux: International Relations Review, 11*(2), 29–37.

Kashwan, P. (2017). *Democracy in the woods*. Oxford University Press.

Lahiri-Dutt, K. (2018). Extractive peasants: Reframing informal artisanal and small-scale mining debates. *Third World Quarterly, 39*(8), 1561–1582.

Lewis, S., & Maslin, M. (2015). Defining the Anthropocene. *Nature, 519*, 171–180.

Littlechild, W., & Stamatopoulou, E. (2014). *Indigenous peoples' access to justice, including truth and reconciliation processes*. Institute for the Study of Human Rights, Columbia University.

Lunstrum, E. (2014). Green militarization: Anti-poaching efforts and the spatial contours of Kruger National Park. *Annals of the Association of American Geographers, 104*(4), 816–832.

Luoma, C. (2023). Reckoning with conservation violence on indigenous territories: Possibilities and limitations of a transitional justice response. *International Journal of Transitional Justice, 17*(1), 89–106.

Mançano Fernandes, B. (2013). Re-peasantization, resistance and subordination: The struggle for land and agrarian reform in Brazil. *Agrarian South: Journal of Political Economy, 2*(3), 269–289.

Margulis, M., Hopewell, K., & Qereshniku, E. (2023). Food, famine and the free trade fallacy: The dangers of market fundamentalism in an era of climate emergency. In I. Scoones, S. Borras, A. Baviskar, M. Edelman, N. L. Peluso, &

W. Wolford (Eds.), *Climate change and critical agrarian studies* (pp. 327–351). Routledge.

Martínez-Torres, M., & Rosset, P. (2010). La Vía Campesina: The birth and evolution of a transnational social movement. *The Journal of Peasant Studies, 37*(1), 149–175.

Martínez-Alier, J. (2011). The EROI of agriculture and its use by the Via Campesina. *Journal of Peasant Studies, 38*(1), 145-160.

Massé, F., Lunstrum, E., & Holterman, D. (2018). Linking green militarization and critical military studies. *Critical Military Studies, 4*(2), 201–221.

McKay, B. (2020). Food sovereignty and neo-extractivism: Limits and possibilities of an alternative development model. *Globalizations, 17*(8), 1386–1404.

Meertens, D. (2015). Discursive frictions: The transitional justice paradigm, land restitution and gender. *Papel Político, 10*(2), 353–381.

Meertens, D. (2016). Justicia de género y tierras en Colombia: desafíos para la era del pos-acuerdo. *European Review of Latin American and Caribbean Studies, 102*, 89–100.

Meger, S. (2016). The fetishization of sexual violence in international security. *International Studies Quarterly, 60*(1), 149–159.

Mudimu, G., Zuo, T., & Nalwimba, N. (2022). Inside an enclave: The dynamics of capitalism and rural politics in a post-land reform context. *The Journal of Peasant Studies, 49*(1), 101–128.

Ní Aoláin, F. (2009). Women, security, and the patriarchy of internationalized transitional justice. *Human Rights Quarterly, 31*(4), 1055–1085.

Ní Aoláin, F., & O'Rourke, C. (2010). Gendered transitional justice and the non-state actor. In M. Reed & A. Lyons (Eds.), *Contested transitions: Dilemmas of transitional justice in comparative experience.* International Center for Transitional Justice.

O'Rourke, C. (2015). Feminist scholarship in transitional justice: A de-politicising impulse? *Women's Studies International Forum, 51*, 118–127.

Page, T. (2010). Can the state create Campesinos? A comparative analysis of the Venezuelan and Cuban Repeasantization programmes. *Journal of Agrarian Change, 10*(2), 251–272.

Palmisano, T., & Wahren, J. (2023). The political economy of extractivism and social struggles in Latin America. In M. Atzeni, D. Azzellini, A. Mezzadri, P. Moore, & U. Apitzsch (Eds.), *Handbook of research on the global political economy of work* (pp. 512–521). Edward Elgar.

Pastor, L., & Santamaría, A. (2021). Experiences of spiritual advocacy for land and territorial itineraries for the Defense of Wiwa women's rights in Postconflict Colombia. *International Journal of Transitional Justice, 15*(1), 86–107.

Philip, J. (2023). Who are we without land? Repeasantization and caste in a village of South India. *Agrarian South: Journal of Political Economy, 12*(4), 488–513.

Pielke, R. (2004). What is climate change? *Energy & Environment, 15*(3), 515–520.

Pimm, S., Jenkins, C., Abell, R., Brooks, T., Gittleman, J., Joppa, L., Raven, P., Roberts, C., & Sexton, J. (2014). The biodiversity of species and their rates of extinction, distribution, and protection. *Science, 344*(6187), 1246752.

Presta, D. (2024). Mujeres, paz y territorio: Construcción de paz en Colombia a través de los enfoques étnico y de género. *Revista Internacional De Derechos Humanos, 14*(2), 9–48.

Rodríguez, L., Pini, B., & Baker, S. (2016). The global countryside: Peasant women negotiating, recalibrating and resisting rural change in Colombia. *Gender, Place & Culture, 23*(11), 1547–1559.

Rodríguez-Garavito, C., & Lam, Y. (2011). *Etnorreparaciones: La justicia colectiva étnica y la reparación a pueblos indígenas y comunidades afrodescendientes en Colombia.* DeJusticia.

Rosset, P., & Muñoz, C. U. (2025). Repeasantization and socio-territorial movements. *The Journal of Peasant Studies, 52*(3), 649–664.

Samper, J. A., Krause, T., & López, J. (2024). "Everyone decided to declare war on the forest": Between territorial peace and pacification in the Colombian Andean-Amazon. *Ecology and Society, 29*(4), 46.

Schulz, P. (2020). Towards inclusive gender in transitional justice: Gaps, blind-spots and opportunities. *Journal of Intervention and Statebuilding, 14*(5), 691–710.

Scoones, I. (2015). *Sustainable livelihoods and rural development.* Practical Action Publishing.

Scott, J. C. (1985). *Weapons of the weak. Everyday forms of peasant resistance.* Yale University Press.

Scott, J. C. (1990). *Domination and the arts of resistance. Hidden transcripts.* Yale University Press.

Scott, J. C. (2009). *The art of not being governed. An anarchist history of upland Southeast Asia.* Yale University Press.

Shanin, T. (1972). *The awkward class; political sociology of peasantry in a developing society: Russia 1910–1925.* Clarendon Press.

Shanin, T. (1987). *Peasants & peasant societies.* Basil Blackwell.

Singh, P., & Sharma, H. (2013). Peasants of Manipur: Agrarian change, land tenure and emerging patterns of re-peasantization in India. *Agrarian South: Journal of Political Economy, 2*(3), 291–314.

Steger, M. (2020). *Globalization: A very short introduction* (5th ed.). Oxford University Press.

van der Ploeg, J. (2018). From de-to repeasantization: The modernization of agriculture revisited. *Journal of Rural Studies, 61*, 236–243.

Vanhaute, E. (2012). Peasants, peasantries and (de)peasantization in the capitalist world-system. In S. Babones & C. Chase-Dunn (Eds.), *Routledge handbook of world-systems analysis: Theory and research* (pp. 313–321). Routledge.

Veltmeyer, H., & Ezquerro-Cañete, A. (2023). Agro-extractivism. *The Journal of Peasant Studies, 50*(5), 1673–1686.
Viaene, L., Doran, P., & Liljeblad, J. (2023). Transitional justice and nature: A curious silence. *International Journal of Transitional Justice, 17*(1), 1–14.
Vila, G. (2022). Natures of concern: The criminalization of artisanal and small-scale mining in Colombia and Peru. *The Extractive Industries and Society, 13*, 101105.
Vila, G. (2025). From minería comunitaria to illegal mining: Indigenous territories and mining formalization in Peruvian Amazonia. In J. A. Gutiérrez & F. Gutiérrez-Sanín (Eds.), *Criminality, political power and conflict. Critical perspectives*. Manchester University Press.
Wallerstein, I. (2000). Globalization, or the age of transition? A long-term view of the trajectory of the world system. *International Sociology, 15*(2), 249–265.
Wolford, W. (2021). The Plantationocene: A Lusotropical contribution to the theory. *Annals of the American Association of Geographers, 111*(6), 1622–1639.
World Bank. (2024). Pathways out of the Polycrisis. In *Poverty, Prosperity, and Planet Report 2024*. International Bank for Reconstruction and Development/ The World Bank.
Yaşın, Z. (2023). The environmentalization of the agrarian question and the agrarianization of the climate justice movement. In I. Scoones, S. Borras, A. Baviskar, M. Edelman, N. L. Peluso, & W. Wolford (Eds.), *Climate change and critical agrarian studies* (pp. 29–59). Routledge.
Ybarra, M. (2012). Taming the jungle, saving the Maya Forest: Sedimented counterinsurgency practices in contemporary Guatemalan conservation. *The Journal of Peasant Studies, 39*(2), 479–502.
Ye, J., van der Ploeg, J., Schneider, S., & Shanin, T. (2020). The incursions of extractivism: Moving from dispersed places to global capitalism. *The Journal of Peasant Studies, 47*(1), 155–183.
Young, L. (2014). A challenging nexus. In R. Laher & K. Sing'Oei (Eds.), *Indigenous people in Africa. Contestations, empowerment and group rights*. African Books Collective.

CHAPTER 5

Contesting the Terms of Agrarian Change: Civil Society, Policy and Law

Abstract Over the last decades, as neoliberal reform advanced and the problems of the peasants became global, transnational peasant movements, such as *La Vía Campesina*, have developed. As these groups demanded social justice in their respective countries, they were not listened to or confronted with political blockages, activating their transnational networks and international allies so they could either put pressure directly on their national government or on their respective governments or other international bodies in order for them to put pressure on the national government in question. These new movements became transnational pushed by the growing globalisation of the political and economic realms, while they articulated their projects in terms of the international human rights law to reflect this new reality. By shifting the terms of the debate through human rights framing strategies, these movements are creating new normative commitments (reflected in UNDRIP and UNDROP) that reinforce the new realities on the ground created through their mobilisation. This is creating a transformative space that could be very useful for future transitional justice processes in the context of agrarian conflict, as will be discussed in the next chapter.

Keywords Neoliberalism • Transnational movements • Structural adjustments • Globalisation • Vía Campesina • UNDRIP • UNDROP • Boomerang effect

J. A. Gutiérrez, *Transitional Justice and Agrarian Conflict*,
https://doi.org/10.1007/978-3-032-25228-9_5

This chapter maps the contemporary landscape of transnational social movements and civil society organisations contesting the terms of agrarian change, situating the emergence of this contemporary activism within societies transitioning to democracy in the 1980s and 1990s and globalisation. During those years, particularly during the 1980s, transition to democracy was a broad term that brought together (rather deceptively) people from across the political spectrum, often with very different notions of what actually transition and democracy meant (Arthur, 2009). This is the context in which many peasant movements that would later go on to contest the terms of agrarian change resorting to human rights framing strategies, emerged. It was later, during the 1990s, that democracy became associated largely with the (neo)liberal project (Whitehead, 1992; Joseph, 1997), but for many in the Global South, the precise meaning of democracy remained a contested issue, with the contents of democracy still hotly disputed (Peeler, 2009).

Indeed, alongside some of the pro-democracy movements mentioned by Teitel in her book, there were multiple other movements that did not share the basic tenets of the liberal peacebuilding paradigm. Together with the emergence of liberal democracy, direct democracy also emerged in Latin America, contesting some of the neoliberal assumptions of the former, but also creating a political space for social movements to demand change from below (Barczak, 2001; Cameron et al., 2012). Peasant and indigenous movements in Brazil, Colombia, Ecuador, Peru or Bolivia, for which freedom and democracy meant access to land by the poor and marginalised rural people and a degree of autonomy to organise their day-to-day lives as they saw fit, were opposed to the liberalisation of the land market to benefit speculators, multinational agribusiness or the landed elites. While many of these social movements had firm roots in predecessors from previous decades, the end of the Cold War shifted the terms of the political debate, and human rights language became an alternative framing for their claims that quickly replaced former ideological commitments (Ignatieff, 2001; Beitz, 2009).

Peasant movements too have used the language of rights to articulate their claims about land (Grajales, 2015). These new movements became transnational, pushed by the growing globalisation of the political and economic realms, while they articulated their projects in terms of the international human rights law to reflect this new reality. By shifting the terms of the debate through human rights framing strategies, these movements are creating new normative commitments that reinforce the new realities on the ground created through their mobilisation. This is creating a transformative space that could be very useful for future transitional justice processes in the context of agrarian conflict, as will be discussed in the next chapter.

5.1 New Local Movements, Organisations and Rural Politics

While peasant movements have been traditionally local movements, often regarded as parochial by the urban social movements (even if their problems were hardly local), over the last decades, transnational and global peasant movements have developed. As neoliberal reform advanced, and the problems of the peasants became global and transnational, peasant movements started to realize that their struggle was no longer one in which they were confronted to local landlords or at most to national government policies; they were confronting much more powerful global forces in both the economic field and politics (Martínez-Torres & Rosset, 2010). The response of the peasant and rural peoples' movement, prompted by both the decentralisation of the state and globalisation experienced under neoliberalism, has been characterised by a contradictory move, at the same time, towards internationalisation or transnationalisation, and localism: 'Today, many agrarian movements have "localized" their struggles in response to partial decentralization, others have focused on "privatized" activities in a manner akin to "state-substitution" on development issues such as social service delivery, while others have "internationalized" their struggles in response to global agrarian restructuring' (Borras et al., 2008, p. 170). Thus, vibrant movements such as *La Vía Campesina*, which have a global reach and represent a considerable force in the international arena, are built over a capillary network of localised organisations that reach millions of rural villages that barely figure in the maps.

This movement has developed policies not only in response to the neoliberal policies that have targeted farmers and peasants across the globe; it also has developed its policies through a critical understanding of the Cold War era attempts, by centrist liberals and left-wing figures, to produce agrarian reforms that very often failed to take the needs, aspirations and visions of development of peasant and rural populations, and were very often imposed on them (Vía Campesina, 2017. See also Scott, 1998, on the failures of the agrarian reforms by the so-called real socialism). As such, the politics of these new transnational rural movements owe a great deal to a history of learned experiences and cannot be considered *only* a response to the conditions on neoliberalisation of the last decades.

Although there is something novel about the transnational turn of the peasant movement as a response to the challenges of this particular period of history, there were precedents dating back to organisations from the 1920s, born in the internationalist fever of those years, such as the communist-oriented and Moscow-aligned Red Peasant International (*Krestintern*) and the populist agrarian International Agrarian Bureau (also known as the Green Peasant International) (van Meurs, 2017). From around the same time is the Associated Country Women of the World (ACWW), a largely British elite-professional organisation, in existence until this day, and besides it, the Catholic farmers (this religion being an important transnational movement in its own right) have been organised for decades in the International Federation of Adult Catholic Farmers' Movements (FIMARC), while more recently another Catholic organisation, the International Movement of Catholic Agricultural and Rural Youth (MIJARC), was also formed (Borras et al., 2008). The International Federation of Agricultural Producers (IFAP), formed in the post-war era and dominated by big farmers, mostly from the Global North, is also still in existence and represents an important transnational political movement for the more conservative farmers' organisations, being the main rival to *La Vía Campesina* (Desmarais, 2007). Despite the different approaches of these organisations, all of them created some level of transnational networks that paved the way for the emergence of the new transnational peasant movement.

While Western rural areas have long been traditionally associated with conservatism, at least since the times of the French Revolution (Jones, 1988), in other parts of the world, such as Latin America, Asia and Africa, the peasantry was associated with mobilisation against colonialism, dictatorships and against the ruling elites (Skocpol, 1982). When we compare the conservative outlook of the IFAP with the militancy and the radical approach of *La Vía Campesina*, there is little wonder that the latter draws most of its political capital from Latin America and Asia, while the former is firmly rooted in Western and Northern Europe. But even in Spain, the peasantry and farmers were at the forefront of the widespread collectivisation experiences in the countryside during the revolutionary experiments of the civil war and the resistance against fascism during 1936–1939 (Leval, 2018). More recently, van der Ploeg (2008) has analysed the rise of new peasantries that have opposed capitalist commodification and the neoliberalisation of agriculture and re-defined a new peasant mode of production through small-scale production that is not fully integrated into the market. He analyses cases of re-peasanisation in the Global South (specifically Perú), but his main focus are cases in Europe (Italy and The Netherlands); these modes of peasant production are described as an alternative to the unsustainable current model of agrarian capitalism, signalling a path to a transition to a post-carbon society.

Together with *La Vía Campesina*, there is a myriad of agricultural unions and fisherfolk organisations that have contributed to raise important issues linked to sustainability and social justice. Some of these movements have managed to create regional networks such as the Asian Peasant Coalition (APC) or the *Coordinadora Latinoamericana de Organizaciones del Campo* (Latin American Coordination of Peasant Organisations, CLOC) and the *Réseaudes Organisations Paysannes et de Producteurs de l'Afrique de l'Ouest* (Network of Peasants' and Producers' Organisations of West Africa, ROPPA). Other movements, such as the International Planning Committee for Food Sovereignty (IPC), which brings together hundreds of small-scale producers' associations, networks, NGOs and farmers' movements, have been created to support the struggle for the realisation of specific policies developed to face the current challenges of the farmers' movements, such as Food Sovereignty, which we will discuss in the next section. While all of these movements struggle with internal contradictions, in the form of class differentiation among peasants, power imbalances between regions (most notably between the Global North and Global South), various political affiliations and ideological differences, and gender inclusion (with women still underrepresented in these organisations, although with great improvements over the years) (Borras et al., 2008), still these movements have managed to articulate a basic political project and mobilise successfully to achieve important landmarks in terms of international frameworks.

5.2 Transnational Peasant Movements: The Case of *La Vía Campesina*

La Vía Campesina (which in Spanish means 'the peasant way') is one of the most remarkable of the international peasant movements in the world today. In their own words, they are 'an international movement which coordinates peasant organisations of small and middle-scale producers, agricultural workers, rural women, and indigenous communities.'[1] Notwithstanding the fact that *La Vía Campesina* was founded in Mons, Belgium in 1993, the main drive for its constitution came from the Global South, with their Spanish language name being a testament to the importance of Latin American organisations in its foundation (Borras et al., 2008). Countries from that region, like Brazil, with massive peasant movements, such as the Landless Rural Workers' Movement (*Movimento dos Trabalhadores Rurais Sem Terra*, MST) and a long history of militancy, activism and political engagement, were in a good position to lead the movement and to help consolidate the network of organisations into a formidable transnational movement with other peasant and farmers' movements in Africa, Asia and Europe. Other movements brought their own particular sets of skills. Asian movements, such as the Indonesian Peasant Union (*Serakat Petani Indonesia*, SPI), brought in their own experience and commitment to normative frameworks to turn many of the goals and aspirations of *La Vía Campesina* into international resolutions, while the Peasant Movement of the Philippines (*Kilusang Magbubukid ng Pilipinas*, KMP) brought in the bulk of farmers and peasant militant networks from that continent. In Europe, organisations like the *Confédération Paysanne*, whose spokesperson is the well-known activist Joseph 'José' Bové, demonstrated that this was a truly global attempt to change a world particularly hostile to peasants as social subjects, pushing alternatives from below. Their positioning in the Global North added visibility and bridges for these Global South movements. The global nature of the movement, and the various skills and knowledges acquired by the various movements that form *La Vía Campesina* in their respective trajectories, have facilitated a global learning and knowledge exchange process, which they call *diálogo de saberes* (or dialogue of knowledges), which informs the shaping of the movement's policies and positions, while on the ground 'peasant to peasant' exchanges also facilitate the development of sustainable agricultural

[1] Taken from their website https://viacampesina.org

systems that turn their back to the 'green revolution' models often promoted by advisors and mainstream agronomist professionals (La Vía Campesina, 2017, p. 36; Nicholson & Borras, 2023).

It is no coincidence that the founding meeting of this movement took place in 1993, at the time in which the Uruguay Round of the General Agreement on Tariffs and Trade (GATT) would pave the way for the creation, 1 year later, of the World Trade Organisation (WTO). The WTO would herald a shift towards a much deeper neoliberal turn that was to dismantle the ways of lives of rural people (peasants, smallholders, farmers, but also pastoralists, fisherfolk and indigenous peoples), drive many of them out of the market and plunge them into poverty (Desmarais, 2007; Nicholson & Borras, 2023). As we have discussed, the agrarian question has changed dramatically over the last decades with the rise of extractivism at a global scale, structural adjustment agreements promoted (in reality imposed) by the IMF, the globalisation of the economy and the subsequent debt crises that shaped the world from the 1980s onwards. As such, the demands of *La Vía Campesina* reflect this reality and are not solely based around redistributive measures when it comes to land, although this, naturally, remains a critical and key objective. Their project, titled *Integral and Popular Agrarian Reform*, actively seeks the redistribution of land and access to credit, but also factors in the distribution of key resources for agriculture, such as water, seeds and biodiversity, together with changes to credit, trade, insurance and education (Munck, 2020). They insist that

> Whereas historically the organisations' proposal for agrarian reform referred particularly to land distribution and to access to productive resources, such as credit, financing, support for marketing of products, amongst others, the **integral** or **genuine** agrarian reform is based on the defence and the reconstruction of territory as a whole, within the framework of Food Sovereignty. The broadening of the object of agrarian reform, from land to territory also broadens the concept of the agrarian reform itself. Therefore, the contemporary proposal for integral agrarian reform does not only guarantee the democratisation of land but also takes into consideration diverse aspects that allow families to have a decent life: water, the seas, mangroves and continental waters, seeds, biodiversity as a whole, as well as market regulation and the end of land grabbing. Furthermore, it includes the strengthening of agroecological production as a form of production that is compatible with the cycles of nature and capable of halting climate change, maintaining

biodiversity and reducing contamination. (Vía Campesina, 2017, p. 5, emphasis in original)

Here, the notion of food sovereignty represents a major contribution of the movement to the universe of rights that the majority of the world has in order to defend themselves from the harm caused by the action and interest of powerful actors on the global stage. Given the massive disruptions to the lives of millions and the rise of famine and deprivation derived from structural adjustments imposed by the IMF and the large-scale deregulation brought about by the WTO, some voices emphasised the need to guarantee food security, that is, to guarantee vulnerable people's access to food. *La Vía Campesina*, by turning the issue from security to sovereignty, identified the structural roots of the problem by questioning the main premise of neoliberal orthodoxy about letting the 'invisible hand' of the market solve the question of food through trade liberalisation and the uneven competition with big agribusiness. By articulating the concept of food sovereignty, they disputed the neoliberal paradigm of the international order by reclaiming the centrality of countries and communities regaining control over the ownership and production of appropriate food, the need to regulate markets to guarantee fairness and quality and the issue of long-term sustainability (see Desmarais, 2007). *La* Via *Campesina* describes it thus,

> We understand that food sovereignty implies redistribution policies, fair and equitable access and control of natural and productive resources (credit, appropriate technology, etc), (…), rural development policies based on agroecological strategies centred on peasant and family farming and traditional fishing; anti-dumping trade policies that favour peasant and indigenous production for local, national and international markets; and complementary public policies, such as health, education and infrastructure for the countryside.
>
> Natural resources must first and foremost be used in the service of food production. Within the context of food sovereignty, agrarian reform benefits the whole of society, giving it healthy, accessible and culturally appropriate food, and social justice. (…) Food sovereignty is based on the human right to food, free determination, indigenous rights to territory and the rights of people to produce food for their subsistence and for local and national markets. (…) The sophisticated knowhow that the indigenous peoples, peasants and fishers have acquired over centuries of interaction with nature provide solutions to the current ecological and social crisis. That is why we are

convinced that indigenous food systems must be given top priority in agrarian reform and that indigenous principles and knowhow must be applied for the benefit of communities (La Vía Campesina, 2017, p. 34)

Another concept made its entry into the previous definition of food sovereignty, which, together with the concept of integral and popular agrarian reform, marks an important contribution to our understanding of rights: the concept of agroecology. Agroecology, which encompasses different forms of traditional agricultural and knowledge systems with newly acquired knowledge, is a central tenet of *La Vía Campesina,* and it is 'not only a means of production, but also as a praxis of change: the building of autonomy from the production systems of the hegemonic model. In this respect, it is a form of resistance and of deconstruction of dependence on commercial seeds, pesticides and fertilisers which are becoming increasingly expensive, and of the possibility of building and·salvaging knowledge which is part of a sustainable relationship between humans and nature, based on ancestral knowledge, culture and territorial diversity' (La Via Campesina, 2017, p. 36). As part of this emphasis in agroecology, peasants are stimulated to exchange seeds, diversify their crops, rotate them, use natural fertilisers and natural ways to control pests, etc. This practical engagement with agriculture is a way to address important rights such as food, health and a healthy environment.

Today, *La Vía Campesina* represents 200 million organised peasants worldwide, making it one of the biggest global civil society organisations on the planet (Nicholson & Borras, 2023). But it would be a mistake to see it as simply bringing together peasants with their ready-made agendas. Through peasant-to-peasant exchange, the dialogue of knowledges and other pedagogical and research tools, most of them firmly anchored in the pedagogy of the oppressed methodologies developed by Brazil's Paulo Freire in the 1960s and participatory methods pioneered in Colombia by Orlando Falso Broda, through their respective educational and research work with rural communities (Freire, 1972; Fals Borda, 2010), *La Vía Campesina* has managed to create new political concepts and ideas and new projects and alternative visions that articulate the traditional practices and knowledges of rural populations—derived from their learning of an extensive history of engagement with the land and the environment—with new knowledges and scientific understandings, in order to face the new challenges posed to rural populations by the current trade, political and economic models (see van der Ploeg, 2008). *La Vía Campesina* has brought together millions and has managed to inspire others into action. Through this movement, peasants have managed to gain sheer leverage in numbers to push for important reforms and new normative frameworks that reflect the plight of the peasant movements and also challenge the dominant economic orthodoxy to favour small agricultural producers and both rural and urban people.

5.3 New Normative Frameworks

Over the last two decades, the United Nations General Assembly (UNGA) has passed important resolutions that reflect the transformative struggles of rural peoples, such as the indigenous, peasants and agrarian workers. We will discuss briefly two paramount UNGA resolutions for the purposes of this book. One is the *Declaration on the Rights of Indigenous Peoples* (UNDRIP), adopted in 2007. The other is the *Declaration on the Rights of Peasants and Other People Working in Rural Areas* (UNDROP), adopted in 2018.

Both received important support from countries from the Global South, including Bolivia, which during the 2000s was an important voice at the international level in the defence of both the indigenous and the peasant populations. Both populations, in many contexts, are one and the same, and often, in the Global South, the distinction between them is purely contextual. Inasmuch as Global South governments actively supported these resolutions, they were the product of decades of protest and mobilisation by transnational indigenous and peasant-led movements, among the latter *La Vía Campesina,* featuring quite prominently, that could exercise serious pressure over national governments together with their key international allies.

It is important to emphasise that both resolutions recognise that the indigenous, but also the peasants and rural workers, have a special relationship with the environment, and both play a key role in preserving biodiversity and in conservation efforts. This reflects the growing awareness on these topics, the product of grassroots pedagogic efforts and decades of mobilisation. Most importantly, both were formulated in a language that draws much from a transitional lexicon, while addressing issues that had been raised by the advocates of transformative justice, such as alternative development, environmental justice and structural transformations, to address the violations of social, economic and cultural rights.

5.3.1 UNDRIP

For centuries, it was believed that the only progressive possible policy in relation to indigenous peoples was their assimilation into what was considered to be proper civilization; this started to change with the proliferation of indigenous movements all over the world during the 1970s, which brought their voices to the fore (Bengoa, 2000; Gómez, 2019). As a result of their mobilisation, the International Labour Organisation (ILO) adopted Convention 169 in 1989, which granted extensive rights to indigenous peoples, but its ratification was resisted by many states, with only 22 countries ratifying it. This led the indigenous movement to look for other avenues to assert their rights. The push for a specific UN resolution on indigenous peoples' rights was the result of the indigenous movement grasping the transformative potential of human rights discourses (despite colonial legacies and narratives) and adopting a framework in which to design a normative framework that could serve as an acceptable starting point for their claims-making (Morgan, 2011).

The resolution, which was approved in 2007, was supported by 143 countries, with four votes against by Western countries with serious problems with their own native populations (Australia, Canada, New Zealand and the United States) and 12 abstentions (Cambou, 2019). All four countries that voted against the resolution eventually reversed their position, giving this resolution, despite its non-binding character, a very strong mandate. UNDRIP marks an important landmark in the recognition of collective rights of the indigenous peoples, including their right to self-determination. In general, this resolution is a very strong reference for 'third generation' human rights (Cambou, 2019; Gómez, 2019). There is also a certain transitional justice edge to the resolution in the sense that it was conceived, very explicitly, as a way to redress the historical violences, dispossession and marginalisation that various indigenous peoples have been subjected to throughout history. With important anti-colonial overtones, the spirit of this declaration, as explicitly stated in the introduction, speaks to some of the socio-economic and developmental concerns of transformative justice. While all of the declaration raise very important questions on the right of indigenous peoples to their own vision of sustainable development, the most important aspects of the resolution, from an agrarian point of view, are Articles 25, 26, 27 and 28, which deal with land rights and the indigenous peoples (UN, 2007).

Article 25, for instance, states that the indigenous peoples' spiritual connection to the land needs to be protected and taken into consideration: 'have the right to maintain and strengthen their distinctive spiritual relationship with their traditionally owned or otherwise occupied and used lands, territories, waters and coastal seas and other resources and to uphold their responsibilities to future generations in this regard'.[2] Article 26 deals with the right of indigenous peoples to land respecting their traditional patterns of ownership and/or use and that states should 'give legal recognition and protection to these lands, territories and resources. Such recognition shall be conducted with due respect to the customs, traditions and land tenure systems of the indigenous peoples concerned'. Article 27 deals with the recognition and adjudication of the rights of the 'indigenous peoples pertaining to their lands, territories and resources, including those which were traditionally owned or otherwise occupied or used', a process that should be conducted with the active participation of the indigenous peoples and according to their rights, customs and laws. Article 28 is about the indigenous peoples' right to appropriate restitution and compensation 'for the lands, territories and resources which they have traditionally owned or otherwise occupied or used, and which have been confiscated, taken, occupied, used or damaged without their free, prior and informed consent'. As can be seen, the language and the topics used by the declaration have strong transformative and restitutive overtones that resonate within certain critical traditions in transitional justice.

While there are still important gaps regarding its implementation, and realities on the ground are still far removed from the lofty goals of the resolution (Côté et al., 2019), UNIDRIP represents an important document that, while not binding on itself, has been adopted seriously by the legislature and judiciary in many countries, becoming an important referent for regional, national and international bodies, giving the indigenous peoples a real leverage to have a say on issues as fundamental as development strategies and policies (Gilbert & Lennox, 2019; Lenzerini, 2019). More importantly, it is a document that has contributed significantly to shifiting the terms of the debate on issues such as land or the environment (Giunta, 2019). Like with many other legal documents, their

[2]The UNDRIP can be found in various languages in the official UN website https://social.desa.un.org/issues/indigenous-peoples/united-nations-declaration-on-the-rights-of-indigenous-peoples. All excerpts are taken from the English version, and the article in question is indicated.

implementation—while in every case far from ideal—seems to go hand in hand with the capacity that communities and people have to come together and mobilise for their implementation. And it is in this process where the political importance of the UNDRIP cannot be understated, for 'indigenous peoples have become subjects of rights under international law rather than objects of protection, thus becoming protagonists of a far-reaching process of expansion of human rights' (Gómez, 2019, p. 10; see also Cambou, 2019). Soon, the path opened by the indigenous movements would be followed by the peasantry and other rural people.

5.3.2 UNDROP

Peasants have actively mobilised for their rights at the highest levels of global politics. Since the inception of *La Vía Campesina*, peasant organisations that before could, at best, merely influence local politics, have found a means with which they can advocate and mobilise for change in instances like the UN. A wide range of social and human rights movements supported *La Vía Campesina* in a long journey that started in 2002 at their regional conference in Jakarta, Indonesia, where they presented a draft titled Declaration on the Rights of Peasants. That this event took place in Indonesia is no coincidence: the Indonesian Peasant Union (*Serakat Petani Indonesia*, SPI), a member organisation of *La* Via *Campesina*, had been for some time a vocal proponent on creating a Charter of Peasant Rights, one that explicitly adopted the human rights frame to address peasant rights, and had, indeed, adopted a Declaration on the Fundamental Rights of Peasants the previous year. While this declaration was thought mostly for Indonesian peasants, they pushed for these principles to be adopted by the international peasant movement to address their global challenges (Shawki, 2014; Vandenbogaerde, 2017).

From 2002, there was a long process of discussion and negotiation between the peasant movement, lawyers, Non-Governmental Organisations (NGOs) and other social movements until a final document was agreed, one which spoke the language of rights in a way that was more compatible with existing legal frameworks (Shawki, 2014). This final document was adopted formally by *La Vía Campesina* in Maputo, Mozambique, in 2008, and then polished the next year in Seoul, Republic of Korea (Vandenbogaerde, 2017). The next step was to institutionalise it as new rights at the UN level through the use of human rights as a framing strategy, an important gamble for a movement that was fully aware of the inherent risks of this strategy, such as co-optation and the undermining of its radical objectives, among others (Claeys, 2015). The declaration of the UNDRIP, around this time, gave real credibility and traction to such a strategy (Edelman & James, 2011).

Around the same time, FAO adopted the 'Voluntary Guidelines on the Responsible Governance of Tenure of Land, Fisheries and Forests in the Context of National Food Security' (VGGT) in 2012, a general voluntary framework about equitable and sustainable tenure and access and governance to land, fisheries and forests, with an eye to promote food security and the progressive realisation of the right to adequate food. In this framework, we find a particular attention paid to rural people, peasants and indigenous, and to the principles of non-discrimination, equality and participation at its core (FAO, 2022). At the same time, the guidelines recognise the centrality that land tenure and governance can have in leading to conflict, during conflict and after conflict (articles 25.1–15.7). The ground was being prepared for the adoption of UNDROP some years later, and the peasantry was no longer just the passive subject of well-intentioned policies from above.

In 2010, after important pressure from the grassroots, through movements of peasant, rural labourers, small farmers, pastoralists and fisherfolk, among others, led by *La Vía Campesina* and allied NGOs placed in a position to influence key international bodies, the UN Human Rights Council gave a mandate to its Advisory Committee to study the issue of the fundamental rights of peasants and other peoples working in rural area. This led to the creation of an open-ended inter-governmental working group in 2013 that oversaw the discussion of what would become UNDROP after 5 years of discussions and advocacy (Golay, 2013). It is important to mention that the core members of the working group were all from the Global South: Bolivia, Cuba, Ecuador and South Africa. This process and the final drafting of UNDROP marked the 'conclusion of a unique exercise in law-making from below' (Claeys & Edelman, 2020, p. 2).

In 2018, the United Nations General Assembly adopted UNDROP with the support of 121 countries, which voted in favour, and 8 votes against (including the United States and the United Kingdom). UNDROP articulates many of the peasant demands, including some related to food sovereignty, agroecology, women's rights and the idea of agrarian reform that *La Vía Campesina* had been agitating for a few decades. The declaration engages with the issue of the civil, political and socio-economic rights of the peasants, including the (collective and/or individual) right to land

and water bodies, with a prominent emphasis on peasant women (UN, 2018). Article 4 declares the need to 'promote their empowerment in order to ensure, on the basis of equality between men and women, that they fully and equally enjoy all human rights and fundamental freedoms and that they are able to freely pursue, participate in and benefit from rural economic, social, political and cultural development'.[3] Here, peasants are defined as a specific subject of rights that needs protection but also the promotion of their culture. Peasants and other people working in rural areas, in Article 26, 'have the right to maintain, express, control, protect and develop their traditional and local knowledge, such as ways of life, methods of production or technology, or customs and tradition. (...) [as well as], individually and/or collectively, in association with others or as a community, to express their local customs, languages, culture, religions, literature and art, in conformity with international human rights standards.'

The spirit of the declaration goes against the grain of the main international trends in terms of trade and the expansion of agri-business, by stating clearly in Article 16 that 'States shall take all appropriate measures to ensure that their rural development, agricultural, environmental, trade and investment policies and programmes contribute effectively to protecting and strengthening local livelihood options and to the transition to sustainable modes of agricultural production. States shall stimulate sustainable production, including agroecological and organic production, whenever possible, and facilitate direct farmer-to-consumer sales'. This is reinforced in Article 17 by adopting a specific stance favouring agrarian reform, another cherished demand of peasant movements: 'Where appropriate, States shall take appropriate measures to carry out agrarian reforms in order to facilitate broad and equitable access to land and other natural resources necessary to ensure that peasants and other people working in rural areas enjoy adequate living conditions, and to limit excessive concentration and control of land, taking into account its social function'.

Among the most interesting contributions in terms of rights to be found in the UNDROP is the explicit mention of 'food sovereignty', a concept developed by the transnational activism of peasant organisations over the past decades. This right is formulated in Article 15, which states that 'Peasants and other people working in rural areas have the right to

[3] The UNDROP can be found in various languages in the official UN website https://digitallibrary.un.org/record/1650694?v=pdf. All excerpts are taken from the English version, and the article in question is indicated.

adequate food and the fundamental right to be free from hunger. This includes the right to produce food and the right to adequate nutrition, which guarantee the possibility of enjoying the highest degree of physical, emotional and intellectual development'. While this article recognises the fact that many of the people suffering from want and hunger today in the world are to be found in rural areas, it also recognises that the rural population is also critical in the struggle against hunger and malnutrition, and this is where the concept of food sovereignty becomes critical. According to the same article:

> Peasants and other people working in rural areas have the right to determine their own food and agriculture systems, recognized by many States and regions as the right to food sovereignty. This includes the right to participate in decision-making processes on food and agriculture policy and the right to healthy and adequate food produced through ecologically sound and sustainable methods that respect their cultures (…) States shall formulate, in partnership with peasants and other people working in rural areas, public policies at the local, national, regional and international levels to advance and protect the right to adequate food, food security and food sovereignty and sustainable and equitable food systems that promote and protect the rights contained in the present Declaration. States shall establish mechanisms to ensure the coherence of their agricultural, economic, social, cultural and development policies with the realization of the rights contained in the present Declaration.

This is an important triumph for the peasant movement that for a decade had been putting pressure for this right to become a reality. However, another important aspect of the declaration that marks a shift from the more old-fashioned understanding of the peasantry is the notion of peasants as critical in the defence of the environment and biodiversity (Alabrese & Savaresi, 2022). This is partly because of the growing awareness of the role of peasants vis-à-vis the environmental crisis of today, which was articulated by *La* Via *Campesina* in their conceptualisation of agroecology, as we have discussed above. This recognition is enshrined in Article 18, which emphasises that 'States shall comply with their respective international obligations to combat climate change. Peasants and other people working in rural areas have the right to contribute to the design and implementation of national and local climate change adaptation and mitigation policies, including through the use of practices and traditional knowledge'. Agroecology here is a key component of these mitigation policies, and the protection of biodiversity also gets another mention in Article 19, dealing with seeds: 'Peasants and other people working in rural areas have the right to maintain, control, protect and develop their own seeds and traditional knowledge'. This article also protects local, traditional knowledge on seeds from unfair intellectual property laws. Biodiversity and sustainability are important parts of the declaration because they have become an important component of the peasant movements' demands and of their political project.

Just like in the case of UNDRIP, there is still a massive gap between the lofty goals and the realities on the ground, together with immense implementation challenges, not least among them the lack of proper monitoring mechanisms and the declaration's lack of actual teeth (Golay, 2022). Most certainly, UNDROP does not represent the radical departure of global capitalism that some people thought it would be (cf., Salomon, 2018), although it represents a certain challenge to the neoliberal dogma that dominated the post–Cold War landscape. But while the risk of institutionalisation and co-optation always looms large in debates around the use of human rights framing strategies (Claeys, 2015), the use of such strategies provides an opportunity for social movements to articulate their aspirations and develop new notions of rights (Monsalve, 2013) that serve as a compass to guide future advances. They establish landmarks in this process, minimums, without stifling the imagination of the movements.

5.3.3 Environmental Justice and Agrarian Justice

Colombia and Ireland are worlds apart. Yet, in both countries, while working on participatory research with peasants and farmers, I heard them bitterly complain about their depiction in mainstream narratives as debased and destructive predators with little concern for nature, without taking into account all the efforts they make in relation to carbon capture by keeping hedgerows and forests, or in shifting to more sustainable patterns of farming (see also Regan & Kenny, 2022). In the case of Colombia, smallholders and peasants in the Amazon region are widely condemned by political elites as drivers of deforestation, with even a whole military offensive, Operation Artemis, orchestrated to secure army control of regions of smallholders' colonisation under a 'green militarisation' logic (Corredor-García & López, 2024).

Certainly, agri-business 'is a major contributor to global warming and climate change by: transporting food all around the world, imposing industrial forms of production (mechanization, intensification, use of agrochemicals, monoculture...), destroying biodiversity and its capacity to capture carbon, converting land and forests into non-agricultural areas, transforming agriculture from an energy producer into an energy consumer' (Martínez-Alier, 2011, p. 146). Large-scale industrial plantation agriculture, with its strong dependence on monoculture, fossil fuels and emissions, chemical fertilisers and unsustainable global markets, has been extremely detrimental to the environment (Wolford, 2021). In particular, soybeans (Fearnside, 2001), palm oil (Shigetomi et al., 2020) and sugar cane have had devastating effects on entire ecosystems (Mintz, 1986; Vega & Gutiérrez, 2019). However, this large-scale model of industrial agriculture is precisely what many of these farmers and peasant movements have been fighting against, even as, paradoxically, the imagination of sectors of the rural population still is captured by market-led entrepreneurial solutions to the problems caused precisely by this market-led unsustainable agricultural model (Camargo, 2022). While indigenous peoples' struggles against environmental dispossession and their role in conservation have long been recognised and discussed in academic and non-academic circles alike (cf., Richmond et al., 2024), the peasants and farmers' movements more recently have started to articulate a discourse, a set of practices and visions that place the environment of the very centre of the definition of what the peasant mode of production is (Claeys & Delgado, 2016).

The agricultural question has been 'greening' and 'environmentalising' for some time, becoming increasingly entangled with the broader ecological question—firstly, because of 'the environmental effects of capitalist development in agriculture'; secondly, because of 'the consequences of rural ecological degradation for capitalist growth'; and finally, because of 'the role of the agrarian classes and groups in the struggle for sustainability, environmental justice or eco-socialism' (Gerber & Veuthey, 2010, p. 475; see also Yaşın, 2023). The articulation of these visions, where new scientific knowledge acquired through research meets with the traditional knowledge acquired through experience on the fields by farmers, has been behind the articulation of agroecology embraced by *La Vía Campesina*. As we have already discussed, in this vision, the defence of the environment and the fight against climate change through the practice of agroecological farming revolves around the utilisation of sustainable methods, cutting down the dependence on fossil fuels and chemical fertilisers, the defence of native seeds and the promotion of local production and consumption of food (Altieri, 1995; Wezel et al., 2020). A comprehensive definition can be summarised as such:

> Agroecology is the integration of research, education, action and change that brings sustainability to all parts of the food system: ecological, economic, and social. It's transdisciplinary in that it values all forms of knowledge and experience in food system change. It's participatory in that it requires the involvement of all stakeholders from the farm to the table and everyone in between. And it is action-oriented because it confronts the economic and political power structures of the current industrial food system with alternative social structures and policy action. The approach is grounded in ecological thinking where a holistic, systems-level understanding of food system sustainability is required. (Gliessman, 2018, p. 599)

Agroecology reclaims the eco-regulatory processes of the traditional peasant mode of production (Benton, 1989) and the energy-efficiency of small-scale agriculture (Martínez-Alier, 2011), while the 'demands for "food sovereignty" from La Via Campesina fit in with complaints against biopiracy, land grabbing and tree plantations, and also with climate change issues, as in the slogan "traditional peasant agriculture cools down the Earth"' (Martínez-Alier et al., 2016, p. 748).

Another dimension of this overlap between the agrarian question and environmentalism is that the indigenous and peasant movements have changed their focus on the struggle for land to the struggle for territory. While the former was usually understood as the physical space, the terrain on which people live, the second has a more political meaning, comprising the relationship with the culture, with the environment, the political organisation and the power of those communities who inhabit the territory (Sauer, 2012; Rosset, 2013; Bauer, 2016). In the words of a peasant activist, 'Territory expresses the identity of a people, it is where the ancestors lived and where they still reside, it means knowledge and ways of knowing ("saberes"), historical memory, and the right of usufruct of the communal resources which properly speaking belong to the Mother Earth' (cited in Rosset, 2013, p. 726).

As this shift towards the idea of territory has progressed, ideas of governance and even self-government have problematised old demands, together with the responsibilities of those in the territory in terms of its protection for future generations and for other forms of life. This idea of territory has been closely linked to current environmental debates, with the indigenous and the peasants playing a key role in reverting centuries of environmental damage and making sure that no further harm to nature is performed in the name of a destructive system that benefits only a marginal, but powerful, segment of the population, to the detriment of the majority (Mantz et al., 2025). Therefore, the idea of the defence of the territory has been closely linked to many environmental struggles, particularly against extractive industries that are experiencing a boom because of the global scramble for critical resources (with the subsequent 'land rush'), from mineral, to rare earths, from fossil fuels to agri-fuels: it is estimated that by 2030 the demand for fossil fuels—already at a record high—will increase by a staggering 45% (Maggio & Cacciola, 2009. See also Peša & Ross, 2021). This has led some to claim we live in a neo-extractivist era in which extractivism has been fused with ideas of political domination projected as national interests, as opposed to the old colonial extractivism (Gudynas, 2009; Burchardt & Dietz, 2014). Needless to say, most of these extractivist activities take place in rural areas—the perspectives of indigenous, peasants and other rural people who have defended their rights to live in their territory and to preserve it represent today a massive buffer against the most destructive tendencies within the system.

Particularly through the struggle against uncontrolled and large-scale extractivism, an alliance has emerged between urban political and environmentalist movements and rural peasant and indigenous movements, bridging two very different perspectives and populations for one common purpose. The case of the struggle against gold mining in Cajamarca, Tolima (Colombia) is a case in question that brought together urban and rural movements that otherwise would have never crossed paths (Dietz, 2019). The demands of the peasant and other rural peoples for agrarian justice are increasingly in convergence with the demands of environmental justice and are starting to be increasingly articulated as such (Mahlatsi, 2018; Martínez-Alier, 2025). Environmental justice focuses on how the environmental impacts and burdens are distributed differentially across the world (Figueroa & Mills, 2001), and most certainly rural populations have been impacted disproportionately by the unsustainability of the present system. On this, indigenous and peasants have also directed their efforts not just to grassroots activism but also towards international instruments like the UN Framework Convention on Climate Change (Claeys & Delgado, 2016). This is all happening at a time when transitional justice processes—which have traditionally overlooked environmental harm as an outcome but also as a source of conflict—are starting to pay more attention to the environment as another victim of conflicts and large-scale violence (Killean & Dempster, 2022; Szoke, 2025) but also as a subject of rights (Gómez-Betancur, 2020; Lyons, 2023), so linking agrarian justice to environmental justice in transitional justice settings is becoming ever more relevant.

5.4 Advocacy Models: The Boomerang Effect

Margaret Keck and Kathryn Sikkink (1998) described the boomerang effect in transnational advocacy. According to this model, when groups demanding social justice in their respective countries were not listened to or were confronted with political blockages, they could activate their transnational networks and international allies so they could either put pressure directly on their national government, or on their respective governments or other international bodies in order for them to put pressure on the national government in question: 'When channels between the state and its domestic actors are blocked, the boomerang pattern of influence characteristic of transnational networks may occur: domestic NGOs bypass their state and directly search out international allies to try to bring pressure on their states from outside' (Keck & Sikkink, 1998, pp. 12–13).

This model was largely developed from the author's research on the transnational advocacy work by human rights and environmentalist organisations that were mushrooming all over the world in the 1990s. Human rights organisations were thriving because of the changes in Latin America, Africa, Asia and Central Europe at the end of the Cold War, which were events also central to the emergence of transitional justice as a field of practice. Environmental organisations had an important momentum around the UN Earth Summit in Rio de Janeiro in 1992 that brought many transnational environmental networks and NGOs with different approaches, some more confrontational than others, together to try to influence the events and environmental policy on a global scale (Willetts, 1996). Other authors have pointed out to similar patterns in transnational advocacy and have called them 'venue shifting' or 'leap frogging' (O'Brien et al., 2000; van Rooy, 2004).

This boomerang effect model captures the need felt by many peasant and rural peoples movements across the globe to activate transnational networks in order to obtain international recognition and legitimacy, even if their national government fails to give them both, and in order to fight back the increasingly neoliberal measures that were being implemented in the countryside through market-led policies and structural adjustment, through ubiquitous free trade agreements and a push towards agribusiness and monoculture of cash crops. These policies were affecting peasants and rural people differentially at the global level, although those worse hit by these policies were those in the Global South. But the mere existence of a global problematic and the willingness of many people around the world to fight back do not automatically mean that the boomerang effect will be put into effect (Borras et al., 2008). Some important preconditions need to be met, and central among them is the pre-existence of some level of networking and relations between national and local organisations from various countries. For organisations in the Global South, the availability of transnational allies, particularly allies in the Global North that may have influence over their own governments, is a *conditio sine qua non*. *La Vía Campesina*, as discussed by Borras et al. (2008), could benefit in their campaigns from two important allies, the Food First Information and Action Network (FIAN), and organisation that has campaigned for decades around social, economic and cultural right, in particular the right to food and the right to land, and the Land Research and Action Network (LRAN), a research network working on issues related to land, environment, trade and food politics. Some development around this time were also critical, such as funders being open to fund 'global programmes' besides traditional country programmes and the development in communications around the time (Skype, emails, text messages, etc.), which were also of benefit to the development of these networks.

However, not all causes are equally susceptible to benefit from the boomerang effect. While human rights or localised environmental campaigns can meet significant success, core areas to global capitalism, such as trade policies or financial institutions, are less likely to be influenced by transnational activism and pressure from below; likewise, powerful institutions such as the G7, the IMF or the World Bank are far more difficult to put pressure on than Global South national governments (Nelson, 2004). According to Marc Edelman (2008, p. 251):

> Certainly state-led agrarian reform, better production conditions for small agricultural producers, food sovereignty and other peasant organization demands are, like trade and financial issues, also less amenable to 'boomerang' international pressures on national governments. The efforts of Vía Campesina and associated organizations, such as FIAN, to employ a rights discourse could begin to give the 'boomerang' greater impact (…). But the

> expansion of the domain of 'rights' to include economic and social rights faces daunting obstacles in an age when the hegemonic conceptions are limited to narrow notions of individual expression and the 'rights' of economic actors in the market.

Other problems have also emerged, though mostly at the local level. Analysing Central American peasant organisations in the course of their transnational activism, Edelman (2008) identifies two sets of distinctive problems. Firstly, he identifies intra-organisational problems such as ideological and political differences between the organisations affecting course of action and framing among other things, to which Borras (2008) also adds class differences between different segments of the peasantry, both nationally and internationally; the dispute over resources, which is a widespread problem wherever there is international funding available, which can have important corrosive effects on cohesion and trust, a problem only exacerbated by over-funding by aid agencies; and the shift from concrete gains to network activism as an end in its own right. Secondly, he identifies external challenges, including the unfavourable economic climate for peasants given the low price of their crops, the financial emphasis of contemporary capitalism and the subsequent decline in bargaining power of rural producers, and in the Central American case in particular (although this is also true in South America and Africa), the massive outmigration and the increasing dependence of communities on remittances.

Despite these massive challenges, *La Vía Campesina* and other transnational movements representing the indigenous population, environmentalists and other grassroots groups were capable of significantly altering the terms of the debate, vis-à-vis very powerful actors, around food, trade and the economy, and to enshrine some of their demands into important resolutions against all odds. The neoliberal orthodoxy, at least when it comes to agrarian issues, is no longer unchallenged and civil society organisations concerned about the right to food, to land, to the territory of indigenous and rural peoples, and the defence of the environment, have important normative documents to back up their claims in the international arena and to articulate them in the language of rights and social justice. More importantly, these documents can be better understood as landmarks in the progress towards a transition to a more inclusive, equitable, peaceful future where millions of people can be free from the forms of direct and structural violence linked to the current accumulation model. While they are still not realities on the grounds, the terms of the debate have shifted massively, and the political significance of these triumphs, even if only at the institutional level for now, cannot be underestimated.

References

Altieri, M. (1995). *Agroecology: The science of sustainable agriculture*. Westview Press.

Alabrese, M., & Savaresi, A. (2022). The UNDROP and Climate Change: Squaring the Circle?. In M. Alabrese, A. Bessa, M. Brunori, & P. Giuggioli (Eds.), *The United Nations' Declaration on Peasant's Rights* (pp. 165–176). Routledge.

Arthur, P. (2009). How "transitions" reshaped human rights: A conceptual history of transitional justice. *Human Rights Quarterly, 31*(2), 321–367.

Barczak, M. (2001). Representation by consultation? The rise of direct democracy in Latin America. *Latin American Politics and Society, 43*(3), 37–59.

Bauer, K. (2016). Land versus territory: Evaluating indigenous land policy for the Mapuche in Chile. *Journal of Agrarian Change, 16*(4), 627–645.

Beitz, C. (2009). *The idea of human rights*. Oxford University Press.

Bengoa, J. (2000). *La emergencia indígena en América Latina*. Fondo de Cultura Económica.

Benton, T. (1989). Marxism and natural limits. An ecological critique and reconstruction. *New Left Review, 178*, 51–86.

Borras, S., Edelman, M., & Kay, C. (2008). Transnational agrarian movements: Origins and politics, campaigns and impact. *Journal of Agrarian Change, 8*(2–3), 169–204.

Burchardt, H.-J., & Dietz, K. (2014). (Neo-)extractivism -a new challenge for development theory from Latin America. *Third World Quarterly, 35*(3), 468–486.

Camargo, A. (2022). Imagined transitions: Agrarian capitalism and climate change adaptation in Colombia. *The Journal of Peasant Studies, 49*(4), 713–733.

Cambou, D. (2019). The UNDRIP and the legal significance of the right of indigenous peoples to self-determination: A human rights approach with a multidimensional perspective. *The International Journal of Human Rights, 23*(1–2), 34–50.

Cameron, M., Hershberg, E., & Sharpe, K. (2012). *New institutions for participatory democracy in Latin America: Voice and consequences*. Palgrave Macmillan.

Claeys, P. (2015). Food sovereignty and the recognition of new rights for peasants at the UN: A critical overview of La via Campesina's rights claims over the last 20 years. *Globalizations, 12*(4), 452–465.

Claeys, P., & Delgado, D. (2016). Peasant and indigenous transnational social movements engaging with climate justice. *Canadian Journal of Development Studies/Revue canadienne d'études du développement, 38*(3), 325–340.

Claeys, P., & Edelman, M. (2020). The United Nations declaration on the rights of peasants and other people working in rural areas. *The Journal of Peasant Studies, 47*(1), 1–68.

Corredor-García, J., & López, F. (2024). The logic of "war on deforestation": A military response to climate change in the Colombian Amazon. *Alternatives: Global Local, Political, 49*(4), 325–343.

Côté, I., Grant, A., Islam, A., McLean, V., Mitchell, M., & Panagos, D. (2019). The global implementation of UNDRIP: A thematic review. *The International Journal of Human Rights, 23*(1–2), 306–330.

Desmarais, A. (2007). *La Vía Campesina. Globalisation and the power of peasants.* Fernwood Publishing.

Dietz, K. (2019). Direct democracy in mining conflicts in Latin America: Mobilising against the La Colosa project in Colombia. *Canadian Journal of Development Studies/Revue canadienne d'études du développement, 40*(2), 145–162.

Edelman, M. (2008). Transnational organizing in agrarian Central America transnational organizing in agrarian Central America: Histories, challenges, prospects. *Journal of Agrarian Change, 8*(2–3), 229–257.

Edelman, M., & James, C. (2011). Peasants' rights and the UN system: Quixotic struggle? Or emancipatory idea whose time has come? *Journal of Peasant Studies, 38*(1), 81–108.

Fals Borda, O. (2010). *Antología.* Universidad Nacional de Colombia.

FAO. (2022). *Voluntary guidelines on the responsible governance of tenure of land, fisheries and forests in the context of National Food Security. First revision.* FAO.

Fearnside, P. (2001). Soybean cultivation as a threat to the environment in Brazil. *Environmental Conservation, 28*(1), 23–38.

Figueroa, R., & Mills, C. (2001). Environmental justice. In D. Jamieson (Ed.), *A companion to environmental philosophy* (pp. 426–438). Blackwell.

Freire, P. (1972). *Pedagogy of the oppressed.* Penguin Books.

Gerber, J.-F., & Veuthey, S. (2010). Plantations, resistance and the greening of the agrarian question in coastal Ecuador. *Journal of Agrarian Change, 10*(4), 455–481.

Gilbert, J., & Lennox, C. (2019). Towards new development paradigms: The United Nations declaration on the rights of indigenous peoples as a tool to support self-determined development. *The International Journal of Human Rights, 23*(1–2), 104–124.

Giunta, A. (2019). Looking back to move forward: The status of environmental rights under the UN declaration on the rights of indigenous peoples. *The International Journal of Human Rights, 23*(1–2), 149–173.

Gliessman, S. (2018). Defining Agroecology. *Agroecology and Sustainable Food Systems, 42*(6), 599–600.

Golay, C. (2013). Legal Reflections on the Rights of Peasants and Other People Working in Rural Areas. First Session of the Intergovernmental Working Group on a United Nations Declaration on the Rights of Peasants and Other People Working in Rural Areas (July 15). Retrieved November 08, 2025, from http://www.ohchr.org/Documents/HRBodies/HRCouncil/WGPleasants/Golay.pdf

Golay, C. (2022). The rights to food and food sovereignty in the UNDROP. In M. Alabrese, A. Bessa, M. Brunori, & P. F. Giuggioli (Eds.), *The United Nations' declaration on peasants' rights* (pp. 134–147). Routledge.

Gómez, F. (2019). The UNDRIP: An increasingly robust legal parameter. *The International Journal of Human Rights, 23*(1–2), 7–21.
Gómez-Betancur, L. (2020). The rights of nature in the Colombian Amazon: Examining challenges and opportunities in a transitional justice setting. *UCLA Journal of International Law and Foreign Affairs, 25*(1), 41–84.
Grajales, J. (2015). Land grabbing, legal contention and institutional change in Colombia. *Journal of Peasant Studies, 42*(3–4), 541–560.
Gudynas, E. (2009). Diez Tesis Urgentes sobre el Nuevo Extractivismo: Contextos y Demandas Bajo el Progresismo Sudamericano Actual. In J. Schuldt, A. Acosta, A. Barandiará, A. Bebbington, M. Folchi, CEDLA, A. Alayza, & E. Gudynas (Eds.), *Extractivismo, Política y Sociedad* (pp. 187–225). CAAP/CLAES.
Ignatieff, M. (2001). *Human rights as politics and idolatry.* Princeton University Press.
Jones, P. (1988). *The peasantry in the French revolution.* Cambridge University Press.
Joseph, R. (1997). Democratization in Africa after 1989: Comparative and theoretical perspectives. *Comparative Politics, 29*(3), 363–382.
Keck, M., & Sikkink, K. (1998). *Activists beyond Borders: Advocacy networks in international politics.* Cornell University Press.
Killean, R., & Dempster, L. (2022). "Greening" transitional justice? In M. Evans (Ed.), *Beyond transitional justice: Transformative justice and the state of the field (or non-field).* Routledge.
La Vía Campesina (2017). *Struggles of La Vía Campesina for agrarian reform and the defense of life, land and territories.* La Vía Campesina.
Lenzerini, F. (2019). Implementation of the UNDRIP around the world: Achievements and future perspectives. The outcome of the work of the ILA Committee on the implementation of the rights of indigenous peoples. *The International Journal of Human Rights, 23*(1–2), 51–62.
Leval, G. (2018). *Collectives in the Spanish revolution.* PM.
Lyons, K. (2023). "Nature" and territories as victims: Decolonizing Colombia's transitional justice process. *American Anthropologist, 125*(1), 63–76.
Maggio, G., & Cacciola, G. (2009). A variant of the Hubbert curve for world oil production forecasts. *Energy Policy, 37*(11), 4761–4770.
Mahlatsi, M. (2018). The peasants revolt: Analysing the role of the democratic state in the struggle for land and environmental justice in Xolobeni, eastern cape, South Africa. *Journal of Public Administration, 53*(2–1), 615–631.
Mantz, F., Frame, M., & Leguizamon, S. (2025). *Grassroots responses to Extractivism.* Bloomsbury.
Martínez-Alier, J. (2011). The EROI of agriculture and its use by the via Campesina. *Journal of Peasant Studies, 38*(1), 145–160.
Martínez-Alier, J. (2025). Agrarian justice and environmental justice. In S. Borras & J. Franco (Eds.), *The Oxford handbook of land politics.* Oxford University Press.

Martínez-Alier, J., Temper, L., Del Bene, D., & Scheidel, A. (2016). Is there a global environmental justice movement? *The Journal of Peasant Studies, 43*(3), 731–755.

Martínez-Torres, M., & Rosset, P. (2010). La Vía Campesina: The birth and evolution of a transnational social movement. *The Journal of Peasant Studies, 37*(1), 149–175.

Mintz, S. (1986). *Sweetness and power: The place of sugar in modern history.* Penguin.

Monsalve, S. (2013). The human rights framework in contemporary agrarian struggles. *Journal of Peasant Studies, 40*(1), 239–290.

Morgan, R. (2011). *Transforming law and institution. Indigenous peoples, the United Nations and human rights.* Ashgate.

Munck, R. (2020). *Social movements in Latin America: Mapping the mosaic.* McGill-Queen's University Press.

Nelson, P. (2004). New agendas and new patterns of international NGO political action. In R. Taylor (Ed.), *Creating a better world: Interpreting global civil society* (pp. 116–132). Kumarian Press.

Nicholson, P., & Borras, S. (2023). It wasn't an intellectual construction: The founding of La via Campesina, achievements and challenges - a conversation. *Journal of Peasant Studies, 50*(2), 610–626.

O'Brien, R., Goetz, A. M., Scholte, J. A., & Williams, M. (2000). *Contesting global governance: Multilateral economic institutions and global social movements.* Cambridge University Press.

Peeler, J. (2009). *Building democracy in Latin America.* Lynne Rienner.

Peša, I., & Ross, C. (2021). Extractive industries and the environment: Production, pollution, and protest in global history. *The Extractive Industries and Society, 8*(4), 100933.

Regan, Á., & Kenny, U. (2022). What do the public want to know about farming and why? Findings from a farmer-initiated public consultation exercise in Ireland. *Sustainability, 14*(9), 5391.

Richmond, C., Coombes, B., & Louis, R. P. (2024). *Because this land is who we are.* Bloomsbury.

Rosset, P. (2013). Re-thinking agrarian reform, land and territory in La via Campesina. *Journal of Peasant Studies, 40*(4), 721–775.

Salomon, M. (2018). *Nihilists, pragmatists and peasants: A dispatch on contradiction in international human rights law* (New York: IILJ Working Paper 2018/5, New York University School of Law).

Sauer, S. (2012). Land and territory: Meanings of land between modernity and tradition. *Agrarian South: Journal of Political Economy, 1*(1), 85–107.

Scott, J. C. (1998). *Seeing Like a State.* Yale University Press.

Shawki, N. (2014). New rights advocacy and the human rights of peasants: La via Campesina and the evolution of new human rights norms. *Journal of Human Rights Practice, 6*(2), 306–326.

Shigetomi, Y., Ishimura, Y., & Yamamoto, Y. (2020). Trends in global dependency on the Indonesian palm oil and resultant environmental impacts. *Scientific Reports, 10*(1), 20624.
Skocpol, T. (1982). What makes peasants revolutionary? *Comparative Politics, 14*(3), 351–375.
Szoke, M. (2025). The green thumb of transitional justice: The consideration of the environmental dimension of armed conflict in truth commissions. *International Journal of Transitional Justice, 19*, 480–496.
UN. (2007). United Nations Declaration on the Rights of Indigenous Peoples (A/RES/61/295).
UN. (2018). United Nations Declaration on the Rights of Peasants and Other People Working in Rural Areas (A/HRC/RES/39/12).
van der Ploeg, J. (2008). *The new peasantries. Struggles for autonomy and sustainability in an era of empire and globalization*. Earthscan.
van Meurs, W. (2017). The red peasant international. In L. van de Grift & A. R. Forclaz (Eds.), *Governing the rural in interwar Europe* (pp. 259–278). Routledge.
van Rooy, A. (2004). *The global legitimacy game: Civil society, globalization and protest*. Palgrave.
Vandenbogaerde, A. (2017). Localizing the human rights council: A case study of the declaration on the rights of peasants. *Journal of Human Rights, 16*(2), 220–241.
Vega, R., & Gutiérrez, J. A. (2019). *Siempre de Pie, Nunca Rendidos. Los Corteros de Caña de Azúcar en el Valle del Cauca, Presencia y Luchas (1860–2015)*. Desde Abajo.
Wezel, A., Herren, B. G., Kerr, R. B., Barrios, E., Gonçalves, A. L. R., & Sinclair, F. (2020). Agroecological principles and elements and their implications for transitioning to sustainable food systems. A review. *Agronomy for Sustainable Development, 40*(6), 40.
Whitehead, L. (1992). The alternatives to "Liberal democracy": A Latin American perspective. *Political Studies, 40*(Special Issue), 146–159.
Willetts, P. (1996). From Stockholm to Rio and beyond: The impact of the environmental movement on the United Nations consultative arrangements for NGOs. *Review of International Studies, 22*(1), 57–80.
Wolford, W. (2021). The Plantationocene: A Lusotropical contribution to the theory. *Annals of the American Association of Geographers, 111*(6), 1622–1639.
Yaşın, Z. (2023). The environmentalization of the agrarian question and the agrarianization of the climate justice movement. In I. Scoones, S. Borras, A. Baviskar, M. Edelman, N. L. Peluso, & W. Wolford (Eds.), *Climate change and critical agrarian studies* (pp. 29–59). Routledge.

CHAPTER 6

Supporting Agrarian Justice in Transition: Towards a Transformative Practice

Abstract While agrarian conflicts and peasants have traditionally been a blind spot of transitional justice, this situation has started to change, thanks to some of the transitional justice experiences we discussed in the previous chapters. This increasing sensitivity around the agrarian dimensions of conflict and peasants is taking place also because of the growing awareness of the economic, social and cultural dimensions of conflict, which had been long neglected, thanks partly to the growing transformative critique of transitional justice. We will now move on to discuss, from the perspective of agrarian justice, what constitutes support for justice in transition and how that support can be provided in practice. The rest of the chapter will emphasise in particular: participation of rural organisations and movements, their voice and their role in agenda setting and the interaction between policies and their quest for justice. This chapter will end by translating how transitional justice—and its various pillars—can incorporate these insights and what can be done in practice to start tackling the agrarian legacies of conflict and repression systematically.

Keywords Agrarian justice • Agrarian movements • Rural participation • Agenda setting • Policies • Truth • Prosecutions • Reparations • Guarantees of non-repetition

J. A. Gutiérrez, *Transitional Justice and Agrarian Conflict*, https://doi.org/10.1007/978-3-032-25228-9_6

Most conflicts have had agrarian dimensions that have been either neglected or insufficiently addressed by transitional justice. Very often, the agrarian dimensions of these conflicts have been neglected by applying a certain prism, borrowed from the new war paradigms and the so-called economic theory of conflict, reducing much conflict in the world to ethnicity or criminality. However, acknowledging these agrarian dimensions is paramount in order to be able to overcome some of the structural causes and mechanisms that have caused violence in the first place, that guarantee its reproduction and that are the basis of future conflict or repression. Most importantly, agrarian conflicts, or the agrarian dimensions of broader conflicts, usually have particular dynamics that relate to structural forms of violence that require an understanding of the political economy in which they fester. Not only are these forms of structural violence important to be addressed in their own right as a source of violations, but they also are what allow other forms of victimisation by creating structural vulnerabilities for entire social groups. Peasants, in this sense, while having participated extensively in transitional justice experiences in the past, have rarely been acknowledged as such, their identity and social category being very often merely background information to understand their violations as members of a particular ethnic group or, more often than not, as simple individuals. The particular experiences of peasants as a social class, in the context of violence and repression, have been almost completely neglected, despite the fact that the violence against peasants (both structural and physical) very often predate and outlive open armed confrontation, being often exacerbated in the course of civil war or dictatorship.

While agrarian conflicts and peasants in general have traditionally been a blind spot of transitional justice, this situation has started to change. In particular, some transitional justice experiences over the last 20 years that we just discussed, such as the Truth Commission report in Kenya or a broad range of transitional justice mechanisms in Colombia, have recognised the particularities of both the agrarian question in conflict and of the victimisation of peasants as a social class or collective. This has started to change, as discussed by Hoddy (2021), because of a more general shift in transitional justice to be more inclusive in terms of the voices that are recognised in their processes and mechanisms, such as women, indigenous, the LGTBI+ community, people with disabilities, etc. Even more recently, transitional justice has started to take seriously the inclusion and the affectations suffered by non-human or other-than-human entities, such as nature, animals or territories.

But this increasing sensitivity around the agrarian dimensions of conflict and peasants in particular is taking place also because of the growing awareness of the economic, social and cultural dimensions of conflict, which had been for long neglected in favour of an almost exclusive focus on civil and political rights. It is no longer the case that the social marginalisation of millions, the constant threat to their livelihoods and the denial of access to basic, often life-saving, services can be regarded as a mere footnote or as background information to other violations such as torture or killings. The field is becoming more aware of the fact that these represent serious violations in their own right, that social, economic and cultural rights are not secondary rights, but rights as important as others, and that usually they also facilitate other forms of victimisation and vulnerability. For those reasons, it is no longer expected that dealing with the violation of social and economic rights is something that will magically happen at some point further down the line, when civil and political rights are fully realised.

We will now move on to discuss, from the perspective of agrarian justice, what constitutes support for justice in transition and how that support can be provided in practice. Here, we want to use the term justice in transition as a practice that moves beyond orthodox transitional justice, and 'Contest[s] continuities of injustice and seek[s] justice in their local environment and with regard to the state. Justice in transition emerges from a particular time and place and in contrast to [ed. orthodox] transitional justice cannot be prescriptively described, but is the product of a highly-contextualised approach to a justice deficit' (Gready & Robins, 2017, p. 2). The rest of the chapter will emphasise in particular: participation of rural organisations and movements; their voice and their role in agenda setting; and the interaction between policies and their quest for justice. This chapter will end by translating how transitional justice—and its various pillars—can incorporate these insights and what can be done in practice to start tackling the agrarian legacies of conflict and repression systematically.

6.1 Participation of Rural Organisations and Movements

Without a doubt, the shift towards a more inclusive approach to 'victims' and to a wider range of social categories in transitional justice, as well as the greater attention paid to social, economic and cultural rights, has taken place because of two important movements bringing about change to the field, one academic in origin, the other coming from the field of practice. On the one hand, the transformative critique has forced important debates in the transitional justice field about the place of social, economic and cultural rights, about the structural and root causes of conflict, about the need to go beyond ideas derived from corrective justice and to move towards ideas of justice that challenge current imbalances of power which are often at the root of the open and physical manifestations of violence and repression. Also, the transformative critique (including calls for transitional justice from the bottom-up or transitional justice from below) has called into question the traditional overreliance of transitional justice on top-down mechanisms and an emphasis on prosecution and retribution. By focusing on process and by focusing on grassroots efforts to right the wrongs suffered by people at the receiving end of violence, authoritarianism and/or repression, the field has directed its gaze towards the practice of social movements to bring about change from a conception of peace and change that is often far richer and more wholesome than the formulas encapsulated in the straitjacket of the liberal peacebuilding or statebuilding paradigms.

On the other hand, and most importantly, from the field of practice, we have that the participation of social movements and organised victims' associations have been able to bring to the fore of the transitional justice agenda the concerns of communities and subaltern groups on the ground, who very often experience egregious forms of marginalisation and denial of economic and social rights that require the field of transitional justice to move beyond the orthodox formulas anchored in the liberal peacebuilding paradigm. It is the collective action of the very people that has been at the receiving end of armed conflict, civil war and repression that has brought to the fore these questions for the transitional justice field. This is a humbling conclusion, but one that reminds us that change rarely comes from above, without significant pressure and mobilisation from below. Where the voice of peasants has been heard the most is where peasants have been organised and have mobilised the most to assert their rights.

The experience of Colombia, in particular, has given an unprecedented prominence to the agrarian question and to peasants, in a way that they won't be so easy to ignore in future transitional justice processes.

The peasants' grassroots participation in various forms of protests and mobilisation, but also in truth commissions, in peace processes, in judicial mechanisms and in various other transitional justice mechanisms available to victims of violence and repression have forced the field to take into consideration these pressing issues. Throughout the various examples discussed here, we see that the participation of rural organisations and peasant movements has been critical for pushing questions related to justice in contexts of agrarian conflict and injustice. Whether in local contexts, such as peasants struggling for agrarian reform and against particular forms of marginalisation, or peasants at the international arena pushing for new normative frameworks to correct the structural injustices of the global system, or using international platforms to put pressure on their own states, we see that peasants have not been standing idle. They have been mobilising for decades on issues related to forms of structural violence that we have discussed and a range of contemporary concerns, such as climate change, that are having and will have a decisive impact on the forms that conflict will assume in the twenty-first century. The problem is that, because of the traditional blind spots and biases of the discipline, scholars and practitioners of transitional justice not always have identified those demands as issues pertinent to justice in transition, or even as justice issues at all.

6.2 Voice and Agenda Setting

And here we can see one of the main contributions of this shift towards the recognition of peasants, of the importance of the social, economic and cultural rights and of the growing sensitivity about the agrarian dimensions of conflict and repression. It has helped us to expand and to broaden our vision of what justice means. Justice no longer can mean (only) people behind bars, public naming and shaming or corrective measures attempting to bring us back to the starting point of violence or repression, to an idyllic pre-conflict situation that usually was never that idyllic in the first place—and this is precisely why conflict happened to begin with! Justice now means the full realisation of all rights, civil and political, but also social, economic and cultural, together with environmental and collective rights such as self-determination and sovereignty. Justice is also about dismantling the structures of colonialism and marginalisation of all categories and groups to make possible that the promise of human rights can take place, that the conditions exist to allow the flourishing of all humans.

Rural organisations and movements have articulated their visions of justice, incorporating pressing issues such as climate justice, while also reclaiming the contested nature of the term 'transition'. Again, there is no pre-determined end to transitions as in the liberal peacebuilding paradigm understanding, which reduced complex processes into the simple formula 'peace = elections + privatisations'. Indeed, social movements and rural movements have opposed free trade agreements, extractivism disguised as development, trade liberalisation and privatisations in the name of justice. They have, likewise, defended democratic freedoms without necessarily sticking to a single universal formula. Their vision of transition goes beyond the G7 version of democracy, and they factor in sustainability, the defence of the commons and a future based around ideas of fraternity and autonomy. Issues like food sovereignty appear as crucial to this vision of justice and, indeed, to the flourishing of our species and of the nature around us. Transitions are highly political and contested, and peasant mobilisations have helped to re-politicise the field and the very idea of transitional justice, moving it away from the (cynical) understanding of it as a neutral technology, while the politics of supposed neutrality conceal the real objectives of powerful actors. This understanding of transitions as processes that are not teleological and not based on pre-determined outcomes (often pre-determined by powerful international and global actors) is not only aligned with the contributions from the transformative justice scholarship, but also by the agonistic approach to transitional justice and peacebuilding, which instead of forcing consensus and monolithic narratives embraces divergence and disagreements as normal aspects of social transitions that do not need to result in violence against the adversary (cf., Murphy & Walsh, 2022; Strömbom & Bramsen, 2022).

These movements not only have managed to set the agenda on important questions related to justice in transition, reclaiming in the process both the concepts of justice and transition. They have also managed to articulate a global voice that respects the many local voices through a process of mobilisation that has autonomy at its very heart. Autonomy here is two things at once. It is, first, a mobilisation mechanism by which the peasants set their own agenda without the leading vanguard of enlightened outsiders, but in solidarity and cooperation with other social sectors that they are in convergence with. Autonomy as a mobilisation mechanism is aligned with the idea of 'radical solidarity' developed by Moore (1966, pp. 475–476), as the autonomous action of peasants in solidarity with one another and against the landlords and other rural elites. Movements such as *La Vía Campesina* have articulated this radical solidarity of peasant movements globally, projecting their voice and demands to the global scale. Autonomy here also means a social project, a radical form of sovereignty that no longer understands the nation-state as the sole locus of sovereignty, but that also devolves an important measure of this sovereignty to the people, to communities on the ground, where people live, build peace and experience participation as democracy in motion. It is both a project and hope that are prefigured in this organisation and in the definitions of their own political project. Having captured our imagination, it has given us the freedom to think of alternative transitions and visions of justice.

6.3 Policies

These grassroots movements have demonstrated an impressive skill to combine calls for reform, with mobilisation on the ground for deep structural change, as well as with the ability of combining corrective, distributive and transformative measures. These experiences have informed the transformative and the bottom-up critiques of transitional justice, both from an intellectual and from a practical perspective. These movements have understood very clearly that the development of policies and frameworks is not an end in itself but a means to advance a much broader project of social and environmental justice. Here, policies are understood as valuable tools to achieve change, and not as if policies were actually the change to be achieved, moving beyond legal fetishism that is very often prevalent in the field.

In particular, the development of new normative frameworks, articulated specifically in terms of justice and in terms of a transition to less violent, more sustainable and just ways of life represents a direct challenge to some of the normative assumptions of orthodox transitional justice. By calling for the protection of traditional livelihoods, the protection of the environment, support for peasant agriculture and smallholding farming and calls for food sovereignty, they call into question the market liberalisation premises of the liberal peacebuilding paradigm, which have informed much of the understandings of orthodox transitional justice. This represents concrete proposals and alternatives that help us move beyond the post–Cold War capture of our political imagination by the neoliberal dogma, which in practice is rarely concerned with peace or justice. By developing these policies, we now have new tools that can be used in transitional justice settings to advance new understandings of justice and new ways to address some of the structural forms of violence that have been prevalent in rural settings and that have opened the doors to other forms of violence in those very same settings.

6.4 Agrarian Justice in Transition

What does all this mean for practitioners and transitional justice scholars? How can we make transitional justice processes more sensitive about the agrarian dimensions and legacies of conflict and repression? Based on our previous discussion, we will now propose, according to the traditional pillars of transitional justice (truth, prosecutions, reparations and guarantees of non-repetition), some ideas on how transitional justice, despite the limitations and blind spots of its more orthodox and narrow versions, can still play a role in engaging with peasants and rural peoples' own agendas. This requires incorporating important aspects of the transformative critique and some of the bottom-up understandings that have emerged over the last decade and a half. While each context will be different, we can have a certain compass that helps us navigate those complexities and ask ourselves the right questions in order to address the agrarian dimensions of conflict and repression.

6.4.1 Truth

The truth, from this perspective, is more than a collection of atrocities and a detailed list of acts of physical violence. We need to understand the patterns of dispossession and the wide range of factors that have made it possible: naked violence, the imposition of alien structures of tenancy and property over customary or traditional ones, the uses of the law and state institutions in facilitating dispossession and the role of business and powerful elite actors in this process. Years ago, when I was conducting research in Putumayo, in Southern Colombia, in an area which had been already researched by a team from one of the official transitional justice institutions, one of the ladies in the focus group said to me, 'It is nice that you let us tell you our side of the story. Because when we told the doctors from Bogotá [the previous team of researchers] that after the paramilitaries finished their massacre in our village, then oil companies showed up, they would shush us and tell us, "we are not here to talk about the oil companies, but about what the paramilitaries did". But we know that it was all linked, that one came after the other'. Revealing the factors behind these patterns can be uncomfortable for the powerful but should be a top priority for Truth Commissions or other truth-finding mechanisms in the transitional justice toolbox.

Indeed, it is important to move beyond an exclusive focus on physical violence and the violation of civil and political rights and start addressing structural and systemic violence systematically. Not only because these forms of violence facilitate very often expressions of physical violence, but because they represent violations of rights and forms of violence in their own right. These are the forms of violence that the peasantry and other rural peoples are routinely exposed to, on a day-to-day basis, as opposed to other, more spectacular but exceptional, forms of physical violence. These require us to engage with the powerful socio-economic structures shaping class, race and gender today, and also with the pervasive legacies of colonialism in much of the world, not as background information but as an intrinsic part of the truth. This also means understanding the damage suffered through dispossession beyond what is quantifiable in monetary terms and understanding as well the impact of dispossession in the social fabric and the collective dimension of these affectations (Walker et al., 2010). Some Truth Commissions, in particular Colombia and Kenya, have advanced in that direction, but it is necessary that this is incorporated as a normal practice, as part of the research agenda of commissions, archives and memorialisation efforts directed towards dealing with the legacies of conflict and repression in the rural world.

6.4.2 *Prosecutions*

Prosecutions can be obfuscating and frustrating for people who have been victimised, even if positive measures such as the flexibilization of the rules of evidence or the inversion of the burden of proof have been introduced in transitional justice to benefit them. Justice, ultimately, is not just about prosecutions, and sectors within the transitional justice field have been consistently moving away from a purely retributive understanding to incorporate a more holistic vision. But without falling into forms of legal fetishism or unrealistic expectations of what can be achieved through retributive justice, for as long as prosecutions are here (and they seem to be here to stay, at least for a long while, cf. McGonigle Leyh, 2016), we need to have a better understanding of the role they could play to advance some of this broader, agrarian justice agenda. First and foremost, because behind the scenes of agrarian conflicts, there are people who profited and benefitted from the structures of repression and violence. More often than not, these are important members of the elites and the dominant classes, with an important foothold in the coalitions of power that sustained both violence and repression, and they need to be held accountable for this.

In the Colombian case, guerrilla leaders, right-wing paramilitaries and some military commanders have been paraded through the dock in various transitional justice settings, while civilians who benefitted from land-grabbing and the politicians who made many of the decisions that led to abuses without ever having to stain their suits with blood are not required to respond in any of those scenarios, except if they want to do it on a voluntary basis. The same can be said about the Gambia, where, despite the well-known land-grabbing practices associated with repression and violence, there is still little recognition of this phenomenon in transitional justice processes, and the debate of what to do to address this issue remains pending. Or in the case of Kenya, where, against common sense, it is expected that a number of political figures who have often benefitted from land injustice will take action to address land injustice and dispossession. Unsurprisingly, little has happened on that front. Here prosecutions could play a role to make sure that there are consequences for the funders, orchestrators and beneficiaries of these forms of violence and that therefore, by holding them accountable, people that become stumbling blocks to structural transformations and change can be removed.

Forms of prosecution that focus exclusively on armed actors—and then exclusively on forms of physical violence and on civil/political violations—can (and very often do) depoliticise the nature of complex conflicts and structures of violence. In these retributive spaces, complex processes of agrarian resistance and politically motivated violence, and the classes, the social structures of oppression and power that stifle them, are metamorphosed into a motley collection of abuses, into a litany of violations and crimes. This narrative is devoid of social and political content, consequently rendering the logics of the actors as socially structured entities (and not just as rational agents or as solipsistic individuals) invisible. Thus, peasants and rural people are reduced merely to 'victims', devoid of agency or primarily portrayed in terms of their violations but not necessarily on their resistance to these violations. What's more, their resistance can be constructed into a violation as well. The 'sterile language' of legal proceedings and 'the legal process does not permit witnesses to tell their own coherent narrative; it chops their stories into digestible parts, selects a handful of parts, and sorts and refines them to create a new narrative—the legal antinarrative' (Mertus, 2003, p. 230).

Staying away from unrealistic expectations from prosecutions and understanding very well the limited but important role they can play, it is important to re-evaluate other venues for public accountability, such as People's Tribunals, modelled in the example of the Russell Tribunal against the Vietnam War in the 1960s (Krever, 2017; Byrnes & Simm, 2018). The Russell Tribunals or the Permanent People's Tribunals are completely absent in Teitel's (2003) genealogy of transitional justice, but initiatives such as these can help advance more transformative forms of transitional justice. These, although lacking the teeth of traditional prosecutions, can have an important moral and ethical weight, can be useful to mobilise public opinion and to raise the visibility of particular violations, and most importantly, can have a more empowering effect upon social movements and civil society organisations working for long-term and transformative change.

6.4.3 *Reparations*

If we are to understand the dynamics of agrarian conflict, we need to move beyond the epistemological individualistic perspectives that very often plague the field. In agrarian contexts, we are not talking just about individuals affected, but we are talking about classes and social groups. Likewise, we are not just talking about civil and political rights; affectations here are different, social and economic in nature, and very often affectations, particularly in countries that have been colonised, can only be grasped from a *long durée* perspective. In agrarian contexts, in the face of this kind of affectations, and given the collective nature of subjects who suffered from these affectations, individual monetary compensation or property restitution are insufficient and often miss the target. While collective forms of reparations need to take priority, they need to address precisely the affectations at the level of the social fabric.

Even though land restitution alone can often be welcome, it is completely insufficient to address the structural forms of violence sustained by land inequality and concentration. The Pinheiro principles (UN, 2005a), in this regard, can provide only some initial steps towards comprehensive policies. Although they address socio-economic rights and introduce a number of very progressive stipulations (right to non-discrimination, right to equality between men and women, participation of the affected people, etc.), restitution—in the exceedingly unlikely scenario that it goes according to plan—brings us back to square one. The same can be said about the 'Basic Principles and Guidelines on the Right to a Remedy and Reparation' (UN, 2005b) and their insistence to restore the victimised people to the original situation before the affectation occurred, which is, in most cases, far from ideal and plagued with vulnerability and power imbalances (Meertens, 2019).

Although in the face of loss, forms of reparation and compensation are always important, lasting responses that lead to sustainable peace in the long term, often will require transformative measures that touch upon structures of inequality and violence. Here grassroots mobilisation needs to coalesce with decisive action from the relevant parties and institutions in long-term processes of change, which are intrinsically political and open to contestation. Without detriment to other forms of reparation, restitution and compensation to individuals that may be decided, these transformative measures address, necessarily, the situation of classes and vast social groups. Here, there is an economy of scale: how viable is it to give individual reparations, for instance, to more than 10 million people officially registered as victims in Colombia? For many people that have suffered from victimisation, reparations can and often ought to be aligned with development and assume a distinctively developmentalist discourse, in the form of infrastructure, access to services and productive and livelihood projects (Gready et al., forthcoming).

6.4.4 *Guarantees of Non-Repetition*

An agrarian perspective on conflict and repression forces us to think about the guarantees of non-repetition beyond traditional mechanisms such as vetting or institutional reform. It also should include dismantling the structures of violence, those causing structural and systemic violence, and those that create the conditions of vulnerability that also make it possible for other forms of physical violence to take place. In agrarian settings, this means engaging seriously with the various dimensions of the land question: governance, tenure, access, register, jurisdiction and legal issues, markets and food sovereignty, etc. It also means to engage with other issues such as security guarantees for agrarian leaders. extractivist policies, together with the long-term effects of climate change and the environmental crisis.

Here, we do not start from scratch. Transnational peasant movements such as *La Vía Campesina* have advanced policies and proposals in this regard, with many local movements already starting to implement them on the ground. They provide both the ideas and the political leverage to make those transformations possible. But it is not only grassroots movements that can provide tools. At an institutional level, UNDROP and UNDRIP, together with the VGGT, can also provide important frameworks and internationally recognised standards that are more amenable to the language and the toolbox of transitional justice to facilitate this process of transition away from agrarian conflict.

Of course, there are no easy fixes here: these forms of transformative change require a much broader political transformation, and it will, necessarily, elicit resistance from powerful sectors who will be eager to defend the *status quo*. This without taking into account the messy local landscapes riddled with local rivalries, difficulties to determine the rightfulness of claims, the problem of secondary occupants, the persistence of violent dynamics, etc., which we have witnessed in restitution (let alone transformation) cases. Here is where we need to remember the intrinsically political nature of transitional justice, but we need to go beyond the narrow liberal peacebuilding paradigm that has for too long been dogmatically associated with it. Social movements on the ground can provide us with a compass but also with the political means to make change happen if we can create meaningful and binding spaces for participation.

References

Byrnes, A., & Simm, G. (2018). *People's tribunals and international law*. Cambridge University Press.

Gready, P., Gutiérrez, J., & Mesa, W. (forthcoming). Rethinking the relationship between development and reparations: Conceptualising transformative reparations from below in Colombia.

Gready, P., & Robins, S. (2017). Rethinking civil society and transitional justice: Lessons from social movements and 'new' civil society. *The International Journal of Human Rights, 21*(7), 956–975.

Hoddy, E. (2021). Peasants' rights and agrarian violence in transitional settings: From transitional justice to transformative agrarian justice. *Journal of Human Rights, 20*(1), 91–109.

Krever, T. (2017). Remembering the Russell Tribunal. *London Review of International Law, 5*(3), 483–492.
McGonigle Leyh, B. (2016). Nuremberg's legacy on transitional justice: Prosecutions are here to stay. *Washington University Global Studies Law Review, 15*, 559–574.
Meertens, D. (2019). *Elusive justice. Women, land rights, and Colombia's transition to peace*. University of Wisconsin Press.
Mertus, J. (2003). The politics of memory and international trials for wartime rape. In P. Gready (Ed.), *Political transition. Politics and cultures* (pp. 227–245). Pluto Press.
Moore, B. (1966). *Social origins of dictatorship and democracy. Lord and peasant in the making of the modern world*. Beacon Press.
Murphy, E., & Walsh, D. (2022). Agonistic transitional justice: A global survey. *Third World Quarterly, 43*(6), 1380–1398.
Strömbom, L., & Bramsen, I. (2022). Agonistic peace: Advancing knowledge on institutional dynamics and relational transformation. *Third World Quarterly, 43*(6), 1237–1250.
Teitel, R. (2003). Transitional justice genealogy (symposium: Human rights in transition). *Harvard Human Rights Journal, 16*, 69–94.
UN. (2005a). Final report of the Special Rapporteur, Paulo Sérgio Pinheiro, 'Housing and property restitution in the context of the return of refugees and internally displaced persons. Principles on housing and property restitution for refugees and displaced persons' (E/CN.4/Sub.2/2005/17).
UN. (2005b). Basic Principles and Guidelines on the Right to a Remedy and Reparation for Victims of Gross Violations of International Human Rights Law and Serious Violations of International Humanitarian Law (A/RES/60/147).
Walker, C., Bohlin, A., Hall, R., & Kepe, T. (2010). *Land, memory, reconstruction, and justice: Perspectives on land claims in South Africa*. Ohio University Press.

CHAPTER 7

Conclusion

Abstract In these concluding remarks, we explain why agrarian justice should become a structural component of transitional justice and an essential component to have a real commitment to non-repetition in many conflicts and repressive contexts. With collective forms of reparation, and their alignment with development, more transformative and redistributive measures should be implemented to alter the landscape of systemic and structural violence, and all the other forms of physical violence interrelated and deriving from those. Policy documents and normative frameworks, together with transnational peasant movements, can contribute to translating these guidelines and aims into real practice on the ground. Participation, binding and meaningful, is key to realise this potential.

Keywords Participation • Collective reparations • Redistributive measures • Development • Policies • Normative frameworks • Transnational movements

Despite being declared an artifact of history so many times, peasants have not gone away. In fact, they have managed to prove the oracles of history wrong by evolving and adapting to the new times, creating in the process one of the most vibrant social movements there is at present. Peasants have fed us all for thousands of years, and they will do it, hopefully, for

J. A. Gutiérrez, *Transitional Justice and Agrarian Conflict*,
https://doi.org/10.1007/978-3-032-25228-9_7

thousands more to come. But their movements have also managed to articulate visions of justice that can inspire us and inform our thought and practice. When looking for alternatives to the orthodox, top-down, neoliberal versions of transitional justice, the transformative critics and their fellow travellers don't need to re-invent the wheel. They just need to look at the practice and programmes of the global, but highly localised, peasant movement to find plenty of sources of inspiration and hope: it is a matter of translating this into transitional language and practices.

Agrarian justice should become a structural and essential component of transitional justice, so it can really live up to its commitments to non-repetition in those conflicts and repressive contexts that have an important rural dimension. Together with the importance of collective forms of reparation, and their alignment with development, more transformative and redistributive measures should be implemented to alter the landscape of systemic and structural violence, and all the other forms of physical violence interrelated and deriving from those. We have enough policy documents and frameworks, plus significant international and transnational peasant movements that can translate these guidelines and aims into real practice on the ground. Participation, binding and meaningful, is key to realise this potential. Participation needs to consider the agenda set by these very movements in their own spaces and territories, with their own voice.

Now I want to come back to the reflection with which I started the book and why this is all, ultimately, about hope. We live in times of uncertainty and dismay—war rages, genocidal violence takes place with pornographic explicitness in real time in front of us, the liberal architecture of the so-called rules-based order (which always allowed some of its VIP members to trample those rules as they pleased) is crumbling, and, as a result, there is a generalised incredulity about the international mechanisms of intervention on which transitional justice has traditionally rested upon (cf., MacGinty, 2025). The so-called forces of good have proven not to be so benign as we thought. They never really were, and the rubble of Gaza bears witness to that. History, however, will not stop. What form the new transitions will take remains to be seen, but amidst all this chaos and unbearable human suffering, hope does not give in. The peasant struggles, and their movements, the policies and frameworks they have influenced and crafted and their enormous resilience have taught us not to expect answers from where they are less likely to come. It is these social movements that are resisting on the streets the brutality of power and the callous silence and complicity of elites, who today, as always, provide us with the moral compass to weather this and future storms. It is they who are giving us the raw materials for new visions of justice in a world in transition.

References

Acosta, M., Castañeda, Á., García, D., Hernández, F., Muelas, D., & Santamaría, Á. (2018). The Colombian transitional process: Comparative perspectives on violence against indigenous women. *International Journal of Transitional Justice, 12*(1), 108–125.

Adepoju, A. (2019). Migrants and refugees in Africa', in Erin Hannah (ed.), *Oxford Research Encyclopedia of Politics.* Oxford University Press. Retrieved February 15, 2026, from https://doi.org/10.1093/acrefore/9780190228637.013.723

Aguirre, C., & Drinot, P. (2017). *The peculiar revolution. Rethinking the Peruvian experiment under military rule.* University of Texas Press.

Ali, J. (2022). *Philippines' Bangsamoro peace process normalization track hits some bumps, United States Institute of Peace*, 6 September. Retrieved December 01, 2025, from https://www.usip.org/publications/2022/09/philippines-bangsamoro-peace-process-normalization-track-hits-some-bumps

Altieri, M. (1995). *Agroecology: The science of sustainable agriculture.* Westview Press.

Andaya, R. (2021). Transformation through normalization: Delineating justice in the Bangsamoro peace process. *Hiroshima Peace Research Journal, 8*, 133–157.

Anderson, D. (2005). *Histories of the hanged: The dirty war in Kenya and the end of empire.* Weidenfeld & Nicolson.

Anrup, R. (2011). *Antígona y Creonte. Rebeldía y Estado en Colombia.* Ediciones B.

Araghi, F. (1995). Global Depeasantization, 1945–1990. *The Sociological Quarterly, 36*(2), 337–368.

J. A. Gutiérrez, *Transitional Justice and Agrarian Conflict*, https://doi.org/10.1007/978-3-032-25228-9

Arango, L., Arias, J., Borras, S., Coronado, S., Díaz, I., Fajardo, D., Ojeda, D., Peña-Huertas, R., Rojas, I., & Serrano, A. (2025). Land grabbing, land dispossession, land rush: What can we learn from Colombia? *The Journal of Peasant Studies, 52*(7), 1632–1665.

Arango, V. J. C. (2023). Morir acribillado buscando la restitución de la tierra: los nueve casos de 2023. *El Espectador*, 28th December.

Arbour, L. (2007). Economic and social justice for societies in transition. *International Law and Politics, 40*(1), 1–27.

Archila, M., & Torres, J. (2009). *Bananeras. Huelga y Masacre, 80 años*. UNAL.

Ariza-Buitrago, I., & Gómez-Betancur, L. (2023). Nature in focus: The invisibility and re-emergence of Rivers, land and animals in Colombia's transitional justice system. *International Journal of Transitional Justice, 17*(1), 71–88.

Artaraz, K., Calestani, M., & Trueba, M. (2021). Introduction: Vivir bien/Buen vivir and post-neoliberal development paths in Latin America: Scope, strategies, and the realities of implementation. *Latin American Perspectives, 48*(3), 4–16.

Arthur, P. (2009). How "transitions" reshaped human rights: A conceptual history of transitional justice. *Human Rights Quarterly, 31*(2), 321–367.

Ashaba, I., & Marijnen, E. (2025). "We are soldiers now": Green militarism and (foreign-assisted) military training in conservation. *International Affairs, 101*(2), 565–582.

Autesserre, S. (2010). Dangerous tales: Dominant narratives on The Congo and their unintended consequences. *African Affairs, 111*, 202–222.

Balint, J., Evans, J., & McMillan, N. (2014). Rethinking transitional justice, redressing indigenous harm: A new conceptual approach. *International Journal of Transitional Justice, 8*(2), 194–216.

Balsari, S., Dresser, C., & Leaning, J. (2020). Climate change, migration and civil strife, current environmental. *Health Reports, 7*, 404–414.

Barczak, M. (2001). Representation by consultation? The rise of direct democracy in Latin America. *Latin American Politics and Society, 43*(3), 37–59.

Barkan, J. (1987). The electoral process and peasant-state relations in Kenya. In F. Hayward (Ed.), *Elections in independent Africa* (pp. 213–237). Westview Press.

Barkan, J. (2008). Will the Kenyan settlement hold? *Current History, 107*(708), 147–153.

Bassett, E. (2017). The challenge of reforming land governance in Kenya under the 2010 constitution. *The Journal of Modern African Studies, 55*(4), 537–566.

Batisai, K., & Mudimu, G. (2021). Revisiting the politics of land recovery among white commercial farmers in Zimbabwe: Implications for transitional justice. *International Journal of Transitional Justice, 15*(2), 370–385.

Bauer, K. (2016). Land versus territory: Evaluating indigenous land policy for the Mapuche in Chile. *Journal of Agrarian Change, 16*(4), 627–645.

Bauluz, L., Yajna, G., & Filip, N. (2020). *Global land inequality* (WID.world WORKING PAPER No. 2020/10).

Beitz, C. (2009). *The idea of human rights*. Oxford University Press.

Bengoa, J. (2000). *La emergencia indígena en América Latina*. Fondo de Cultura Económica.

Benton, T. (1989). Marxism and natural limits. An ecological critique and reconstruction. *New Left Review, 178*, 51–86.

Berg, R. (1986). Sendero Luminoso and the peasantry of Andahuaylas. *Journal of Interamerican Studies and World Affairs, 28*(4), 165–196.

Bergquist, C. (1986). *Coffee and conflict in Colombia, 1886–1910*. Duke University Press.

Bernstein, H. (2008). Agrarian questions from transition to globalisation. In H. A. Lodhi & C. Kay (Eds.), *Peasants and globalisation: Political economy, rural transformation and the agrarian question* (pp. 239–261). Routledge.

Bernstein, H. (2010). *Class dynamics of agrarian change*. Fernwood Publishing.

Bernstein, H., & Byres, T. (2001). From peasant studies to agrarian change. *Journal of Agrarian Change, 1*(1), 1–56.

Betancur-Alarcón, L., & Krause, T. (2020). Reaching for the mountains at the end of a Rebelocracy: Changes in land and water access in Colombia's highlands during the post-peace agreement phase. *Frontiers in Environmental Science, 8*, 546821.

Biddolph, C. (2024). Queering the global governance of transitional justice: Tensions and (Im)possibilities. *International Journal of Transitional Justice, 18*(2), 281–298.

Boesten, J. (2014). *Sexual violence during war and peace. Gender, power, and post-conflict justice in Peru*. Palgrave Macmillan.

Boesten, J., & Wilding, P. (2015). Transformative gender justice: Setting an agenda. *Women's Studies International Forum, 51*, 75–80.

Bonilla, L. (2025). Contra los PDET, la promesa monumental del Acuerdo de Paz que nunca aterrizó. *El Espectador*, 1st May.

Boone, C. (2011). Politically allocated land rights and the geography of electoral violence: The case of Kenya in the 1990s. *Comparative Political Studies, 44*(10), 1311–1342.

Borras, S. (2009). Agrarian change and peasant studies: Changes, continuities and challenges–an introduction. *The Journal of Peasant Studies, 36*(1), 5–31.

Borras, S. (2023). Politically engaged, pluralist and internationalist: Critical agrarian studies today. *The Journal of Peasant Studies, 50*(2), 449–489.

Borras, S., Edelman, M., & Kay, C. (2008). Transnational agrarian movements: Origins and politics, campaigns and impact. *Journal of Agrarian Change, 8*(2–3), 169–204.

Borras, S., Scoones, I., Baviskar, A., Edelman, M., Peluso, N. L., & Wolford, W. (2023). Climate change and agrarian struggles. In I. Scoones, S. Borras, A. Baviskar,

M. Edelman, N. L. Peluso, & W. Wolford (Eds.), *Climate change and critical agrarian studies* (pp. 1–28). Routledge.

Boutros-Ghali, B. (1992). An agenda for peace: Preventive diplomacy, peacemaking, and peacekeeping. Report of the Secretary-General, UN Doc. A/47/277-S24111, 17 June.

Browne, B. (2023). *Transitional (in)justice and enforcing the peace on Palestine*. Palgrave Macmillan.

Buendia, R. (2006). Mindanao conflict in The Philippines: Ethno-religious war or economic conflict? In A. Croissant, M. Beite, & S. Kneip (Eds.), *The politics of death: Political violence in Southeast Asia* (pp. 147–187). Lit Verlag Berlin.

Bueno-Hansen, P. (2018). The emerging LGBTI rights challenge to transitional justice in Latin America. *International Journal of Transitional Justice, 12*(1), 126–145.

Buijtenhuijs, R. (2000). Peasant wars in Africa: Gone with the wind? In D. Bryceson, C. Kay, & J. Mooij (Eds.), *Disappearing peasantries? Rural labour in Africa, Asia and Latin America* (pp. 112–122). ITDG.

Burchardt, H.-J., & Dietz, K. (2014). (Neo-)extractivism -a new challenge for development theory from Latin America. *Third World Quarterly, 35*(3), 468–486.

Byrnes, A., & Simm, G. (2018). *People's tribunals and international law*. Cambridge University Press.

Caballero, V. (1986). La Crisis de las Empresas Asociativas en el Agro Puneño. In V. Gómez, B. Revesz, E. Grillo, & R. Montoya (Eds.), *Perú: El Problema Agrario en Debate* (pp. 123–151). SEPIA.

Cahill-Ripley, A. (2014). Foregrounding socioeconomic rights in transitional justice: Realising justice for violations of economic and social rights. *Netherlands Quarterly of Human Rights, 32*(2), 183–213.

Camargo, A. (2022). Imagined transitions: Agrarian capitalism and climate change adaptation in Colombia. *The Journal of Peasant Studies, 49*(4), 713–733.

Cambou, D. (2019). The UNDRIP and the legal significance of the right of indigenous peoples to self-determination: A human rights approach with a multidimensional perspective. *The International Journal of Human Rights, 23*(1–2), 34–50.

Cameron, M., Hershberg, E., & Sharpe, K. (2012). *New institutions for participatory democracy in Latin America: Voice and consequences*. Palgrave Macmillan.

Carastathis, A. (2016). Interlocking Systems of Oppression. In N. Rodríguez, W. Martino, J. Ingrey, & E. Brockenbrough (Eds.), *Critical concepts in queer studies and education. An international guide for the twenty-first century*. Palgrave Macmillan.

Caro, J., & Vidal, A. (2012). The worker's massacre of 1928 in the Magdalena Zona Bananera-Colombia. An unfinished story. *Memorias: Revista Digital de Historia y Arqueología desde el Caribe, 9*(18), 22–54.

Carpenter, C. (2005). "Women, children and other vulnerable groups": Gender, strategic frames and the protection of civilians as a transnational issue. *International Studies Quarterly, 49*(2), 295–334.

Castel-Branco, C., Cramer, C., & Hailu, D. (2001). *'Privatization and economic strategy in Mozambique', WIDER discussion Paper, no. 2001/64.* UNU-WIDER.

CEV. (2022). *There is future if there is truth. Call for great peace (final report). Declaration of the Commission for the Clarification of truth, coexistence and non-repetition.* CEV.

Chagnon, C., Durante, F., Gills, B., Hagolani-Albov, S., Hokkanen, S., Kangasluoma, S., Konttinen, H., Kröger, M., LaFleur, W., Ollinaho, O., & Vuola, M. (2022). From Extractivism to global Extractivism: The evolution of an organizing concept. *The Journal of Peasant Studies, 49*(4), 760–792.

Chapman, C. (2011). Transitional justice and the rights of minorities and indigenous peoples. In P. Arthur (Ed.), *Identities in transition: Challenges for transitional justice in divided societies* (pp. 251–270). Cambridge University Press.

Christie, K. (1986). *Oligarcas, Campesinos y Política en Colombia.* Universidad Nacional.

CINEP. (2015). La política de restitución de tierras. Una oportunidad para acercar al Estado y la sociedad civil en una meta común: la dignidad de las víctimas del despojo y el abandono de tierras', *Programa por la Paz* (October).

Claeys, P. (2015). Food sovereignty and the recognition of new rights for peasants at the UN: A critical overview of La via Campesina's rights claims over the last 20 years. *Globalizations, 12*(4), 452–465.

Claeys, P., & Delgado, D. (2016). Peasant and indigenous transnational social movements engaging with climate justice. *Canadian Journal of Development Studies/Revue canadienne d'études du développement, 38*(3), 325–340.

Claeys, P., & Edelman, M. (2020). The United Nations declaration on the rights of peasants and other people working in rural areas. *The Journal of Peasant Studies, 47*(1), 1–68.

CNMH. (2013). *¡Basta Ya! Colombia: Memorias de Guerra y Dignidad.* CNMH.

CNMH. (2014). *Guerrilla y Población Civil.* CNMH.

Collier, P. (2000). Rebellion as a quasi-criminal activity. *Journal of Conflict Resolution, 44*(6), 839–853.

Collier, P., & Hoeffler, A. (1998). On economic causes of civil wars. *Oxford Economic Papers, 50*(4), 563–573.

Collins, P. H. (2015). Intersectionality's definitional dilemmas. *Annual Review of Sociology, 41*, 1–20.

Collins, P. H. (2019). *Intersectionality as critical social theory.* Duke University Press.

Comissão Nacional da Verdade. (2014). *Relatorio da CNV: Volume II—Textos Tematicos.* Comissão Nacional da Verdade.

Commission for Reception, Truth and Reconciliation in Timor-Leste. (2005). *Chega! The report of the Commission for Reception, truth and reconciliation in Timor-Leste (CAVR)*. Commission for Reception, Truth and Reconciliation.

Coronel-Ferrer, M. (2012). To share or divide power? Minorities in autonomous regions, the case of the autonomous region in Muslim Mindanao. *Ethnic and Racial Studies, 35*(12), 2097–2115.

Corredor-García, J., & López, F. (2024). The logic of "war on deforestation": A military response to climate change in the Colombian Amazon. *Alternatives: Global Local, Political, 49*(4), 325–343.

Côté, I., Grant, A., Islam, A., McLean, V., Mitchell, M., & Panagos, D. (2019). The global implementation of UNDRIP: A thematic review. *The International Journal of Human Rights, 23*(1–2), 306–330.

Cowie, R., Bouchet, P., & Fontaine, B. (2022). The sixth mass extinction: Fact, fiction or speculation? *Biological Reviews, 97*, 640–663.

Crabtree, J. (2002). The impact of neo-liberal economics on Peruvian peasant agriculture in the 1990s. *Journal of Peasant Studies, 29*(3–4), 131–161.

Cramer, C., & Richards, P. (2011). Violence and war in agrarian perspective. *Journal of Agrarian Change, 11*(3), 277–297.

Crenshaw, K. (1989). Demarginalizing the intersection of race and sex: A black feminist critique of antidiscrimination doctrine, feminist theory and antiracist politics. *University of Chicago Legal Forum, 1*, 139–167.

Crenshaw, K. (1991). Mapping the margins: Intersectionality, identity politics, and violence against women of color. *Stanford Law Review, 43*(6), 1241–1299.

Crutzen, P. (2002). Geology of mankind - the Anthropocene. *Nature, 415*, 23.

CVR. (2003). *Comisión de la Verdad y Reconciliación. Informe Final.* CVR.

Daly, S. (2016). *Organized violence after civil war.* Cambridge University Press.

DANE. (2024). *Resultados para población campesina. Encuesta Nacional de Calidad de Vida (ECV) 2023. Boletín Técnico.* DANE.

Darby, P. (2009). Rolling Back the Frontiers of empire: Practising the postcolonial. *International Peacekeeping, 16*(5), 699–716.

Davidson, B. (1981). *The people's cause.* Longman.

De Greiff, P. (2020). The future of the past: Reflections on the present state and prospects of transitional justice. *International Journal of Transitional Justice, 14*(2), 251–259.

de la Cadena, M. (2000). *Indigenous mestizos: The politics of race and culture in Cuzco, Peru, 1919–1991.* Duke University Press.

Degregori, C. (1990). *Ayacucho 1969–1979. El surgimiento de Sendero Luminoso.* IEP.

Degregori, C. (1998). Harvesting storms: Peasant Rondas and the defeat of Sendero Luminoso in Ayacucho. In S. Stern (Ed.), *Shining and other paths. War and Society in Peru, 1980–1995* (pp. 128–157). Duke University Press.

Degregori, C. (2012). *How difficult it is to be god. Shining path's politics of war in Peru, 1980–1999*. University of Wisconsin Press.

del Pino, P. (1996). Tiempos de Guerra y de Dioses: Ronderos, Evangélicos y Senderistas en el Valle del Rio Apurímac. In C. Iván, J. de Gregori, P. Coronel, & d. P. y. O. Starn (Eds.), *Las Rondas Campesinas y la Derrota de Sendero Luminoso* (pp. 117–188). IEP.

Dercon, S., & Gutiérrez-Romero, R. (2011). Triggers and characteristics of the 2007 Kenyan electoral violence. *World Development, 40*(4), 731–744.

Desmarais, A. (2003). The Vía Campesina: Peasant women on the frontiers of food sovereignty. *Canadian Woman Studies/les cahiers de la femme, 23*(1), 140–145.

Desmarais, A. (2009). *La Vía Campesina: Globalization and the power of peasants*. Pluto Press.

Díaz, A. (1969). *Ayacucho: Hambre y Esperanza*. Waman Puma.

Dietz, K. (2019). Direct democracy in mining conflicts in Latin America: Mobilising against the La Colosa project in Colombia. *Canadian Journal of Development Studies/Revue canadienne d'études du développement, 40*(2), 145–162.

Dietz, T., Shwom, R., & Whitley, C. (2020). Climate change and society. *Annual Review of Sociology, 46*, 135–158.

Duffy, R., Massé, F., Smidt, E., Marijnen, E., Büscher, B., Verweijen, J., Ramutsindela, M., Simlai, T., Joanny, L., & Lunstrum, E. (2019). Why we must question the militarisation of conservation. *Biological Conservation, 232*, 66–73.

Edelman, M. (2000). The persistence of the peasantry. *NACLA Report on the Americas, 33*(5), 14–19.

Edelman, M. (2008). Transnational organizing in agrarian Central America transnational organizing in agrarian Central America: Histories, challenges, prospects. *Journal of Agrarian Change, 8*(2–3), 229–257.

Edelman, M. (2022). ¿Qué es un campesino? ¿Qué son los campesinados? Un breve documento sobre cuestiones de definición. *Revista Colombiana de Antropología, 58*(1), 153–173.

Edelman, M., & James, C. (2011). Peasants' rights and the UN system: Quixotic struggle? Or emancipatory idea whose time has come? *Journal of Peasant Studies, 38*(1), 81–108.

Edelman, M., Oya, C., & Borras, S. (2013). Global land grabs: Historical processes, theoretical and methodological implications and current trajectories. *Third World Quarterly, 34*(9), 1517–1531.

Eguren, F. (1990). La Reforma agraria y el nuevo orden en el campo peruano. In Á. Fernández & A. Gonzalés (Eds.), *La Reforma Agraria Peruana, 20 años después*. Centro de Estudios Sociales Solidaridad.

Elkins, C. (2005). *Britain's gulag: The brutal end of empire in Kenya*. Jonathan Cape.

Eriksson-Baaz, M., & Stern, M. (2013). *Sexual violence as a weapon of war? Perceptions, prescriptions, problems in The Congo and beyond*. Zed.
Evans, M. (2019). *Transitional and transformative justice. Critical and international perspectives*. Routledge.
Evans, M. (2022). *Beyond transitional justice: Transformative justice and the state of the field (or non-field)*. Routledge.
Fajardo, D. (1985). La Violencia 1946-1964: Su Desarrollo y su Impacto. In *Once Ensayos sobre la Violencia*. CEREC.
Fajardo, D. (2014). *Las Guerras de la Agricultura Colombiana, 1980–2010*. ILSA.
Fajardo, D. (2015). Estudio sobre los Orígenes del Conflicto Social Armado, Razones de su Persistencia y sus Efectos más Profundos en la Sociedad Colombiana. In C. H. d. C. y. s. Víctimas (Ed.), *Contribución al Entendimiento del Conflicto Armado en Colombia* (pp. 361–419). Desde Abajo.
Fajardo, L., Gamboa, J. C., & Villanueva, O. (1999). *Manuel Quintín Lame y los Guerreros de Juan Tama*. Nossa y Jara.
Fals Borda, O. (2010). *Antología*. Universidad Nacional de Colombia.
FAO. (2022). *Voluntary guidelines on the responsible governance of tenure of land, fisheries and forests in the context of National Food Security. First revision*. FAO.
FAO. (2023). *The status of women in Agrifood systems*. FAO.
Fearnside, P. (2001). Soybean cultivation as a threat to the environment in Brazil. *Environmental Conservation, 28*(1), 23–38.
Ferro, J. G., & Uribe, G. (2002). *El Orden de la Guerra*. CEJA.
Fick, C. (1990). *The making of Haiti: The saint Domingue revolution from below*. The University of Tennessee Press.
Figueroa, R., & Mills, C. (2001). Environmental justice. In D. Jamieson (Ed.), *A companion to environmental philosophy* (pp. 426–438). Blackwell.
Freire, P. (1972). *Pedagogy of the oppressed*. Penguin Books.
Fundación Paz y Reconciliación. (2024). *Los Decepcionantes Números de la Restitución de Tierras en Tiempos de Petro*, 22nd April. Retrieved July 22, 2024, from https://www.pares.com.co/post/los-decepcionantes-n%C3%BAmeros-de-la-restituci%C3%B3n-de-tierras-en-tiempos-de-petro
Furedi, F. (1989). *The Mau Mau war in perspective*. Ohio University Press.
Gaitán, G. (1984). *La lucha por la tierra en la década del 30*. El Ancora.
Garcia, R. (2021). *Disrupting cycles of discontent. Transitional justice and prevention in The Philippines*. International Center for Transitional Justice.
García, R. (2022). La política de memoria en Colombia. El relato histórico del Centro nacional de Memoria. *Pasado y Memoria, 25*, 375–398.
Gerber, J.-F., & Veuthey, S. (2010). Plantations, resistance and the greening of the agrarian question in coastal Ecuador. *Journal of Agrarian Change, 10*(4), 455–481.
Gilbert, J., & Lennox, C. (2019). Towards new development paradigms: The United Nations declaration on the rights of indigenous peoples as a tool to

support self-determined development. *The International Journal of Human Rights, 23*(1–2), 104–124.

Gilhodes, P. (1970). Agrarian struggles in Colombia. In R. Stavenhagen (Ed.), *Agrarian problems and peasant movements in Latin America* (pp. 407–452). Anchor Books.

Giunta, A. (2019). Looking back to move forward: The status of environmental rights under the UN declaration on the rights of indigenous peoples. *The International Journal of Human Rights, 23*(1–2), 149–173.

Glasson, A. (2020). The militarisation of conservation in Africa. In S. Russell, A. Tschudin, S. Buchanan-Clarke, C. Moffat, & L. Coutts (Eds.), *Extremisms in Africa (volume 3)* (pp. 29–51). Good Governance Africa.

Golay, C. (2013). Legal Reflections on the Rights of Peasants and Other People Working in Rural Areas. First Session of the Intergovernmental Working Group on a United Nations Declaration on the Rights of Peasants and Other People Working in Rural Areas (July 15). Retrieved November 08, 2025, from http://www.ohchr.org/Documents/HRBodies/HRCouncil/WGPleasants/Golay.pdf

Golay, C. (2022). The rights to food and food sovereignty in the UNDROP. In M. Alabrese, A. Bessa, M. Brunori, & P. F. Giuggioli (Eds.), *The United Nations' declaration on peasants' rights* (pp. 134–147). Routledge.

Gold, A. (1978). The Nandi in transition: Background to Nandi resistance to the British 1895-1906. *Kenya Historical Review, 6*(1–2), 84–104.

Gómez, F. (2019). The UNDRIP: An increasingly robust legal parameter. *The International Journal of Human Rights, 23*(1–2), 7–21.

Gómez-Betancur, L. (2020). The rights of nature in the Colombian Amazon: Examining challenges and opportunities in a transitional justice setting. *UCLA Journal of International Law and Foreign Affairs, 25*(1), 41–84.

Góngora-Mera, M. (2019). The ethnic chapter of the 2016 Colombian peace agreement and the afro-descendants' right to prior consultation: A story of unfulfilled promises. *The International Journal of Human Rights, 23*(6), 938–956.

González, J., & Bueno-Hansen, P. (2021). The promise and perils of mainstreaming Intersectionality in the Colombian peace process. *International Journal of Transitional Justice, 15*(3), 553–575.

González, L. (2025). *Entre la Impunidad y la Resistencia: Tendencias Recientes en el Asesinato de Líderes Sociales en Colombia*. Indepaz.

Gorman, S. (1982). *Post-revolutionary Peru. The politics of transformation*. Westview Press.

Gott, R. (1973). *Rural guerrillas in Latin America*. Penguin.

Gradoni, L., & Pasquet, L. (2022). Voice under domination: Notes on the making and significance of the United Nations declaration on the rights of peasants. *European Journal of International Law, 33*(1), 39–64.

Grajales, J. (2011). The rifle and the title: Paramilitary violence, land grab and land control in Colombia. *The Journal of Peasant Studies, 38*(4), 771–792.

Grajales, J. (2015). Land grabbing, legal contention and institutional change in Colombia. *Journal of Peasant Studies, 42*(3–4), 541–560.

Gready, P., Gutiérrez, J., & Mesa, W. (forthcoming). Rethinking the relationship between development and reparations: Conceptualising transformative reparations from below in Colombia.

Gready, P., & Robins, S. (2014). From transitional to transformative justice: A new agenda for practice. *International Journal of Transitional Justice, 8*(3), 339–361.

Gready, P., & Robins, S. (2017). Rethinking civil society and transitional justice: Lessons from social movements and 'new' civil society. *The International Journal of Human Rights, 21*(7), 956–975.

Gready, P., & Robins, S. (2019). *From transitional to transformative justice.* Cambridge University Press.

Gready, P., & Robins, S. (2020). Transitional justice and theories of change: Towards evaluation as understanding. *International Journal of Transitional Justice, 14*(2), 280–299.

Gready, S. (2022). The case for transformative reparations: In pursuit of structural socio-economic reform in post-conflict societies. *Journal of Intervention and Statebuilding, 16*(2), 182–201.

Gudynas, E. (2009). Diez Tesis Urgentes sobre el Nuevo Extractivismo: Contextos y Demandas Bajo el Progresismo Sudamericano Actual. In J. Schuldt, A. Acosta, A. Barandiará, A. Bebbington, M. Folchi, CEDLA, A. Alayza, & E. Gudynas (Eds.), *Extractivismo, Política y Sociedad* (pp. 187–225). CAAP/CLAES.

Guillerot, J. (2019). *Reparations in Peru: 15 years of delivering redress.* Queens University Belfast.

Guillerot, J. (2021). *Alive in the demand for change. Transitional justice and prevention in Peru.* ICTJ.

Gutierrez, E., & Borras, S. (2004). *The Moro conflict: Landlessness and misdirected state policies.* East-West Center.

Gutiérrez, F., Acevedo, T., & Viatela, J. (2007). *'Violent liberalism? State, conflict and political regime in Colombia, 1930–2006', crisis states research Centre working Paper no. 19.* London School of Economics.

Gutiérrez, J. (2016). Participatory action research (PAR) and the Colombian peasant reserve zones: The legacy of Orlando Fals Borda. *Policy & Practice, 22*, 59–76.

Gutiérrez, J. (2018). Insurgent Institutions: Refractory communities, armed insurgency and institution-building in the Colombian conflict (PhD Dissertation: University College Dublin).

Gutiérrez, J. (2020). Toward a new phase of guerrilla warfare in Colombia? The reconstitution of the FARC-EP in perspective. *Latin American Perspectives, 47*(5), 227–244.
Gutiérrez, J. (2021). "Whatever we have, we owe it to coca" insights on armed conflict and the coca economy from Argelia, Colombia. *International Journal of Drug Policy, 89*, 103068.
Gutiérrez, J. (2025a). Rebel governance: A matter of time. *Civil Wars, 5*, 1–26.
Gutiérrez, J. (2025b). Greedy peace-makers. Post-FARC-EP trajectories from political crime to politicised common crime. In J. Gutiérrez & F. Gutiérrez-Sanín (Eds.), *Criminality, political power and conflict. Critical perspectives* (pp. 177–204). Manchester University Press.
Gutiérrez, J., Hoddy, E., McGill, D., del Pilar, R., Peña-Huertas, I. V.-T., & Muriel, D. (2023). *Justicia transformativa y conflicto agrario. Elementos para un debate necesario*. USTA.
Gutiérrez-Sanín, F., & Vargas, J. (2017). Agrarian elite participation in Colombia's civil war. *Journal of Agrarian Change, 17*(4), 739–748.
Gutiérrez-Sanín, F. (2015). Agrarian inequality and civil war revisited. *Geography Compass, 9*(8), 423–431.
Gutiérrez-Sanín, F. (2019). *Clientelistic warfare*. Peter Lang.
Gutiérrez-Sanín, F. (2020). *¿Un nuevo ciclo de la guerra en Colombia?* Debate.
Gutiérrez-Sanín, F. (2025). *Tierra, Guerra, Política*. Debate.
Gutiérrez-Sanín, F., Machuca, D., & Cristancho, S. (2019). ¿Obsolescencia programada? La implementación de la sustitución y sus inconsistencias. *Análisis Político, 97*, 136–160.
Gutiérrez-Sanín, F., Marín, M., Machuca, D., Parada, M., & Rojas, H. (2020). Paz sin garantías: el asesinato de líderes de restitución y sustitución de cultivos de uso ilícito en Colombia. *Estudios Socio-Jurídicos, 22*(2), 361–418.
Gutiérrez-Sanín, F., & Parada, M. (2022). *Las Deudas de la Paz*. Observatorio de Tierras.
Haastrup, T., & Hagen, J. (2021). Racial hierarchies of knowledge production in the women, peace and security agenda. *Critical Studies on Security, 9*(1), 27–30.
Haldemann, F. (2022). *Transitional justice for foxes. Conflict, pluralism and the politics of compromise*. Cambridge University Press.
Hall, D. (2013). Primitive accumulation, accumulation by dispossession and the global land grab. *Third World Quarterly, 34*(9), 1582–1604.
Harvey, D. (2003). *The new imperialism*. Oxford University Press.
Hecht, L., & Michalowski, S. (2012). *The economic and social dimensions of transitional justice*. Essex Transitional Justice Network.
Hilton, R. (1973). *Bond men made free. Medieval peasant movements and the English rising of 1381*. M. Temple Smith Ltd..
Hobsbawm, E. (1959). *Primitive Rebels*. Norton &.

Hobsbawm, E. (1973). Peasants and politics. *The Journal of Peasant Studies, 1*(1), 3–22.
Hobsbawm, E. (1986). Murderous Colombia. *New York Review of Books*, 20 November.
Hoddy, E. (2021a). Peasants' rights and agrarian violence in transitional settings: From transitional justice to transformative agrarian justice. *Journal of Human Rights, 20*(1), 91–109.
Hoddy, E. (2021b). Transformative justice in practice: Reflections on the pastoral land commission during Brazil's political transition. *Journal of Human Rights Practice, 13*(2), 339–356.
Hoddy, E., & Gready, P. (2020). From agency to root causes: Addressing structural barriers to transformative justice in transitional and post-conflict settings. *Contemporary Social Science, 15*(5), 561–576.
Humphreys, J., & Smith, M. L. R. (2014). The "rhinofication" of south African security. *International Affairs, 90*(4), 795–818.
Huneeus, A., & Rueda, P. (2021). Territory as a victim of armed conflict. *International Journal of Transitional Justice, 15*(1), 210–229.
ICG. (2023). *Southern Philippines: Making peace stick in the Bangsamoro*. International Crisis Group.
Ignatieff, M. (2001). *Human rights as politics and idolatry*. Princeton University Press.
IPCC. (2023). *Climate change 2023 synthesis report. Summary for policymakers. A report of the intergovernmental panel on climate change*. IPCC.
IPES-Food. (2024). *Land Squeeze: What is driving unprecedented pressures on global farmland and what can be done to achieve equitable access to land?* Retrieved February 27, 2026, from https://ipes-food.org/wp-content/uploads/2024/05/LandSqueeze.pdf
Jackson, W. (2016). Settler colonialism in Kenya, 1880–1963. In E. Cavanagh & L. Veracini (Eds.), *The Routledge handbook of the history of settler colonialism* (pp. 231–246). Routledge.
James, C. L. R. (2001). *Black Jacobins*. Penguin.
Jansen, K., Vicol, M., & Nikol, L. (2022). Autonomy and repeasantization: Conceptual, analytical, and methodological problems. *Journal of Agrarian Change, 22*(3), 489–505.
Jenkins, C. (1982). Why do peasants rebel? Structural and historical theories of modern peasant rebellions. *American Journal of Sociology, 88*(3), 487–514.
JEP. (2023). *JEP firma convenio con la URT para luchar contra la impunidad en cuanto al despojo de tierras durante el conflicto armado (Comunicado 146)*, 11 December. Retrieved January 21, 2026, from https://www.jep.gov.co/Sala-de-Prensa/Paginas/-jep-firma-convenio-con-la-urt-para-luchar-contra-la-impunidad-en-cuanto-al-despojo-de-tierras-durante-el-conflicto-armado.aspx
Jones, B., & Bernath, J. (2017). *Resistance and transitional justice*. Routledge.

Jones, E. (2021). Capital and control: Neocolonialism through the militarization of African wildlife conservation. *Flux: International Relations Review, 11*(2), 29–37.

Jones, P. (1988). *The peasantry in the French revolution.* Cambridge University Press.

Jopson, T. (2023). Moro women's participation and legitimation in the Bangsamoro peace process. *Journal of Current Southeast Asian Affairs, 42*(2), 143–167.

Joseph, R. (1997). Democratization in Africa after 1989: Comparative and theoretical perspectives. *Comparative Politics, 29*(3), 363–382.

Kaldor, M. (2001). *New & old wars.* Polity.

Kanogo, T. (1987). *Squatters and the roots of Mau Mau.* Ohio University Press.

Kaplan, O. (2025). Development for peace in Colombia: Experiences with PDETs in El Carmen and Cartagena del Chairá. *Journal of Peacebuilding & Development, 20*(3), 439–448.

Kashwan, P. (2017). *Democracy in the woods.* Oxford University Press.

Keck, M., & Sikkink, K. (1998). *Activists beyond Borders: Advocacy networks in international politics.* Cornell University Press.

Kenyan Human Rights Commission. (2001). *The right to return: The internally displaced persons and the culture of impunity in Kenya.* KHRC.

Kershaw, G. (1997). *Mau Mau from below.* James Currey.

Killean, R., & Dempster, L. (2022). "Greening" transitional justice? In M. Evans (Ed.), *Beyond transitional justice: Transformative justice and the state of the field (or non-field).* Routledge.

Kloop, J., & Lumumba, O. (2017). Reform and counter-reform in Kenya's land governance. *Review of African Political Economy, 44*(154), 577–594.

Knight, P. (1975). New forms of economic Organization in Peru: Towards workers' self-management. In A. Lowenthal (Ed.), *The Peruvian experiment* (pp. 350–401). Princeton University Press.

Knight, P. (1976). Social property in Peru: The political economy of predominance. *Economic Analysis and Workers' Management, 10*(3–4), 167–195.

Krever, T. (2017). Remembering the Russell Tribunal. *London Review of International Law, 5*(3), 483–492.

Kritz, N. (1995). *Transitional justice: How emerging democracies reckon with former regimes (3 volumes).* United States Institute of Peace Press.

Lahiri-Dutt, K. (2018). Extractive peasants: Reframing informal artisanal and small-scale mining debates. *Third World Quarterly, 39*(8), 1561–1582.

Lambourne, W. (2009). Transitional justice and Peacebuilding after mass violence. *International Journal of Transitional Justice, 3*(1), 28–48.

Lambourne, W. (2014). What are the pillars of transitional justice? *The United Nations, civil society and the justice cascade in Burundi', Macquarie Law Journal, 13*, 41–60.

Larsen, R., Dimaano, F., & Pido, M. (2019). Can the wrongs be righted? Prospects for remedy in the Philippine oil palm agro-industry. *Development and Change, 50*(5), 1373–1397.

Leech, G. (2011). *The FARC. The longest insurgency*. ZED Books.

LeGrand, C. (1986). *Frontier expansion and peasant protest in Colombia, 1830–1936*. University of New Mexico Press.

Lenzerini, F. (2019). Implementation of the UNDRIP around the world: Achievements and future perspectives. The outcome of the work of the ILA Committee on the implementation of the rights of indigenous peoples. *The International Journal of Human Rights, 23*(1–2), 51–62.

Leo, C. (1981). Who benefited from the million-acre scheme? Toward a class analysis of Kenya's transition to independence. *Canadian Journal of African Studies/Revue Canadienne des Études Africaines, 15*(2), 201–222.

Leo, C. (1984). *Land and class in Kenya*. University of Toronto Press.

Leval, G. (2018). *Collectives in the Spanish revolution*. PM.

Lewis, S., & Maslin, M. (2015). Defining the Anthropocene. *Nature, 519*, 171–180.

Leys, C. (1971). Politics in Kenya: The development of peasant society. *British Journal of Political Science, 1*(3), 307–337.

Linares, M. (2021). *Setting an agenda for sustainable peace. Transitional justice and prevention in Colombia*. ICTJ.

Lindsay-Poland, J. (2018). *Plan Colombia: U.S. ally atrocities and community activism*. Duke University Press.

Littlechild, W., & Stamatopoulou, E. (2014). *Indigenous peoples' access to justice, including truth and reconciliation processes*. Institute for the Study of Human Rights, Columbia University.

Lonsdale, J., & Berman, B. (1979). Coping with the contradictions: The development of the colonial state in Kenya, 1895–1914. *The Journal of African History, 20*(4), 487–505.

Lucas, K. (2001). *We will not dance on our grandparents' tombs*. LAB.

Lundy, P., & McGovern, M. (2008). Whose justice? Rethinking transitional justice from the bottom up. *Journal of Law and Society, 35*(2), 265–292.

Lunstrum, E. (2014). Green militarization: Anti-poaching efforts and the spatial contours of Kruger National Park. *Annals of the Association of American Geographers, 104*(4), 816–832.

Luoma, C. (2023). Reckoning with conservation violence on indigenous territories: Possibilities and limitations of a transitional justice response. *International Journal of Transitional Justice, 17*(1), 89–106.

Lyons, K. (2023). "Nature" and territories as victims: Decolonizing Colombia's transitional justice process. *American Anthropologist, 125*(1), 63–76.

MacGinty, R. (2025). The liberal peace is over and it is not coming back: Hybridity and the emerging international peace system. *Third World Quarterly, 46*(16), 1999–2018.

MacGinty, R., & Richmond, O. (2013). The local turn in peace building: A critical agenda for peace. *Third World Quarterly, 34*(5), 763–783.

Macher, S. (2023). *Las Recomendaciones de la CVR 20 Años Después.* CNDDHH.

Maddison, S., & Shepherd, L. (2014). Peacebuilding and the postcolonial politics of transitional justice. *Peacebuilding, 2*(3), 253–269.

Maggio, G., & Cacciola, G. (2009). A variant of the Hubbert curve for world oil production forecasts. *Energy Policy, 37*(11), 4761–4770.

Mahlatsi, M. (2018). The peasants revolt: Analysing the role of the democratic state in the struggle for land and environmental justice in Xolobeni, eastern cape, South Africa. *Journal of Public Administration, 53*(2–1), 615–631.

Mançano Fernandes, B. (2013). Re-peasantization, resistance and subordination: The struggle for land and agrarian reform in Brazil. *Agrarian South: Journal of Political Economy, 2*(3), 269–289.

Manning, C. (2003). Local level challenges to post-conflict Peacebuilding. *International Peacekeeping, 10*(3), 25–43.

Mantz, F., Frame, M., & Leguizamon, S. (2025). *Grassroots responses to Extractivism.* Bloomsbury.

Margulis, M., Hopewell, K., & Qereshniku, E. (2023). Food, famine and the free trade fallacy: The dangers of market fundamentalism in an era of climate emergency. In I. Scoones, S. Borras, A. Baviskar, M. Edelman, N. L. Peluso, & W. Wolford (Eds.), *Climate change and critical agrarian studies* (pp. 327–351). Routledge.

Mariagrazia, A., & Savaresi, A. (2022). The UNDROP and climate change: Squaring the circle? In M. Alabrese, A. Bessa, M. Brunori, & P. F. Giuggioli (Eds.), *The United Nations' declaration on peasants' rights* (pp. 165–176). Routledge.

Martínez, P. (2013). *The victims and land restitution law in Colombia in context. An analysis of the contradictions between the agrarian model and compensation for the victims.* FDCL.

Martínez-Alier, J. (2011). The EROI of agriculture and its use by the via Campesina. *Journal of Peasant Studies, 38*(1), 145–160.

Martínez-Alier, J. (2025). Agrarian justice and environmental justice. In S. Borras & J. Franco (Eds.), *The Oxford handbook of land politics.* Oxford University Press.

Martínez-Alier, J., Temper, L., Del Bene, D., & Scheidel, A. (2016). Is there a global environmental justice movement? *The Journal of Peasant Studies, 43*(3), 731–755.

Martínez-Torres, M., & Rosset, P. (2010). La Vía Campesina: The birth and evolution of a transnational social movement. *The Journal of Peasant Studies, 37*(1), 149–175.

Marx, K. (1999). *Capital.* Oxford University Press.

Mason, D. (2004). *Caught in the crossfire. Revolutions, repression, and the rational peasant.* Rowman & Littlefield.

Massé, F., Lunstrum, E., & Holterman, D. (2021). Linking green militarization and critical military studies. *Critical Military Studies, 4*(2), 201–221.
Matos, J., & Mejía, J. (1980). *La reforma agraria en el Perú*. IEP.
McAuliffe, P. (2011). Transitional justice's expanding empire: Reasserting the value of the paradigmatic transition. *Journal of Conflictology, 2*(2), 32–44.
McAuliffe, P. (2017). *Transformative transitional justice and the malleability of post-conflict states*. Edward Elgar.
McAuliffe, P., & Schwöbel-Patel, C. (2018). Disciplinary matchmaking: Critics of international criminal law meet critics of Liberal Peacebuilding. *Journal of International Criminal Justice, 16*(5), 985–1009.
McClintock, C. (1984). Why peasants rebel: The case of Peru's Sendero Luminoso. *World Politics, 37*(1), 48–84.
McClintock, C. (1989). Peru's Sendero Luminoso rebellion: Origins and trajectory. In S. Eckstein (Ed.), *Power and popular protest. Latin American social movements* (pp. 61–101). University of California Press.
McEvoy, K., & McGregor, L. (2008). *Transitional justice from below. Grassroots activism and the struggle for change*. Bloomsbury.
McGill, D. (2017). Different violence, different justice? Taking structural violence seriously in post conflict and transitional justice processes. *State Crime Journal, 6*(1), 79–101.
McGill, D. (2019). Tackling structural violence through the transformative justice framework. In M. Evans (Ed.), *Transitional and transformative justice, critical and international perspectives* (pp. 36–53). Routledge.
McGonigle Leyh, B. (2016). Nuremberg's legacy on transitional justice: Prosecutions are here to stay. *Washington University Global Studies Law Review, 15*, 559–574.
McKay, B. (2020). Food sovereignty and neo-extractivism: Limits and possibilities of an alternative development model. *Globalizations, 17*(8), 1386–1404.
Meertens, D. (2015). Discursive frictions: The transitional justice paradigm, land restitution and gender. *Papel Político, 10*(2), 353–381.
Meertens, D. (2016). Justicia de género y tierras en Colombia: desafíos para la era del pos-acuerdo. *European Review of Latin American and Caribbean Studies, 102*, 89–100.
Meertens, D. (2019). *Elusive justice. Women, land rights, and Colombia's transition to peace*. University of Wisconsin Press.
Meger, S. (2016). The fetishization of sexual violence in international security. *International Studies Quarterly, 60*(1), 149–159.
Meléndez, C. (2007). Los conflictos después del conflicto. Desestructuración del sistema político y conflictos sociales después de la violencia. In F. Reátegui (Ed.), *Conflictos sociales y respuestas del Estado: del orden interno a la protección de los derechos* (pp. 47–54). IDEHPUPC.

Merino, R. (2021). Buen vivir and the making of indigenous territories in the Peruvian Amazon. *Latin American Perspectives, 48*(3), 136–151.

Merino, R. (2023). Lost in transition: Explaining authoritarianism in Peru. *International Journal of Transitional Justice, 17*(3), 480–488.

Mertus, J. (2003). The politics of memory and international trials for wartime rape. In P. Gready (Ed.), *Political transition. Politics and cultures* (pp. 227–245). Pluto Press.

Michalowski, S., Sánchez, N., Marín, D., Jiménez, A., Martínez, H., Domínguez, V., & Arroyave, L. (2018). *Entre coacción y colaboración. Verdad judicial, actores económicos y conflicto armado en Colombia*. Dejusticia.

Migdal, J. (1974). *Peasants, politics, and revolution. Pressures toward political and social change in the third world*. Princeton University Press.

Miguel, E. (2004). Tribe or nation? National building and public goods in Kenya and Tanzania. *World Politics, 56*(3), 327–362.

Milton, C. (2007). At the edge of the Peruvian truth commission: Alternative paths to recounting the past. *Radical History Review, 98*, 3–33.

Mintz, S. (1986). *Sweetness and power: The place of sugar in modern history*. Penguin.

Molano, A. (1994). Algunas Consideraciones sobre Colonización y Violencia. In A. Machado (Ed.), *El Agro y la Cuestión Social* (pp. 27–41). Tercer Mundo.

Molloy, I. (1985). Revolution in The Philippines: The question of an alliance between Islam and communism. *Asian Survey, 25*(8), 822–833.

Molloy, S. (2023). Conceptualising the transformative justice potential of peace processes. *The International Journal of Human Rights, 27*(2), 307–334.

Monsalve, S. (2013). The human rights framework in contemporary agrarian struggles. *Journal of Peasant Studies, 40*(1), 239–290.

Montiel, C., Rodil, R., & de Guzman, J. (2012). The Moro struggle and the challenge to peace building in Mindanao, southern Philippines. In D. Landis & R. Albert (Eds.), *Handbook of ethnic conflict* (pp. 71–89). Springer.

Moore, B. (1966). *Social origins of dictatorship and democracy. Lord and peasant in the making of the modern world*. Beacon Press.

Morgan, R. (2011). *Transforming law and institution. Indigenous peoples, the United Nations and human rights*. Ashgate.

Mudimu, G., Zuo, T., & Nalwimba, N. (2022). Inside an enclave: The dynamics of capitalism and rural politics in a post-land reform context. *The Journal of Peasant Studies, 49*(1), 101–128.

Munck, R. (2020). *Social movements in Latin America: Mapping the mosaic*. McGill-Queen's University Press.

Munive, J. (2011). A political economic history of the Liberian state, forced labour and armed mobilization. *Journal of Agrarian Change, 11*(3), 357–376.

Murphy, E., & Walsh, D. (2022). Agonistic transitional justice: A global survey. *Third World Quarterly, 43*(6), 1380–1398.

Muvingi, I. (2009). Sitting on powder kegs: Socioeconomic rights in transitional societies. *International Journal of Transitional Justice, 3*(2), 163–182.

Nagy, R. (2012). Centralizing legal pluralism? Traditional justice in transitional settings. In C. Sriram, J. García-Godos, J. Herman, & O. Martin-Ortega (Eds.), *Transitional justice and Peacebuilding on the ground: Victims and ex-combatants* (pp. 81–99). Routledge.

Nagy, R. (2013). The scope and bounds of transitional justice and the Canadian truth and reconciliation commission. *International Journal of Transitional Justice, 7*(1), 52–73.

Navarrete-Cruz, Á., Birkenberg, A., & Birner, R. (2023). Agrarian change and land dispossession linked to the armed conflict in Colombia - a review. *Third World Quarterly, 44*(7), 1526–1545.

Ndungú, C. (2014). *Lessons to be learned: An analysis of the final report of Kenya's Truth, Justice and Reconciliation Commission.* ICTJ Briefing, Retrieved November 10, 2025, from https://www.ictj.org/sites/default/files/ICTJ-Briefing-Kenya-TJRC-2014.pdf

Nelson, P. (2004). New agendas and new patterns of international NGO political action. In R. Taylor (Ed.), *Creating a better world: Interpreting global civil society* (pp. 116–132). Kumarian Press.

Ní Aoláin, F. (2009). Women, security, and the patriarchy of internationalized transitional justice. *Human Rights Quarterly, 31*(4), 1055–1085.

Ní Aoláin, F., & O'Rourke, C. (2010). Gendered transitional justice and the non-state actor. In M. Reed & A. Lyons (Eds.), *Contested transitions: Dilemmas of transitional justice in comparative experience.* International Center for Transitional Justice.

Nicholson, P., & Borras, S. (2023). It wasn't an intellectual construction: The founding of La via Campesina, achievements and challenges - a conversation. *Journal of Peasant Studies, 50*(2), 610–626.

O'Brien, R., Goetz, A. M., Scholte, J. A., & Williams, M. (2000). *Contesting global governance: Multilateral economic institutions and global social movements.* Cambridge University Press.

O'Rourke, C. (2015). Feminist scholarship in transitional justice: A de-politicising impulse? *Women's Studies International Forum, 51*, 118–127.

Olivari, W. (2015). El problema de la tierra. El caso peruano: un análisis comparativo. *Cultura Latinoamericana, 22*(2), 19–40.

Olivera, Ó. (2008). *Nosotros Somos la Coordinadora.* Fundación Abril.

Olsen, T., Payne, L., & Reiter, A. (2010). *Transitional justice in balance: Comparing processes, weighing efficacy.* United States Institute of Peace Press.

OPAPRU. (2025). *GPH, MILF launch Transitional Justice Roadmap to address historical grievances in Bangsamoro*, Office of the Presidential Adviser on Peace, Reconciliation and Unity (OPAPRU), 9 December, Retrieved February 27,

2026, from https://peace.gov.ph/2025/12/gph-milf-launch-transitional-justice-roadmap-to-address-historical-grievances-in-bangsamoro/

Ortiz, C. (1985). *Estado y Subversión en Colombia*. CEREC.

Oxfam. (2017). *Snapshots of inequality*. Oxfam.

Page, T. (2010). Can the state create Campesinos? A comparative analysis of the Venezuelan and Cuban Repeasantization programmes. *Journal of Agrarian Change, 10*(2), 251–272.

Paige, J. (1975). *Agrarian revolution. Social movements and export agriculture in the underdeveloped world*. The Free Press.

Paige, J. (2020). *Indigenous revolutions in Ecuador and Bolivia, 1990–2005*. The University of Arizona Press.

Palacios, M. (2011). *¿De Quién es la Tierra?* Fondo de Cultura Económica.

Palmer, D. (1986). Rebellion in rural Peru: The origins and evolution of Sendero Luminoso. *Comparative Politics, 18*(2), 127–146.

Palmer, D., & Bolívar, A. (2011). *Peru's shining path: Recent dynamics and future prospects*. WHEMSAC/Florida International University.

Palmisano, T., & Wahren, J. (2023). The political economy of extractivism and social struggles in Latin America. In M. Atzeni, D. Azzellini, A. Mezzadri, P. Moore, & U. Apitzsch (Eds.), *Handbook of research on the global political economy of work* (pp. 512–521). Edward Elgar.

Paris, R. (2004). *At war's end: Building peace after civil conflict*. Cambridge University Press.

Pastor, L., & Santamaría, A. (2021). Experiences of spiritual advocacy for land and territorial itineraries for the Defense of Wiwa women's rights in Postconflict Colombia. *International Journal of Transitional Justice, 15*(1), 86–107.

Peeler, J. (2009). *Building democracy in Latin America*. Lynne Rienner.

Peña-Huertas, R., Parada, M., Abril-Bonilla, N., Uribe-Larrota, L., Jiménez-Nicholls, C., & Nieto-Cruz, V. (2021). Collective ownership and land restitution: A new opportunity for afro-Colombian communities. *International Journal of Transitional Justice, 15*(1), 230–241.

Peña-Huertas, R., Ruiz, E., Parada, M., Zuleta, S., & Álvarez, R. (2017). Legal dispossession and civil war in Colombia. *Journal of Agrarian Change, 17*(4), 759–769.

Peša, I., & Ross, C. (2021). Extractive industries and the environment: Production, pollution, and protest in global history. *The Extractive Industries and Society, 8*(4), 100933.

Peters, K., & Richards, P. (2011). Rebellion and agrarian tensions in Sierra Leone. *Journal of Agrarian Change, 11*(3), 377–395.

Peterson, J. (2014). *Building a peace economy? Liberal Peacebuilding and the development-security industry*. Manchester University Press.

Pfeiffer, S. (2015). Building up a peace infrastructure for Colombia: lessons from implementing the Victims Law. Norwegian Peacebuilding Resource Centre. NOREF Report October 2015.

Philip, J. (2023). Who are we without land? Repeasantization and caste in a village of South India. *Agrarian South: Journal of Political Economy, 12*(4), 488–513.

Pielke, R. (2004). What is climate change? *Energy & Environment, 15*(3), 515–520.

Pimm, S., Jenkins, C., Abell, R., Brooks, T., Gittleman, J., Joppa, L., Raven, P., Roberts, C., & Sexton, J. (2014). The biodiversity of species and their rates of extinction, distribution, and protection. *Science, 344*(6187), 1246752.

Pinheiro, L., & Rosset, P. (2024). Conceptions and practices of autonomy among indigenous and peasant movements in Latin America. *Latin American Perspectives, 51*(4), 100–121.

Pinkeviciute, J. (2025). The limits of participation without economic justice in Peacebuilding: A study of Colombia. *Journal of Peacebuilding & Development, 21*, 52–69.

Pizarro, E. (1991). *Las FARC (1949–1966) de la Autodefensa a la Combinación de Todas las Formas de Lucha*. IEPRI/Tercer Mundo.

PNUD. (2011). *Colombia Rural: Razones para la esperanza. Informe Nacional de Desarrollo Humano 2011*. PNUD.

Popkin, S. (1979). *The rational peasant: The political economy of rural Society in Vietnam*. University of California Press.

Presta, D. (2024). Mujeres, paz y territorio: Construcción de paz en Colombia a través de los enfoques étnico y de género. *Revista Internacional De Derechos Humanos, 14*(2), 9–48.

Pugh, M., Cooper, N., & Turner, M. (2008). *Whose peace? Critical perspectives on the political economy of Peacebuilding*. Palgrave Macmillan.

Putzel, J. (1992). *A captive land: The politics of agrarian reform in The Philippines*. CIIR.

Regan, Á., & Kenny, U. (2022). What do the public want to know about farming and why? Findings from a farmer-initiated public consultation exercise in Ireland. *Sustainability, 14*(9), 5391.

Restrepo, J., & Bernal, A. (2014). *La Cuestión Agraria: Tierra y Posconflicto en Colombia*. Debate.

Rettberg, A. (2010). Global markets, local conflict: Violence in the Colombian coffee region after the breakdown of the international coffee agreement. *Latin American Perspectives, 37*(2), 111–132.

Reyes, A. (2009). *Guerreros y Campesinos*. Norma.

Riaño, P., & Uribe, M. V. (2016). Constructing memory amidst war: The historical memory Group of Colombia. *International Journal of Transitional Justice, 10*(1), 6–24.

Richani, N. (2013). *Systems of Violence. The political economy of war and peace in Colombia*. SUNY Press.

Richmond, C., Coombes, B., & Louis, R. P. (2024). *Because this land is who we are*. Bloomsbury.

Richmond, O. (2011). *A post-liberal peace*. Routledge.

Ríos, S. (2023). The fragmentation of historical memory in Colombia. In A. Bazin, E. Hébert, V. Rosoux, & E. Sangar (Eds.), *Memory fragmentation from below and beyond the state. Uses of the past in conflict and post-conflict settings*. Routledge.

Rodil, R. (1994). *The Minoritization of the indigenous communities of Mindanao and the Sulu archipelago*. Philippine Edition.

Rodríguez, L., Pini, B., & Baker, S. (2016). The global countryside: Peasant women negotiating, recalibrating and resisting rural change in Colombia. *Gender, Place & Culture, 23*(11), 1547–1559.

Rodríguez, S. (2010). Política del testimonio y reconocimiento en las comisiones de la verdad guatemalteca y peruana: En torno a la figura del "indio subversivo". *Revista Crítica de Ciências Sociais, 88*, 23–55.

Rodríguez-Garavito, C., & Lam, Y. (2011). *Etnorreparaciones: La justicia colectiva étnica y la reparación a pueblos indígenas y comunidades afrodescendientes en Colombia*. DeJusticia.

Roht-Arriaza, N., & Mariezcurrena, J. (2006). *Transitional justice in the 21st century -beyond truth versus justice*. Cambridge University Press.

Rosset, P. (2013). Re-thinking agrarian reform, land and territory in La via Campesina. *Journal of Peasant Studies, 40*(4), 721–775.

Rosset, P., & Muñoz, C. U. (2025). Repeasantization and socio-territorial movements. *The Journal of Peasant Studies, 52*(3), 649–664.

Rubiano, M., Vélez, M. A., & Arenas, P. (2022). *¿Cómo va la implementación del PNIS en las Zonas de Manejo Especial?* CESED, Universidad de los Andes.

Ruiz, E., Peña-Huertas, R., Parada-Hernández, M., Lozano, A., Triana, B., & Valencia-Herrera, M. (2021). Who owns what in Macondo? The Flexibilization of the rules of evidence in land restitution in Colombia. *International Journal of Transitional Justice, 15*(1), 26–46.

Ruiz, M. (2023). *El cascarón y la semilla. Lecciones de la negociación con las Autodefensas Unidas de Colombia*. ICTJ.

Salomon, M. (2018). *Nihilists, pragmatists and peasants: A dispatch on contradiction in international human rights law* (New York: IILJ Working Paper 2018/5, New York University School of Law).

Samper, J. A., Krause, T., & López, J. (2024). "Everyone decided to declare war on the forest": Between territorial peace and pacification in the Colombian Andean-Amazon. *Ecology and Society, 29*(4), 46.

Sánchez, G. (1977). *Las Ligas Campesinas en Colombia*. Tiempo Presente.

Sánchez, N. (2021). The promised land of transitional justice. *International Journal of Transitional Justice, 15*(1), 242–251.

Sauer, S. (2012). Land and territory: Meanings of land between modernity and tradition. *Agrarian South: Journal of Political Economy, 1*(1), 85–107.

Schubiger, L. (2021). State violence and wartime civilian agency: Evidence from Peru. *The Journal of Politics, 83*(4), 1383–1398.

Schulz, P. (2020). Towards inclusive gender in transitional justice: Gaps, blind-spots and opportunities. *Journal of Intervention and Statebuilding, 14*(5), 691–710.

Scoones, I. (2015). *Sustainable livelihoods and rural development.* Practical Action Publishing.

Scott, J. C. (1976). *The moral economy of the peasant.* Yale University Press.

Scott, J. C. (1977). Hegemony and the peasantry. *Politics and Society, 7*(3), 267–296.

Scott, J. C. (1985). *Weapons of the weak. Everyday forms of peasant resistance.* Yale University Press.

Scott, J. C. (1990). *Domination and the arts of resistance. Hidden transcripts.* Yale University Press.

Scott, J. C. (1998). *Seeing Like a State.* Yale University Press.

Scott, J. C. (2009). *The art of not being governed. An anarchist history of upland Southeast Asia.* Yale University Press.

Sehmi, A. (2024). Legacies of colonial violence in contemporary transitional justice: Memories of Mau Mau, the "Kapenguria six" and the "Ocampo six" in Kenya. *International Journal of Transitional Justice, 18*(1), 32–48.

Selby, J. (2013). The myth of liberal peace-building. *Conflict, Security & Development, 13*(1), 57–86.

Shanin, T. (1972). *The awkward class; political sociology of peasantry in a developing society: Russia 1910–1925.* Clarendon Press.

Shanin, T. (1987). *Peasants & peasant societies.* Basil Blackwell.

Sharp, D. (2013). Interrogating the peripheries: The preoccupations of fourth generation transitional justice. *Harvard Human Rights Journal, 26*, 149–178.

Sharp, D. (2014). *Justice and economic violence in transition.* Springer.

Shawki, N. (2014). New rights advocacy and the human rights of peasants: La via Campesina and the evolution of new human rights norms. *Journal of Human Rights Practice, 6*(2), 306–326.

Shigetomi, Y., Ishimura, Y., & Yamamoto, Y. (2020). Trends in global dependency on the Indonesian palm oil and resultant environmental impacts. *Scientific Reports, 10*(1), 20624.

Simmons, E. (2016). *Meaningful resistance. Market reforms and the roots of social protest in Latin America.* Cambridge University Press.

Singh, P., & Sharma, H. (2013). Peasants of Manipur: Agrarian change, land tenure and emerging patterns of re-peasantization in India. *Agrarian South: Journal of Political Economy, 2*(3), 291–314.

Skocpol, T. (1979). *States and social revolutions.* Cambridge University Press.

Skocpol, T. (1982). What makes peasants revolutionary? *Comparative Politics, 14*(3), 351–375.

Slye, R. (2017). Putting the J into the TRC: Kenya's truth justice and reconciliation commission. In M. Swart & K. van Marle (Eds.), *The limits of transition: The south African truth and reconciliation commission 20 years on* (pp. 282–307). Brill.

Slye, R. (2018). *The Kenyan TJRC. An outsider's view from the inside.* Cambridge University Press.

Soto, L. (2020). En medio de la incredulidad, Duque apuesta por nueva estrategia de sustitución de coca, La Silla Vacía, 17 July. Retrieved March 23, 2025, from https://www.lasillavacia.com/silla-nacional/en-medio-de-la-incredulidad-duque-apuesta-por-nueva-estrategia-de-sustitucion-de-coca/

South African Truth and Reconciliation Commission. (1998). Truth and Reconciliation Commission of South Africa Report Vol. 5, Chapter 1 Analysis of Gross Violations of Human Rights (South African Truth and Reconciliation Commission 1998) 11, para 48.

Starn, O. (1991). Missing the revolution: Anthropologists and the war in Peru. *Cultural Anthropology, 6*(1), 63–91.

Starn, O. (1998). Villagers at arms: War and counterrevolution in the central-South Andes. In S. Stern (Ed.), *Shining and other paths. War and Society in Peru, 1980–1995* (pp. 224–257). Duke University Press.

Steger, M. (2020). *Globalization: A very short introduction* (5th ed.). Oxford University Press.

Stern, S. (1987). *Resistance, rebellion, and consciousness in the Andean peasant world, eighteenth to twentieth centuries.* University of Wisconsin Press.

Strömbom, L., & Bramsen, I. (2022). Agonistic peace: Advancing knowledge on institutional dynamics and relational transformation. *Third World Quarterly, 43*(6), 1237–1250.

Szoke, M. (2025). The green thumb of transitional justice: The consideration of the environmental dimension of armed conflict in truth commissions. *International Journal of Transitional Justice, 19*, 480–496.

Tan, S. (1995). *The socioeconomic dimension of Moro secessionism.* University of the Philippines Center for Integrative and Development Studies.

Tapia, C. (1997). *Las Fuerzas Armadas y Sendero Luminoso. Dos Estrategias y un Final.* IEP.

Teitel, R. (2000). *Transitional justice.* Oxford University Press.

Teitel, R. (2003). Transitional justice genealogy (symposium: Human rights in transition). *Harvard Human Rights Journal, 16*, 69–94.

Teló, F., Gasparotto, A., de Medeiros, L., & Fernandes, R. (2021). Land and transitional justice in Brazil. *International Journal of Transitional Justice, 15*(1), 190–209.

Theidon, K. (2006). Justice in transition: The micropolitics of reconciliation in Postwar Peru. *Journal of Conflict Resolution, 50*(3), 433–457.

Theidon, K. (2022). Reproductive warfare: Enforced sterilizations in Peru. In N. Hirschmann & D. Thomas (Eds.), *Citizenship on the edge: Sex/gender/race. Democracy, citizenship, and constitutionalism* (pp. 228–240). University of Pennsylvania Press.

Thomson, F. (2011). The agrarian question and violence in Colombia: Conflict and development. *Journal of Agrarian Change, 11*(3), 321–356.

Throup, D. (1987). *Economic & Social Origins of Mau Mau*. Ohio University Press.

Tilly, C. (1987). Conflict, resistance and collective action versus capitalization and Statemaking. In T. Shanin (Ed.), *Peasants & peasant societies* (pp. 340–342). Basil Blackwell.

TJRC. (2017). *TJRC Land Report: Dealing with the Past and Land Dispossession*. Retrieved December 01, 2025, from https://cdn.viiworksdemo.com/pdf/snrz-TJRC%20Land%20Report%20PPT.pdf

Torelly, M. (2018). Assessing a late truth commission: Challenges and achievements of the Brazilian National Truth Commission. *International Journal of Transitional Justice, 12*(2), 194–215.

UN. (2004). Report of the Secretary-General, 'The rule of law and transitional justice in conflict and post-conflict societies' (S/2004/616).

UN. (2005a). Final report of the Special Rapporteur, Paulo Sérgio Pinheiro, 'Housing and property restitution in the context of the return of refugees and internally displaced persons. Principles on housing and property restitution for refugees and displaced persons' (E/CN.4/Sub.2/2005/17).

UN. (2005b). Basic Principles and Guidelines on the Right to a Remedy and Reparation for Victims of Gross Violations of International Human Rights Law and Serious Violations of International Humanitarian Law (A/RES/60/147).

UN. (2007). United Nations Declaration on the Rights of Indigenous Peoples (A/RES/61/295).

UN. (2018). United Nations Declaration on the Rights of Peasants and Other People Working in Rural Areas (A/HRC/RES/39/12).

UN. (2023). Guidance Note of the Secretary General on Transitional Justice: A Strategic Tool for People, Prevention and Peace (OHCHR).

UNAL. (2017). *Caracterización Comunidad FARC-EP. Resultados Generales*. Universidad Nacional de Colombia.

UNICEF. (2024). *Levels & trends in child mortality. Report 2023*. UNICEF.

UNODC. (2020). *PNIS, Monitoreo a la implementación del Plan de Atención Inmediata -componente familiar, Informe No. 23*. UNODC.

Unruh, J. (2010). Land rights and peacebuilding: Challenges and responses for the international community. *International Journal of Peace Studies, 15*(2), 89–125.

Unruh, J., & Abdul-Jalil, M. (2021). Housing, land and property rights in transitional justice. *International Journal of Transitional Justice, 15*(1), 1–6.

van der Ploeg, J. (2008). *The new peasantries. Struggles for autonomy and sustainability in an era of empire and globalization.* Earthscan.

van der Ploeg, J. (2018). From de-to repeasantization: The modernization of agriculture revisited. *Journal of Rural Studies, 61*, 236–243.

van Meurs, W. (2017). The red peasant international. In L. van de Grift & A. R. Forclaz (Eds.), *Governing the rural in interwar Europe* (pp. 259–278). Routledge.

van Rooy, A. (2004). *The global legitimacy game: Civil society, globalization and protest.* Palgrave.

Vandenbogaerde, A. (2017). Localizing the human rights council: A case study of the declaration on the rights of peasants. *Journal of Human Rights, 16*(2), 220–241.

Vanelli, F., & Ochoa, D. (2022). Territorial peace: Land governance and sustainable peacebuilding. *International Journal of Urban Sustainable Development, 14*(1), 368–387.

Vanhaute, E. (2012). Peasants, peasantries and (de)peasantization in the capitalist world-system. In S. Babones & C. Chase-Dunn (Eds.), *Routledge handbook of world-systems analysis: Theory and research* (pp. 313–321). Routledge.

Vanhaute, E., & Bernardi, C. (2024). The global enclosure and the remaking of peasantries, 1870–1950. *The Historical Journal, 67*(4), 785–802.

Vargas, J., & Uribe, S. (2017). State, war, and land dispossession: The multiple paths to land concentration. *Journal of Agrarian Change, 17*(4), 749–758.

Vega, R., & Gutiérrez, J. A. (2019). *Siempre de Pie, Nunca Rendidos. Los Corteros de Caña de Azúcar en el Valle del Cauca, Presencia y Luchas (1860–2015).* Desde Abajo.

Vega, R., & Rodríguez, E. (1990). *Economía y Violencia.* Universidad Distrital Francisco José de Caldas.

Vellema, S., Borras, S., & Lara, F. (2011). The agrarian roots of contemporary violent conflict in Mindanao, southern Philippines. *Journal of Agrarian Change, 11*(3), 298–320.

Veltmeyer, H., & Ezquerro-Cañete, A. (2023). Agro-extractivism. *The Journal of Peasant Studies, 50*(5), 1673–1686.

Verwimp, P. (2011). The 1990–92 massacres in Rwanda: A case of spatial and social engineering? *Journal of Agrarian Change, 11*(3), 396–419.

Verwimp, P. (2013). *Peasants in power. The political economy of development and genocide in Rwanda.* Springer.

Viaene, L., Doran, P., & Liljeblad, J. (2023). Transitional justice and nature: A curious silence. *International Journal of Transitional Justice, 17*(1), 1–14.

Vianni, W. (2016). Jomo Kenyatta: War, land, and politics in Kenya. In E. Obadare & W. Adebanwi (Eds.), *Governance and the crisis of rule in contemporary Africa* (pp. 97–117). Palgrave Macmillan.

Vila, G. (2022). Natures of concern: The criminalization of artisanal and small-scale mining in Colombia and Peru. *The Extractive Industries and Society, 13*, 101105.

Vila, G. (2025). From minería comunitaria to illegal mining: Indigenous territories and mining formalization in Peruvian Amazonia. In J. A. Gutiérrez & F. Gutiérrez-Sanín (Eds.), *Criminality, political power and conflict. Critical perspectives.* Manchester University Press.

Villarreal, J. (2021). The historical relationship between agrarian reforms and internal armed conflicts: Relevant factors for the Colombian post-conflict scenario. *Land Use Policy, 101*, 105138.

Voyvodic, C. (2024). The fog of war: Development, conflict narratives, and civilian victimisation in Colombia. *Third World Quarterly, 45*(9), 1497–1516.

Walker, C., Bohlin, A., Hall, R., & Kepe, T. (2010). *Land, memory, reconstruction, and justice: Perspectives on land claims in South Africa.* Ohio University Press.

Wallerstein, I. (2000). Globalization, or the age of transition? A long-term view of the trajectory of the world system. *International Sociology, 15*(2), 249–265.

Wesche, P. (2019). Business actors, paramilitaries and transitional criminal justice in Colombia. *International Journal of Transitional Justice, 13*(3), 478–503.

Wezel, A., Herren, B. G., Kerr, R. B., Barrios, E., Gonçalves, A. L. R., & Sinclair, F. (2020). Agroecological principles and elements and their implications for transitioning to sustainable food systems. A review. *Agronomy for Sustainable Development, 40*(6), 40.

Whitehead, L. (1992). The alternatives to "Liberal democracy": A Latin American perspective. *Political Studies, 40*(Special Issue), 146–159.

Wickham-Crowley, T. (1992). *Guerrillas & revolution in Latin America.* Princeton University Press.

Wiener, J. (1975). The Barrington Moore thesis and its critics. *Theory and Society, 2*, 301–330.

Willetts, P. (1996). From Stockholm to Rio and beyond: The impact of the environmental movement on the United Nations consultative arrangements for NGOs. *Review of International Studies, 22*(1), 57–80.

Wolf, E. (1969). *Peasant wars of the twentieth century.* Harper and Row.

Wolff, R. (1970). Economic aspects of British colonialism in Kenya, 1895 to 1930. *The Journal of Economic History, 30*(1), 273–277.

Wolford, W. (2021). The Plantationocene: A Lusotropical contribution to the theory. *Annals of the American Association of Geographers, 111*(6), 1622–1639.

World Bank. (2017). *Land: territory, domain, and identity. A report submitted by the WB-IOM technical team to the Transitional Justice and Reconciliation Commission (TJRC).* Retrieved November 29, 2025, from https://openknowledge.worldbank.org/server/api/core/bitstreams/124f3544-3e59-5992-8347-828324797e51/content

World Bank. (2024). Pathways out of the Polycrisis. In *Poverty, Prosperity, and Planet Report 2024.* International Bank for Reconstruction and Development/ The World Bank.

World Bank. (2025). Poverty & inequality update. October 2025.

Yaşın, Z. (2023). The environmentalization of the agrarian question and the agrarianization of the climate justice movement. In I. Scoones, S. Borras, A. Baviskar, M. Edelman, N. L. Peluso, & W. Wolford (Eds.), *Climate change and critical agrarian studies* (pp. 29–59). Routledge.

Ybarra, M. (2012). Taming the jungle, saving the Maya Forest: Sedimented counterinsurgency practices in contemporary Guatemalan conservation. *The Journal of Peasant Studies, 39*(2), 479–502.

Ye, J., van der Ploeg, J., Schneider, S., & Shanin, T. (2020). The incursions of extractivism: Moving from dispersed places to global capitalism. *The Journal of Peasant Studies, 47*(1), 155–183.

Young, L. (2014). A challenging nexus. In R. Laher & K. Sing'Oei (Eds.), *Indigenous people in Africa. Contestations, empowerment and group rights.* African Books Collective.

Zamosc, L. (1986). *The agrarian question and the peasant movement in Colombia.* Cambridge University Press.

Zamosc, L. (2001). Peasant struggles of the 1970s in Colombia. In S. Eckstein (Ed.), *Power and popular protest* (pp. 102–131). University of California Press.

Index[1]

[1] Note: Page numbers followed by 'n' refer to notes.

J. A. G. Danton, *Transitional Justice and Agrarian Conflict*,
https://doi.org/10.1007/978-3-032-25228-9

The manufacturer's authorised representative in the EU is Springer Nature Customer Service Centre GmbH, Europaplatz 3, 69115 Heidelberg, Germany. If you have any concerns regarding our products, please contact ProductSafety@springernature.com

Printed and bound by CPI Group (UK) Ltd, Croydon, CR0 4YY
17/09/2026
02218454-0005